RENAISSANCE

OR

RUIN

THE FINAL SAGA OF A ONCE GREAT CHURCH

Britt Minshall

Renaissance Institute Press

St. Augustine, FL, 32084

Copyright © 1994 by Dr. Britt Minshall

All rights reserved. Written permission must be secured from the publisher to use or reproduce any part of this book, except for brief quotations in critical reviews or articles.

Published by the Renaissance Institute Press
division of
the Renaissance Institute of American Churches
24 Cathedral Place, St. Augustine, FL, 32084

All Scripture quotations are from The Holy Bible: the New King James Version. Copyright © Thomas Nelson Publishers.

ISBN 0-9642773-0-1

Library of Congress Catalog Card Number 94-68169

Printed in the USA by
Morris Publishing
3212 East Hwy 30 • Kearney, NE 68847

ACKNOWLEDGMENTS

Especially to the memory
of my mother and father:
Frances and Melvin Minshall.
Though they now reside with Jesus
they enable this ministry to continue.

SPECIAL TRIBUTE

To these heroes of the church from our age. These dedicated prophets have long worked to discover the causes of failure in our churches. They have exhorted our congregations to change. They have attempted to warn us of the disastrous results of continuing business as usual - of living in blissful ignorance. Most of our congregations have, to date, not heeded their cries. May God bless their courage.

- Lyle E. Schaller
- Leonard I. Sweet
- Bishop Richard B. Wilke
- Loren B. Mead and the men and women of the Alban Institute
- The hundreds of pastors and lay leaders in the local church who have stood for right and for the life of the church as God's house of prayer; an open place where all persons may come to find love and strength.

NOTICE

The case studies in this book are presented for teaching purposes and not for the purpose of judgment. All of these parables and stories are fictitious; figments of the author's imagination. Any resemblance to any person, church, place or situation is strictly coincidental.

SPECIAL THANKS

To the following special people, all volunteers at the Institute, may I offer my deepest thanks for your work in the production of this book.

Kathy Minshall
Leslie Wilson
Gail Wright
Betsey Lawrence
Rev. James O'Brien
Trina Curtis

RENAISSANCE or RUIN

TABLE OF CONTENTS

Prelude i

Chapter I
The Tribal House 1

Chapter II
Power in the Church 19

    Power in the Past 19

    Power in the Present 25

    Very Best Friends 45

Chapter III
The Powers that Be 49

    The Power Personality 53

    The Tools of Power 66

    Power at Work 67

Chapter IV
Power, Power, Who's Got the Power 77

    Power vs. Authority 78

    Pillars of Authority 83

Pejorative Power...........,........................90

The Power of "NO"...............................94

The Unloving Personality.....................99

Chapter V
The Power or The Glory...111

Faith or Fear..118

Leadership Not Power.........................123

Chapter VI
What Is This Thing You Are Doing..............................129

The Change Agent...............................129

Managers From Hell............................133

By Whose Authority.............................141

Chapter VII
God Will Be With You..147

Defining Leadership............................154

Requirements For Church
  Leadership.....................................158

Methods and
  Means...162

Intervenor As Change
  Agent..167

    The Internal Leadership
        Factor..179

Chapter VIII
Stand Before God For The
People...187

    Hard Pan...187

    Leadership vs. Hard Pan.....................192

    The Proactive Leader..........................198

    As Leadership Develops.....................210

Chapter IX
Bring The Difficulties To God......................................215

    The Dysfunctional Church..................220

    Process Planning...............................227

    The Healthy Church..........................234

Chapter X
Teach Them The Statutes
Show Them How To Walk...................................247

    Teach Them The Statutes
      (Developing Leadership)...............250

    Ten Commandments Of Leadership...255

    Show Them How To Walk.................271

    Adaptable Leadership Theory.............275

Chapter XI
The Work They Must Do 291

The Basics Of Strategic Planning..........296

The Process Of Strategic Planning..........303

Getting Started...................................306

    Step One - Planning The Process   306

Chapter XII
Growing Into Glory 321

Planning Team's Agenda........................321

    Step Two - Scanning Values   321

    Step Three - The Mission Statement   336

    Step Four - Strategic Business Modeling   351

    Step Five - Performance Audit and Gap Analysis   359

    Step Six - Integrated Organizational Action Plan   362

    Step Seven - Plan for Problems   366

    Step Eight - Implementation   368

Chapter XIII
Select Able People 373

Recognizing Able Leaders........................377

Opening Closed Leader Systems..................381

Something From Nothing........................384

Postlude..391

Bibliography..404

PRELUDE

Success Becomes Failure

During the winter of 1947 the prospects in the city of Arlington were bleak for Roy Peterson. He could not foresee himself as ever making a "success" of his life. It was post World War II; factories were in the process of retooling and had not begun to take on new people. The economy was stagnant, but held out the hope that "once things are up and running, and these GI's get their college degrees, things will begin to hum!"

Roy, however, had no industrial skills. He was an insurance salesperson, and very few people were buying insurance. It was during this bleak period that Roy caught a glimpse of what was destined to be a new industry - mutual investment funds.

In 1947 these "mutual funds" were such a new commodity that they were almost unregulated. Therefore Roy, with few resources, was able put together a consortium of backers creating a mutual fund under the name "The Thomas Jefferson Fund." Within two years, Roy and his agents were on the street selling "shares" in the mutual fund at an astonishing rate.

During the 1950's, as the economy grew exponentially, so to did "The Jefferson." Roy and his board, it seemed, had the golden touch. Everyone was happy - sales agents, share holders, and executives. Thanks to the almost unlimited and consistent growth in the wealth of our nation, by 1975 The Jefferson boasted assets that topped $205,000,000. and a group of six diversified funds.

Then something unexpected happened.

Investment capital needed by large firms, banks, and the government became desperately short in supply. It was an investors paradise. Anyone possessing large amounts of cash realized unheard of profits as interest rates grew from 6.6% in 1972 to as high as 14.8% in 1978.

Roy and his board had cash, lots of cash, so much that they no longer had to exert themselves to find new customers. By simply investing their reserves, speculated the fund managers, they could realize an unheard-of return. Current shareholders would be well served and the board could "make a killing."

There was only one hitch. In order to maximize their return they would need to "downsize" The Jefferson, retaining only a skeleton staff to manage the wealth. Consequently the decision was made to "dump" the sales and marketing divisions. The company would keep placing ads in Investors' Daily and the Wall Street Journal, but this was more a matter of form than function - an effort to appear as if they were still a growing concern.

In reality, if a prospective investor were to circumvent the detailed inquiry procedure, becoming interested in spite of mediocre ads, the prospective client would be handled by mail. In other words, new customers would not be courted; if they made it through the front door and insisted on being made a shareholder, the existing structure would reluctantly acquiesce to their presence.

The Jefferson was on a roll, and roll it did. The fund managers didn't need to proclaim success any longer; it was everywhere. The doors closed and the company settled into an eternal life of riches and wealth without exertion.

Unfortunately, Roy and his board had forgotten a basic law of the universe:

> Organisms and entities only continue to exist as long as they fulfill a function, and continue to interact with their environment.

Nothing in creation will long exist as a closed non-producing system.

The Jefferson no longer sold mutual funds, it only invested money for the gain of insiders. Rather than having continual interaction with the world around them, they became closed and inwardly focused. As a result, the infusion of new capital dried up and, unnoticed by the board, the money market slowly, surreptitiously shifted. The return on investments decreased. The Jefferson had only "old money" and that was losing its value.

By the time the directors realized their situation, it was too late. Their investments were in the wrong places, their marketing staff was long gone, their market share was at near zero, and no one was interested in the fund any longer.

On December 16, 1989 the company ceased its business activities, distributed the remaining capital to its few shareholders, and closed its doors forever. It had not failed from failure; it had failed by prospering.

Success had killed The Jefferson.

This same threat hangs ominously over the heads of General Motors, IBM, and the most venerable of institutions, the mainstream American church. All these groups have fallen into the trap that accompanies great achievement:

> *Success in doing what they were created to do had encouraged them to stop doing the very thing that made them thrive.*

The Jefferson assumed that its business was making money - it wasn't. Its real business was to invest money for as many people as possible, thus creating wealth from the continual exchange of capital. In a similar manner, GM began to assume its job was to manufacture cars - not so; its task was to create and sell innovative transportation to an ever growing number of people.

During this same period of America's Golden Era (1940-1980), our churches determined that their task was to provide a fellowship center for members to gather securely under God's protection. NOT!

> **The Church's task is to continually reach out into all the world, helping as many people as possible find peace, joy, and righteous living by coming to know Jesus Christ as their Lord and Savior.**

Several decades ago, the leaders of America's mainline congregations decided that our churches had enough people and resources to carry out their perceived purpose - *providing a place of fellowship and care for their own.* In accepting this premise - we, like The Jefferson, then fired our promotional staff, closed our doors, placed obstacles to entering our community of faith, and closed the Kingdom of God.

This is not a new phenomenon in the church. Jesus found the same situation abounding in the Palestine of the first century. Matthew records the Son of God addressing this issue head on, as he spoke in Jerusalem to the "stakeholders" of the Jewish ecclesiastical community of his day. He said,

> Woe unto you, scribes and Pharisees, you are all hypocrites! For you shut up and closed the kingdom of heaven to your fellow human beings: for you neither go in yourself nor will you allow others to enter.[1]

Nothing in the universe will continue to live and thrive if it ceases to function in the role for which it was created. This is no less true for the church than it was for the now defunct W. T. Grant Company, A&P Supermarkets or the Jefferson Fund. The role of the church in society is now, and has always been, to move out from itself, out into the world, sharing the good news that is the Gospel of Jesus Christ.

The church is in possession of a "pearl of great price,"[2] a valuable message that ✦ it must openly share with all, and in doing so, ✦ it will find life.

> ✦ **It is Not**
>
> ✦ **So It Won't.**
>
> **It will surely die.**

Why This Book

Renaissance or Ruin will probably make you angry. If you're a pastor or a long term lay member of a mainline Protestant church it will most likely make you "mad as hell." I've written Renaissance or Ruin with that response in mind. It

---

[1] Matthew 23:13, para.
[2] Matthew 13:46.

v

is my hope the anger generated will be directed toward solving the problem, rather than defending the status quo.

For too long concerned lay and clergy leaders, have prophetically called for change and issued warnings to the people of our mainline churches. These warnings have been replete with factual information and validating data; however, the warnings have gone unheeded.

Many pastors are fearful of bringing the warnings to their congregations in the same prophetic manner of their issue. As a pastor, for over a decade, I can attest to the extreme pressure pastors are under, having to depend on a group of people for your basic support - all the while being charged with the task of delivering corrective messages the group wishes not to hear. In many cases when clergy have tried to do justice to the warnings, delivering them with the urgency they command, a syndicate of clerical hierarchy and powerful local lay officials have joined forces to brand these attempts at reform as "panic preaching or overkill."

Would-be reformers are labeled as trouble-makers and either transferred to lesser charges or are isolated and censored in vocational opportunities. In either case with a good taste of institutional reprimand under their belts, these protagonists either leave the system or repent and kept their mouths shut.

Some literature has found its way to the laity.[3] Many readers of this type of material, however, are the very core leaders whose main interest has been to maintain the status quo. Lay leaders who wish to see the problems of the dying

---

[3]   Richard B. Wilke, <u>And Are We Yet Alive? The Future of the United Methodist Church</u>, (Nashville, Abington Press, 1986), 9-28, 31-32. This most notable of these efforts sold well in excess of 70,000 copies many of which were used as study guidelines. Unfortunately, it was aimed at the UMC to the exclusion of other groups and even then less than one in a hundred United Methodists purchased the book.

church addressed are, like their clergy partners, chastised or ignored. These "heroes of the faith" often leave the fold and join one of the more conservative fast growing churches, or far worse, abandon the church once and for all.

Twenty million families have left our once great denominational churches in this manner!

Yet, even as I write, our leaders chose to remain in blissful ignorance and the church continues to die. This book will show you how *power* is being used in the local church in a pejorative[4] way, to keep the church a closed dying system.

How The Book Works

As you read this book you will forfeit forever the luxury of thinking that our church is drying up due to demographic or cultural changes. This book will not permit the blame to be placed upon anyone but ourselves.

Renaissance and Ruin asks real questions and issues life altering challenges:

1. Do we have the faith to invite God back into our churches. To trust God in all things? Obey God in all things?

2. Do we have the "guts" to take a critical look at ourselves? Very little change can be effected until we've had the courage to see ourselves as we really are.

---

[4] Throughout, I shall take literary license with the word pejorative, which means to decrease in value or degrade, particularly in the case of a word whose value is lessened in certain usage. Power, I postulate, is a good and productive force, given by God to the church for use in ministry. Many in the church are using it in a harmful way, thus pejorating it.

3. Do we have the courage to jeopardize friendships in order to create change?

4. Do we have the boldness to lay aside our fear of outsiders, our racial prejudices, and cultural biases?

5. Are we willing to drastically alter our methods of operation: the way we minister in our community, and style of our worship?

Renaissance or Ruin targets three areas:

- **POWER.** You will see how power is being used to destroy your church. You will learn how to recognize those who wield it, and how to circumvent these efforts at congregational control. The Holy Spirit will invite you to convert evil pejorative power into godly Productive Power.

- **LEADERSHIP.** You will discover the difference between managers and leaders. You will learn the secrets of the most successful leaders in the world and how to use their system. You will be invited to convert your church from failure-assuring crisis management to a dynamic of Proactive Leadership that guarantees your success.

- **STRATEGIC PLANNING.** You will be guided through the process step by step. It has succeeded in world class corporations; it is modified here for the church. No more great plans with no completion. Your congregation will be led into the Twenty-first century as a reinvented, regenerated, and redirected ministering community of faith.

Hear God's promise:

IF your congregation will fall in love with God with all its heart, mind, spirit, and resources, IF you will love and be open to all persons in the world around you, IF you will follow carefully the flow of this book - *you cannot help but see the rebirth of a living, growing, ministering church of Jesus Christ.*

The destiny of your church is in your hands. You only have two choices. It's either

RENAISSANCE OR RUIN.

Epilogue

On Christmas Sunday, 1993, two mainstream churches in the City of Arlington held their final services and closed their doors forever. On that same day, just six blocks away, The Church of the Savior (a charismatic - fundamentalist fellowship) hosted 1500 people at its inaugural service held in the newly acquired church building at 2006 Arlington Expressway, the former headquarters of the Thomas Jefferson Investment Group.

CHAPTER I

THE TRIBAL HOUSE

The rain falls in a light drizzle as a small group of older people huddle together under the overcast March sky. The scene looks like a funeral, complete with the sobs of mourners; yet missing are the coffin and the body of the departed. None the less, a funeral it is.

These people have gathered at the corner of Broad and Potter streets in this once great industrial city to witness the de-consecration of a Christian Church. As the presbyters say the prescribed words, bulldozers and wrecking crews stand ominously by as the Third Presbyterian Church is ushered out of existence.

This is a far different saga than the one played out just ninety-five years earlier. On May 17, 1896, four hundred elated members and another 400 delighted well-wishers assembled at the dedication of this then new church building. And what a building it was! State of the art Sturtevant Heating and Cooling Systems provided central heating and fresh air. The church boasted magnificent stained glass windows, hand-crafted by the soon to be famous Edward Colgate Company, and gas lighting fixtures, carved from imported Mexican onyx by Reinhold G. Ledig of Philadelphia, lined the freshly plastered walls.[1]

These avant-garde and somewhat pretentious amenities, however, where not the reason for such jubilation. It was the four hundred and eleven active members, the forty-two dedicated Sabbath School teachers and their two hundred pupils that assured such hope for the future.

All this is now changed. There is no such hope being shared today. Standing before the dilapidated buildings all exultation is gone.

- *Gone are the children*
- *Gone are the people*
- *Gone is the mission.*

The names of the people, gathered to say good-bye on this winter day in 1991, reflect their Scottish ancestors who worked so diligently to build this mighty church of God. There were the Walkers, the Sweeneys, the Magees, the MacLoeds and the MacClures. And so it is in the sadness of this farewell event, amidst the din of city noise, one can almost hear the strains from a tartan clad piper, as *Amazing Grace* echoes off

---

[1] All new and innovative in 1896.

the hills of Glen Carnon and from the walls of Castle Wellie.[2]

Any expedition leading to an understanding of the contemporary local church in America must begin far from the little white clapboard church of postcard fame, far from the sound of the steeple bells ringing out across village and stream. Far, too, from the deserted urban churches whose bell towers silently dot the landscape of every American city. For most of us this vision of the church is the pictorial embodiment of all that symbolizes home and peace. To understand how the modern congregation[3] functions, however, we must turn our calendar back four thousand years. Our trip will take us several thousand miles to the east of Broad and Potter Streets in Chester, Pennsylvania - indeed beyond the Scottish highlands.

We find ourselves on the banks of a central European river, perhaps the Dnieper or the Danube. Here, in the second millennium B.C., humankind is emerging from the shadows of unknown Neolithic history. The Battle Axe people have merged with the more sophisticated Beaker people, and the

---

[2] Located in the north central mountains and east coast lowlands of Scotland, respectively.

[3] Congregation, throughout this book, will be understood to refer to churches of congregational and quasi congregational polity. Mainline denominations fitting this description would include, but not be limited to, United Church of Christ, Presbyterian, United Methodist, American and Southern Baptist, Disciples of Christ and Episcopal. The focus of this book is toward churches of European ancestry in an effort to show historical connection with contemporary group behavior. Churches rising from other cultural and racial traditions, however, will also be able to identify with behavior patterns featured in this book.

result is the forming of the Celtic race, soon to be the dominant people of prehistoric Europe.

Prior to this time, a common race, with a more or less common tongue, inhabited Europe from the Irish Sea to the Indus River. Over time, and impacted by geography, these people slowly developed separately in culture and language. These Indo-European ancestors were the fathers and mothers of not only the Celts (Gauls to the Romans), but also to the original Latin speakers (pre-Etruscan), the Slavs, the Scots, the Germans, the Anglo-Saxons and to the Indian speakers of Sanskrit.[4]

It can be theorized that some cataclysmic event in central Europe, perhaps a flood, began the process of pushing these common Indo-European people apart, eventually to settle in separate areas, scattering from this "tribal-center" like rays of a star in every direction. While the core of the mother tongue remained, as people were isolated by geographical barriers, variations in tongues developed leading to cultural separation and language barriers. In the end this resulted in universal fear of the now separated clans people, distrust of the strange and a systemic paranoia. This xenophobia manifested itself in dread of the "people from the other side of the mountain."

---

[4]   Robert McGrum, William Cran, and Robert MacNeil, The Story of English, (New York, Penguin Books, 1986), 50-56.

Renaissance or Ruin

About the time the pre-Hebrews were moving south from Asia Minor, and fully 800 years before the Eustruscans arrived on the shores of Europe, probably from the Middle East, the white-skinned, red-haired and blond people of Central Europe were evolving first into the Uretice, Tumulus, and Urnfield cultures of the Bronze age. These became the tribes and the first permanent settlers of historic Europe. It is from their ideology and philosophy of life that our history and current lifestyle began to be emerge.

These Celtic European people, called the Haldstatt and La Tene cultures of the eighth through the sixth century B.C., began to develop into warlike and identifiable tribal peoples who were to continue to war with the advancing civilization of the Greeks and Romans, as well as with each other. During this era horsemen began pushing into central Europe from the east. Simultaneously, Mediterranean cultures began to systematize and civilize their cultures and formed power spheres using the Mediterranean Sea as their common foundation. These two forces started a gradual westward movement of the Celts following the rivers of Europe and resulted in the final, and to date, permanent division of the central Indo-European peoples. Out of this movement (that had really begun in the 3500 to 2500 B.C. period with the break off of the Indo-Iranian, Hittite, Greek and Italic peoples) there now arose the tribes of Western Europe.

By the coming of the Christian era, the Celts occupied only a fringe of their original territory; mainly Ireland, southern France (Gaul), Scotland, and southern Britain. The Angles, the Saxons, and the Jutes occupied West Germany, the Burguins occupied eastern France, while the Franks settled in northern France. The tribes of the Frisians settled in Belgium, and the Teutonic people, while subject to invasions, made Prussia their home.[5]

Much more movement took place in much this same manner, as is well documented in books dealing with the history of Europe. The only reason for the telling of any of this story is to dispel several false beliefs that seriously impact the church today. First, it would be helpful to see the church in the light of the function it serves for the people who populate it. Theologically, we present the church as the house of God open to all people, but in reality it is the "tribal house" of an ethnic people seeing themselves as under siege. The difference between how we see ourselves theologically, and what we are culturally, is so much at odds that we must examine this area carefully.

Long before Christianity or modern nationhood came to the European tribespeople, one can picture small enclaves of people isolated from other tribes only a few miles distant, around the river bend or in the next valley. These semi-nomadic people seeking to become permanent residents of

---

[5] Nora Chadwick, The Celts, (London, Penguin Books, 1991), 40-50.

their own valley were few in number (each village may have boasted less than fifty people). Life was harsh and unpredictable. As a result of these precarious conditions, each tribe, seeking a degree of security established at its center, the altar to its own god. Often sheltered in a cathedral of trees, this sanctuary became the center of the community. These gods had strange and different names: Belemus, Torroz Trigaranus, Esus, Epona, Rosmerter, Sucillos, Monhony or Regda,[6] to name but a few.

With warring invaders often traversing the mountains, each village in a tribe could easily succumb to extinction or at least permanent displacement on a regular basis. As invaders landed upon the shore, men would be killed (often decapitated and their heads collected), women would be raped, and taken into servitude and children carried off as slaves. In this milieu one can understand a race collectively incorporating a high fear level into its socio-psyche particularly a fear of outsiders.

The place where "the god" was kept became the final inner bastion of sanctity. The last thing of a people to be violated would be the god's "tribal house." Understandably, that grove or that hill became the rallying point of defense, the last huddling point of a besieged people.

During times of peace this same sacred clearing became the assembly place to elect the chief, bury the elders and present the newborn to the community, celebrating paternal

---

[6] Chadwick, 152-162.

acceptance. This "tribal house" came to reflect the very existence of the people of that particular village. When outsiders did enter this place, it usually meant the tribe had ceased to exist - *the invaders had won.*

The second important feature to note is the size of these bands of mutually isolated tribes that developed all over Europe. The number of persons in a single tribe was continually impacted by the geography. Because of valleys, river separations, and ocean estuaries (the English Channel, Irish Sea, Baltic Sea, Bay of Finland, the North Sea) these once culturally united people continued to develop in isolation from one another. Instead of becoming a mixed people, seeking a common hierarchy, as did the Mediterranean dwellers whose mutual existence bordered on and depended on a common sea, these northern Europeans developed into small enclaves seeking their security in an independent governing mode and a tribal village model. Hierarchy became suspect. Any movement to merge lone villages or tribes together for common defense was perceived as a threat. One can see the ghost of this "mixed society" fear in the elections of 1992 to form a common Europe. The Danes turned down the Maastricht Treaty in June of that year and other nations came to the brink of doing the same thing.

The impact on the American church, formed by immigrant successors of these tribespeople from this two thousand years of isolationism, is evident. The tribal house of the first millennium B.C. served as a repository of the tribe's culture and society, as well as the community's validation and protection under a deity. The tribal house also reflected the commitment of the small tribal village to the concept of government and the managing of affairs in a small community independent of other peoples.

The mainline Protestant church, the successor to the ancient tribal house, relates little to Jesus' commandment for the church "to preach and teach the Gospel to all creatures." The mid-eastern, Mediterranean based culturalization that created Paul's mindset and therefore impacted his writings, would have embraced no understanding of northern European tribalism. Paul's letters, which formed the basis of the western church, were accepted into a Greco-Roman hierarchically based world. The "people uniting culture" set forth in his epistles envisioned a church open to all people, international in make-up, and governed by an apostolic central authority. Such became the standard in the evolving Roman Catholic Church.

One may cry "we're Americans, we're all one people - a melting pot." Sociologists, however, discount that belief at once. The mainline church of today reflects the last 2,000 years of its evolution. The Presbyterian church on a Chicago corner is a direct transplant of the Scots tribe people of the loch country of Scotland. The Methodists are an odd mixture of lower-born English, mainly from north of the Danelaw, predominantly Anglo-Saxon; a remnant of invading Vikings

(Danes), and leftover Brits (Celts) living outside the culturally "in" areas of Romanized London, Oxford, and the South Country of England. Those from the latter locations are today's high Anglicans (Episcopal) or Roman Catholics. The farther north in England you travel, the farther away from Roman-Mediterranean influence you go, and the more "congregational" the churches become. This is due to the influence upon the lives of the Viking invaders of the geographical separating effect of the fjords of their homeland.

If, for instance, your ancestors came from the area near Boston, Lincolnshire, England, when they emigrated they carried their tribal philosophy to the new world with them. They then naturally give their new city the name Boston, and made sure their churches were separatist and congregational. Their sons and daughters settled Massachusetts and pioneered west to Ohio, which is the reason the congregational branch of the U.C.C. is so predominant in New England and Ohio. In the mid-Atlantic area where the Church of England, Roman Catholics and Methodists had their greatest influence, most congregations adopted the Roman idea of stronger central authority. For this reason congregationalists of all brands, including Baptist, have had little success along the mid-Atlantic seaboard states. These analogies go on and on and are too numerous to cover in detail. The crux of the matter, however, is to illustrate the importance of examining our operating philosophy in the light of where our church ancestors came from rather than living in ignorance, thinking that our church follows some kind of universally accepted Biblical model. We who enter the third millennium of the Christian era will need, in a real cathartic way, to examine ourselves much as a counselor of the dynamics school would look at a client with a crippling psychopathology. Such an examination reveals our church communities to be isolationist, separatist, and exclusionary. While our churches have been publicly hanging out the welcome sign to everyone, in truth we do not want every person. Many don't want most newcomers! Some of our congregations don't want any at all. As a people, we have been reared (English), or raised (Viking & German), for over two thousand years to keep the tribe small, to be suspicious of the people from the other side of the mountain and, above all to protect from desecration the tribal house where the god lives. As an etymological study of our language betrays our heritage, so also does our mono-racial church tell a story of exclusion.

Move that culture clique into a modern community and you will find your church. You'll find a xenophobic congregation rife with fear (fear of displacement, fear of loss of control). You'll find a congregation whose people feel that their lands are being invaded by Blacks, Latins, Orientals, and other culturally different people pouring across "their" borders. The tribal house is once again besieged by outsiders. The natural reaction of the human organism when threatened this way is to pull inward, to throw barricades up around itself, and to bury its head in denial.

It is difficult to do this in everyday life. We need to enter the world to work, we must go to school and shopping centers that are integrated and public. In the church, however, we can find sanctuary. Here we can react in a defensive isolationist way in relative safety. In this, our tribal house, we, not the government, the employer, or social political correctness, can control what happens.

Most churches in America, fully 95%, are "one-celled" units.[7] These churches number up to 125 people and will always maintain that level until, due to changes in neighborhood demographics and attritional patterns, the numbers decline to dangerously low levels. At this point the one-celled unit will cease to exist.

For two centuries, as the tides of immigrants washed upon the American shore, each successive group found its own niche and settled in, near to but separate from the other immigrating tribespeople. Out of this phenomenon came the myth of America the melting pot. Descendants of the first English settlers felt safe because the newly arrived Irish settled on the

---

[7] One-celled units refer to groups or congregations numbering less than 100 people. These tightly knit long-term groups usually boast one leader, and the very relationship factor inherent in this configuration is its most important draw. Carl Dudley refers to these congregations as "single celled" and explores their personality at length in his 1982 book Making the Small Church Effective, published by Abingdon Press, Nashville.

Renaissance or Ruin

other side of Boston and Philadelphia and Baltimore. These newcomers moved into the leftover and less desirable areas and founded churches under the names of their patron saints, safely segregated from the Italians who settled in still another section of town. The groups were assigned to parishes by Rome and these tribal houses became culture centers far from the shores of the homelands. Here, the priests spoke their language and knew their stories.

Most other communities both in and outside the city formed around other churches. These were northern Europeans, so the assigned parish model didn't apply. Theirs were smaller churches. Most Reformed churches were German in theology, organization, and often language. Still other churches were built near the farms of Swedish yeomen. These were Swedish Evangelical Lutheran and peopled entirely by Swedes. Here, as in the urban parish, was the repository of the "back home" culture.

Each group had its own section of the city or their own side of the mountain. All were civil to each other as long as no one interfered with any of the others. By way of example, Protestant/Catholic marriage was viewed at least as derogatorily as a black/white union would have been in the 1950's and 1960's. In the past twenty years, however, a monumental change has taken place.

The little parish or neighborhood church can no longer expect to perpetuate itself with the children of its children.

They have moved away. The great European immigration has ceased and the neighborhood is being infiltrated by hordes of other peoples. The hope during the 1960's and 70's was that the children who had moved away by the millions to distant cities would find another ethnic church just like the one back in their "valley" or in the parish from whence they had come. In this way each tribal house would be able to continue with some other village's offspring; but no such luck. These children moved away during the era of the 1950's and 60's as the world was changing to a modern secular lifestyle. During this period the church was supplying "answers to questions that fewer and fewer people (were) asking."[8] Religion and church were therefore considered trivial by the children of the immigrants. One entire generation, and then a second, moved away from "back home" and dropped out of the church of their ancestors. The little churches fell into disrepair, many were boarded up.

The congregations that did survive became more and more gray, attended by older congregants; everything had changed for the mainline Protestant church. Much of the same thing happened in the urban Catholic church. It is estimated that only one out of five children reared as a Roman Catholic between 1950 and 1970 is still active in the Roman Catholic church. The Catholic parishes, however, have been able to survive and in some cases prosper by being able to allow for racial

---

[8] Harvey Cox, Religion In the Secular City, (New York, Simon and Schuster, 1984),159.

hegemony to take place in an orderly manner as the neighborhood changed. Protestants have almost never tried or succeeded at this.

Historically, these mainline churches were considered the leaders of the church establishment in the U.S. For example, from 1870 to 1889, 70,000 new congregations had been founded by these inheritors of the northern European tribal system. By 1970 all had changed. As the grandchildren of the immigrants began to return to church they didn't seek out the now old and dilapidated church that spoke the old ethnic message they no longer sought or understood. During the 1970's mainline denominations founded less than 4% of the new churches. In this same period new interdenominational and sub-culture churches were growing, with 72% of their membership being reported as converts from the former mainline churches.[9]

Leonard Sweet highlights this problem when he writes:

> One example: The United Methodist Church boasts the best-trained, hardest-working, most motivated clergy it has ever seen. But The United Methodist Church is getting fewer and fewer results from its clergy than ever before. Why? Because we are geared up for a world-we-have-lost ministry. We are captivated by a world-that-is-no-more syndrome. Our appeals and ambitions center in

---

[9] Lyle E. Schaller, It's a Different World, (Nashville, Abingdon Press, 1988), 50-81.

"recapturing what we have lost" rather than in stepping forward to meet the challenges of what we have gained. The United Methodist Church's stubborn identity anxieties, its inappropriate displays of anger, its self-mutilation and suicide attempts, its tendency to push away those who love it, its impulsivity and frantic efforts to avoid abandonment, are only a few indications that the church itself may be afflicted with continuing borderline behavior.

The church does not have the option of standing safely by and watching these changes take place without taking part. One of the cardinal planks in quantum theory is that it is impossible to be an observer.[10]

We of the mainline church are indeed more interested in a *"world-that-is-no-more"*. We cling tenaciously to our old country culture hoping a few more immigrants from back home will stumble through our doors.

The first step in recovery from dysfunction, then, is to examine our church and own it for what it is. We may be astonished to find it is not a lighthouse of the resurrected Jesus standing in a world of hurting people seeking to save the lost. We may discover it to be a tribal house filled with the trinkets of a dead civilization whose main function is to provide a place for the tribal villagers from a long forgotten land to get together to hear their language and tell their stories. It is,

[10] Sweet, 26.

however, a place where we can feel safe and secure, a place where we can feel important. Its chief purpose, in other words, is as a place to meet in order to meet.

Secondly, we must acknowledge that the primary force, effort and power of the church is being expended to keep the tribal house safe, isolated and closed to outsiders. It is NOT the open inviting "house of prayer" that our conference ministers and bishops tell us it is when they visit. We aren't a loving, ministering embodiment of our God, but rather we are stalwart defenders of the status quo of a now departed culture. We are committed to trying to keep alive, as long as possible, that which is dead, and dead forever.

In reality, very little, if anything, has changed in the function of the tribal house since its altar was used to worship the god of the bull Tervos Trigaranus three thousand years ago. Some may long to return to the god of the bull who promised to keep the tribal house safe from outsiders; at least then they could be true to their mission. Conversely, Jesus, the would-be occupant of the altars, died to give our altars away to anyone who comes through the front doors. Jesus taught that our closed tribal houses were to be open houses of prayer for all people.[11] He told us to reach out from sanctuary, to preach and teach the Gospel to all persons, and to invite them in to live with us (make disciples), baptizing them into our body, in

---

[11]   Mark 11:17

the name of the Father, the Son, and the Holy Ghost.[12]

TRIGGER POINTS

1. What is the ethnic or racial history of the denomination to which you belong?

2. Who were the founding families of your local church?

3. From what country or area did these founders immigrate?

4. Are there any currently active members who are directly descended from these founders?

5. Are there any ethno-cultural patterns or events that have become part of the life of your church? What meaning do these have for others of your community?

6. Do you believe your church is known throughout the community by its ethnic identity or by its broad social appeal?

7. How much effort is being expended to keep your church the "way it has always been?"

---

[12] Matthew 28:19

CHAPTER II

POWER IN THE CHURCH

Power In The Past

It was a cold dark morning in February of 1555. Mary was Queen of England and protector of the Catholic faith. Bishop John Hooper of Gloucester, a Protestant cleric, was being chained to a stake in the town square within sight of his cathedral, he was about to be burned for the crime of "irritating" Catholic bishops. As he burned for three quarters of an hour, he delivered his most powerful sermon. John Foxe describes the scene:

> When he was black in the mouth and his tongue swollen that he could not speak, yet his lips went till they were shrank from the gums; and he did knock his fists with his hands until one of his arms fell off, and then knocked still with the other, what time the fat, water, and blood dropped out at his fingers' ends, until by renewing of the fire his strength was gone and his hand did clinch fast in knocking to the iron upon his breast. So immediately bowing forward, he yielded up his spirit.

Hundreds of other men and women, including the famous cleric Thomas Cramner, died in the horrible carnage during Mary's reign.[1] Not only clergy, but many laymen and laywomen also gave their lives as martyrs for Protestantism and the Bible between 1553 and 1558. As six Protestant laymen were being burned at Colcester they could be seen clapping their hands. Shortly after, a twenty-two year old blind Joan Waste of Derby cited Bible verses as she died in the flames. Cealy Ornes of Norwich sang the song of another woman from scripture, "My soul doth magnify the Lord,"[2] as she was put to death.

The tables soon turned, however, as is inevitable in power struggles, and the Catholics fared little better during the ensuing reign of the Protestants under Elizabeth. Over a hundred newly arrived Catholic priests from France were tortured or burned. Jesuit Edmund Campion, a Fellow of St. John's College, Oxford, was tortured so badly, "He walked like an elephant" as he was led to be quartered. As he was being cut apart while still alive he noticed his fingernails had been removed. As the executioner pulled the entrails from the screaming victim's body a drop of blood fell on the head of Henry Walpole who, having witnessed such a carnage, instantly

---

[1] John Foxe, Foxes's Book of Martyrs, ed. G. A. Williamson (London 1965). Quoted in David L. Edwards, Christian England Vol. 2, From the Reformation to the 18th Century, (Grand Rapids, Wm. B. Eerdmans Publishing Co, 1984), 18-20.
[2] Edwards, 20.

had a conversion experience, became a Jesuit, and was later martyred himself.

Horrified? I hope! And all this in the church of the "First Born of God." If these were the only examples of "power gone sour" in ecclesiastical history they wouldn't carry the significance they do; unfortunately, there are many more.

History is replete with stories of human beings who came into contact with the institutional church of their age and suffered at its hands. The power of the ecclesiastical authorities[3] of the ancient Israelis came to bear against Jeremiah. As he prophesied against the infidelity of the people toward God, Poshkur, the priest who was the chief governor of the temple (dean of the temple), struck Jeremiah, had him flogged, then thrown into prison.[4]

Six hundred years later another Jewish rabbi, speaking prophetically, threatened the contemporary religious establishment. This Jesus of Nazareth condemned the hypocritical behavior of the religious leaders. He criticized both the high church coterie clustered around the temple (Sadducees) and the low church party of the local synagogue (Pharisees). These "inner ring"[5] power holders of the first

---

[3] It would be wrong to use the term "power of the church." However, the operations of power in the prototypical "church" or ecclesiastical institutions of the old testamental period were identical in that the power exerted was generated from and delivered through a theological community.
[4] Jeremiah 20:1-3.
[5] A term used by C. S Lewis to indicate a social power bloc or clique.

Christian century's ecclesiastical institution bound themselves to civil interest to act out their power struggles.[6] Jesus' entire ministry was haunted by these power players and their political maneuvering as they attempted to discredit and/or execute Him.

In the end, the very highest religious authority, Caiaphas, the high priest and Annas, the former holder of that office, brought Jesus before the Sanhedrin, the highest ecclesiastical body in the land. With methods that were to become archetypical for the torture chambers of the Middle Ages, the man of Nazareth was questioned, beaten and tortured for hours. By enlisting the Roman government through the auspices of Governor Pontious Pilate, himself an unknown power hungry political player, and the local establishment of the indigenous people whose power was wielded by Herod, the power play was completed, and Jesus was dragged through the streets and hung on the cross.

What an amazing similarity to a morning fifteen hundred years later as the Protestant authorities dragged twelve Catholic monks through the streets of Oxford, England to be burned at the stake. Other examples of power struggles in the church resulting in death and horror aren't limited to the Middle East or to the British Isles. Many of the early popes vying for supreme authority were accused of poisoning rivals and having critics murdered. The infamous Spanish

---
[6] Mark 3:6.

Renaissance or Ruin

Inquisitions began in 1391 with a social purge ostensibly to rid the church of half-hearted Christians, "Marranos" (the name means pig), who had once been Jewish but who had converted to Christianity. The charge was levied by "real" Christians that these converts had only changed religions to become part of mainstream society. It is worth noting that once the restrictions against these former Jews were lifted, they became successful beyond expectations at business pursuits. It was then, after their success, that the cry of condemnation went out from the local churchmen.

The power "of" the church was beginning once again to be power "in" the church and was being politically manipulated for personal profit or gain, rather than being used in society for reform and justice. By 1498 when Pope Sixtus IV officially issued the Bull empowering the Inquisition, the Christian populace of Spain was thirsty for blood, thanks to the hate-filled preaching and political maneuvers of Rev. Thomas DeTorquemada. The thousands of innocent recent Jewish converts, and later lifelong Christians, that were imprisoned or killed were to become some of the most notable victims of power in the church. The last victim of the "Holy Office" perished in 1826 and the Inquisition was abolished, over the protest of the religious establishment of Spain. Queen Isabella II ended the 350 years of "power gone sour" on July 15, 1834.[7]

---

[7] Ceal Roth, The Spanish Inquisition, (New York, Norton Co., 1964), 267.

Three hundred and fifty years during which the people of hate had powered the church of love.

Calvin, the Protestant theologian, legally murdered Servetus, the Catholic evangelist[8], in 1553 in Geneva, thus enshrining Calvin's power. "Peaceful" pilgrims fresh from their own persecution in England burned innocent women to death at Salem, Massachusetts, and a lay power block of a Southern Baptist congregation in Florida worked feverishly behind the scenes to discredit and fire their preacher of 13 years - the one that the rank and file "just adored." On and on the power *of* the church goes "sour" and becomes power *in* the church, destined for evil use. Throughout most of the history these political maneuverings and the resulting use of power for political gain have been wielded by persons in high places, often against other persons in high places. While many of the examples cited above do affect lay people, many more incidents were, in the past, relegated to cloistered walls and holy halls. Now, however, that has changed as the seat and organization of power has changed in the church.

Any renaissance of true Christianity in the church is contingent upon this force being openly identified, understood and dealt with. Power no longer nails people to stakes for burning; now it kills our congregations and destroys well-meaning men and women of faith, lay and clergy alike.

---

[8] Kenneth Scott Latourette, A History of Christianity, (New York, Harper & Row, 1953), 759.

The stench of burning bodies has been replaced by the sound of clanging padlocks, but in the end society will suffer just the same.

Power in The Present

In his second letter to Theophilus, the writer of Acts pens the final words of the ascending Christ.

> But you shall receive power when the Holy Spirit has come upon you; and you shall be witnesses to Me in Jerusalem, and in all Judea and Samaria, and to the end of the earth.[9]

The power referred to by Paul was to be different in three basic ways from the power that any of the voyeurs to this event had known previously. First, it was to come directly from God; second, it was to be selfless; and third, it was to be expended righteously.

Prior to the above commission from Christ, power was abundantly present in the lives of His followers. Christ did not breathe on them that they should receive power for the first time. These disciples had always held and used power of one type or another in their secular and religious lives. Power is everywhere, the planet on which we live is a living energy converter, the universe is forever an exploding, expanding

---

[9] Acts 1:8, NKJV (All Biblical quotations contained in this work were taken from the New King James Version of the Holy Bible, (Nashville, Thomas Nelson Publishers, 1983).

dynamo. Every human being from the youngest infant to the oldest great grandparent is a living, energy filled creature, a power driven organism. What then was the Son of God leaving behind? How was it to be a new thing?

First, let's look at power in the sense of the physical sciences to see what power is and how it's supposed to work. Picture a familiar scene from the past. A giant, steam powered, stamping press in a turn-of-the-century foundry. The huge steam belching machine has three basic components: the fire chamber (energy center), the boiler (power center) where water becomes steam and is projected , and finally the press (the implement or action center) which is moved up and down by the force of the escaping, directed steam. Every system known in our universe works essentially in this fashion:

1. Fueled by kinetic energy,

2. Converted to usable power, given force or thrust which,

3. Acts upon an implementing drive to activate a tool, resulting in the completion of a work.

Social systems contain approximately the same components which work in about the same manner. In all groups, be they called church, club, department, or firm, there are basically three levels of actors within any human relational organism. We can label these as:

1. *People* (employees or members) provide the energy,

2. *Leaders* (executives or local lay leadership) provide energy focus or power direction, and

3. *Implementors* (machines, agents, or missionaries/local ministers and workers) become the tools.

The work completed in business is the production of product; in the church it is ministry. Every church works this way and every people system works the same way - energy = *people*, power = *leaders*, implementors = *ministers*[10].

Another similarity between the giant stamping machine and the church rests in the fact that each requires an outsider to operate. The machine cannot run inertially without an outside person to watch its gauges and open and close its valves. This machinist or operator may have the grease of the instrument ground down to his/her bones and may live in mind and spirit for the privilege of working with the machine, but this person can never be part of the machine. If operators were ever to succeed in becoming part of their machines, they would lose their usefulness in the scheme of things. The church also

---

[10]   Minister within the context of this work is understood to mean any person who actively serves God in any capacity whatsoever, whether ordained clergy or layperson.

boasts such an outsider, whose job it is to gauge its progress and to keep its fire lit. This operative is given the designation of *intentional outsider* by social scientists; we in ecclesiastical circles usually see this person as the pastor[11]. Unfortunately, this person almost always becomes part of the community (machine), most often as "the one and only" implementor. When this happens, the pastor loses his or her effectiveness as intentional outsider. Both the operator of the stamping machine and the pastor, or some other intentional outsider, must remain in close proximity to the system, but outside it, in order for the systems to perform at maximum efficaciousness.

There is a vital difference, however, between the church and any other system. God breathed upon the church that it might receive the power of the Holy Spirit. The club, the factory and the firm did not receive that blessing. The church is different in that it is not purely a social organization, it is the body of Christ. The result is then that while all energy systems work similarly, the power exerted by the church that accepts this blessed incarnation becomes exponential (greater than the sum of its parts). A local church might, for example, consist of a body of powerless, poor, undereducated people, but if they allow the Holy Spirit to be the life force, being therefore incarnate with the presence of God, a kind of synergy develops. The force and power emanating from earthly beings

---

[11] Lyle E. Schaller, <u>Community, Organization, Conflict and Reconciliation</u>, (Nashville, Abingdon, 1966), 44.

Renaissance or Ruin

undergoes a metamorphosis, becoming that which can change the face of the earth. Remember, however, that the blessing can only be present in a body that is surrendered to God. It can no longer be subject to the laws of social endeavor, but rather must imitate the body of Christ, selfless in mission and purpose, and willing to expend itself, its buildings, its privileged seclusion to create a loving, righteous world.

Power in the physical system is a natural force. It can be used either *productively* or *pejoratively*[12]. Judgment regarding its overall use is rendered by the society in which it is deployed and by successive generations. For example, the development of atomic energy during the 1940's and the power derived from it was neither good or bad. When, however, this atomic power was used as the implementing force in the A-bomb it became, to the military establishment, a great and wonderful gift. When that power exploded over Hiroshima, Japan in 1945 it became an evil disaster to the Japanese people. History has increasingly begun to judge the use of this power by the U.S. in a negative light. Therefore, in just thirty years this energy source and its power in usage, first seen as a possible boon to the world, later became an instrument of mass

---

[12] I will use "pejorative" in connection with destructive power throughout this book in order to create an <u>alliteration</u>. I take this liberty with a word that traditionally means "to lessen the value of...," normally applied to the value of words. Power, however, like verse, has no value in and of itself, but only in connection with its use. Therefore, power, like words, used to bring harm, loss, and/or pain to innocent people can be said to be power that has "pejorated."

29

killing. It has moved from neutral to productive = *ends war*, on to pejorative = *killed thousands*, and finally on to extreme evil, condemned by the civilized world as an act of genocide.

Within a social system, power itself begins no less neutrally. The responsibility for assessing the quality of its use falls to the group, community, generation and successors on whom the power was exerted and from whose ranks the power wielders rose. As stated, power is ubiquitous in every system, both physical and social. Here, as in the physical system, it can be used *productively* to create, grow, learn, heal, or build, or it can be used *pejoratively* to kill, regress, harm, promote ignorance, or destroy.

In the church setting power is often seen as a modern idolatry, a living incarnation; not of God, but of evil. "Power (in this social setting) promises,

- I will name you

- I will define you

- I will tell others who you are

- And I will start today"

writes Cheryl Forbes in her book <u>The Religion of Power</u>.[13] She feels that in our quest to change the world we have "accommodated our theology" to that of the world. She

---

[13] Cheryl Forbes, <u>The Religion of Power</u>, (Grand Rapids, Zondervan Publishing House, 1983), 18.

examines the "power of positive thinking" and the highest achiever under its influence, Robert Schuller, in theological terms. She sees his Crystal Cathedral as a purveyor of power, as a "modern Tower of Babel." The ideas of sacrifice, commitment, service and discipline have been replaced by "doing your own thing" or "fulfilling your gifts."[14] She does admit that power is "basic to human nature" and that power's bottom line is "power over people."[15]

While religious people (A) deny that power is wielded in their churches, they would even more vehemently, (B) deny that power as exercised in their churches is power over people. In both of these assumptions, which form the basic concepts of our social thought processes, may lie a big part of our current inability to handle power and leadership problems in our churches as well as in the rest of the social system. Jeffrey Pfeffer, one of the nation's leading experts on power, politics, and group dynamics states that while power has been known and observed since the beginning of time, its study has not been systematized due to a certain sense of sinfulness we place on both politics and power. The very definition of power would mean that the church could not easily own up to the politics of power being present among its rolls.

---

[14] Forbes, 107-109.
[15] Forbes. 45.

Power has been defined as:

> A relation among social actors in which one social actor (A), can get another social actor (B), to do something that (B) would not otherwise have done. Power becomes defined as force...force sufficient to change the probability of (B)'s behavior...[16]

Another expert on the subject, James MacGregor Burns, views the power process:

> As one in which power holders (P), possessing certain motives and goals, have the capacity to secure changes in the behavior of a respondent (R), human or animal, and in the environment, by utilizing resources in their power base, including factors of skill, relative to the targets of the power-wielding and necessary to secure such changes.[17]

By these or any other definition, power in the social sense is the power of one person over another.

The church must deny the presence of political power as power over people because of its incompatibility with the teachings of Jesus. The very words of Jesus prohibit political power of the above sort to be practiced among his followers.[18]

---

[16] Jeffrey Pfeffer, Power in Organizations, (Boston, Pitman Publishing, Inc., 1981), 2-3.

[17] James MacGregor Burns, Leadership, (New York, Harper & Row, 1978), 13.

[18] Authority is power that has legitimated and is accepted within a social setting. For a complete examination see Max Weber, The Theory of Social and Economic Organization, (New York, Free Press, 1947).

Renaissance or Ruin

Mark records the words of Jesus:

> You know that those who are considered rulers over the Gentiles lord it over them, and their great ones exercise authority over them. Yet it *shall not* be so among you; but whoever desires to become great among you shall be your servant.
>
> And whoever of you desires to be first shall be slave of all.[19]

In the first verse, Jesus acknowledged that the ruling system of the world outside the church of God was one in which political power and physical force, if necessary, were widely known and used as the method of operating social structures. "Lord it over them," or "lordship" as it was translated in the King James Version, is taken from the word κατακυριευω *(katakurieuo)* in the Greek, the root of which means "control, subjugate, or exercise power and dominion over." This is much in line with the definition of power examined above. Then, in the second part of the verse, Jesus strictly prohibits such behavior among those inside the church of God. He continues by offering himself as an archetype for church authority. He says, "For even the Son of Man did not come to be served, but to serve and to give His life as a ransom for many."[20] Keeping true to His word He did finally give His life as a ransom. This teaching is further validated by such scriptural vignettes as, "If

---

[19] Mark 10:42-44, NKJV.
[20] Mark 10:45, NKJV.

anyone desires to be first, he shall be last of all and servant of all,"[21] and again, "For whoever exalts himself will be abased, and he who humbles himself will be exalted."[22] There are more. In fact, the entire life of Jesus as portrayed throughout the three synoptic Gospels and almost all of John is seen as one not exercising power over anyone, not even the evil ones who opposed him. Yet while not openly brandishing power Jesus, filled with God's glory and power, was seen as one who epitomized the authority of God.

It is easy to see from reviewing the teachings of Jesus why the church is so reticent in denying the widespread existence of political power forces at work in the local church and throughout the denominational systems. One may ask why after two thousand years is this phenomenon just now becoming such a matter of concern for local leaders. Examples of pejorative power being wielded to the detriment of society and the church have already been cited from hundreds of years ago. I believe there are two reasons. First, the seat of power has moved down into the local church, your church. Second, the day-to-day power being exerted has greater efficacy in a more speedy fashion than ever before.

The stories cited above of political power, pejoratively used to create horror in the church, all emanate from power sources hierarchically placed. Chief priests, deans, popes,

---

[21] Mark 9:35,NKJV.
[22] Luke 14:11,

Renaissance or Ruin

archbishops, bishops, and archdeacons became involved in forcing their will upon their contemporaries and peers. In many instances lay people were pulled into the struggle and became victims along with the lesser priests and parish monks who had been traditionally the victims of the carnage that resulted from these upper level power struggles. Still, however, the struggle for power and authority was centered in high places. Many local parish priests and other incidental victims were unaware of what was going on.

In the Holy Roman Empire (Germany) during the sixteenth century The One Hundred Years War between Protestants and Catholics was typical of this pattern. The rule of civil law in the empire was structured so that whatever religion the reigning monarch of a particular political division or duchy was, the people would be that same religion. As a ruler was killed, deposed or died of natural causes he would be supplanted with another. Therefore a peasant in the valley or the vicar of a small village church in the Black Forest may have been shifted from one religion to another on a yearly basis as the power struggle played out, Protestant to Catholic and Catholic to Protestant, throughout the bloody Hundred Years War.

Thanks to American democracy and American civil law, congregational control of one sort or another is almost universally practiced in the United States. Thanks to local congregational control, ecclesiastical power, formerly generated in the cathedral and the bishoprics, now lives in the administrative board room or the parlor where the church council meets. This trend is now beginning to appear even in the Roman Catholic church which has traditionally seen itself as inexorably apostolic with almost total control emanating from the Vatican. However, beginning with the German Catholics in Brooklyn, New York and Boston as early as the 1880's, an undeniable clamor was heard in American Catholicism to have power shared at the local level. Only the great migration of Italian Catholics at the turn of the century forestalled the Roman church's march toward tighter congregational control (Germans followed the northern European model, the Italians followed the Roman model). Today, however, subsequent to Vatican II, the power of the Vatican has been weakened and hierarchical power is coming closer to being vested securely in the United States Conference of Catholic Bishops. Pope John Paul II leads a conservative move attempting to strip the local diocese of their fledgling power while the publication <u>Catholic World Report</u> champions this regressive cause. This reverse power shift, however, cannot succeed - the power module is rolling in the opposite direction.

On the local level, parish councils are exercising much greater authority over decisions in each diocese than ever before. Formerly, priests were sent to the local parish church with no consideration or thought to the congregation. No

Renaissance or Ruin

longer is that done. Any bishop doing that today would risk a real rebellion from the pews. With declining membership resulting in money becoming a scarce resource, parishioners now realize that the purse strings of the "church international" are being controlled in the parish council meeting. The administration of the church no longer rides solely on the authority of its clergy alone, but now meat-cutters, teachers, parents, and car salesmen have become the power center of the church. Even here one cannot expect a smooth transfer of power as it descends through the church. Any observer can sense in Catholic writings and pronouncements the desperate attempt of the clergy and the Vatican to re-exert clerical authority. This, however, is a lost cause and the Roman Church can expect a monumental shift in its power complex within the next decade.

While the Roman Church is just now beginning to feel this shift, mainline Protestants are caught firmly in its grip. In the United Church of Christ, for example, congregational autonomy has become so strong that it is deemed almost a sin for a local parishioner to view the General Synod's policies as praiseworthy. Conference workers and executives painfully realize that their livelihood is 100% dependent on ever shrinking funds from the local parish. Therefore, if the "politically correct" thing to do in the local church becomes to "dump" the General Synod, then that will be done. And if, as is the case in one U.C.C. state conference, it becomes politically expedient to no longer fund the denomination in a particular area, keeping the money at the conference level, then that will be done. In the example cited above as in the Roman Church, dwindling membership has resulted in shrinking revenue. A situation then develops rendering revenue as the primary source of power consideration at all levels of the church. God, authority, mission, and message all become secondary. The main activity of all persons concerned becomes the raising of funds, resulting in money and its holders as the only base consideration for decisions. In this climate the local church can become as a child who has all kinds of independence and power, but with little or no accountability.

This shifting of power from upper seats to the local church, based on the scarcity of capital at the higher level, is an excellent example of the *Strategic Contingency Theory*.[23] This view of social organization sees power as something that accrues to individual companies, departments, or in this case, a point in the church structure, the local church lay administration (cadre or sponsors). This is the place where the allocation of a scarce resource (in this case cash) is decided. According to the tenets of this theory, power rarely organizes around abundant resources. After all, if there is a plethora of an item, the holding or controlling of that item does little to

---

[23] D. J. Hinkson, C. R. Hinings, C. A. Lee, R. E. Satineck, J. M. Pennings. "A Strategic Contingency Theory of Intra Organizational Power". Administrative Science Quarterly. June 1971, 216-229.

enhance the importance of its owner or controller. Additionally, both environmental conditions and the core players of an organization need to agree on the importance of a particular need in order for the fulfiller of that need to receive power.

Across the length and breadth of the mainline church money has become critical due to the lack of it in the system. Today most local churches can barely meet their own needs, let alone pass money upward to support denominational programs and executives. The once asset rich Roman Church can no longer depend on the appraised value of its art treasures to seat its power at upper levels. As a priest friend recently said, "In this day and age who would pay $10,000,000 for a 400 square foot Michelangelo to hang in their living room?" His statement illustrates that, here too, the scarce resource becomes the strategic contingency in a cash poor environment.[24]

In between the purely local power model of the congregational system and the totally hierarchical power model of the Catholic Church we find the United Methodist Church, whose hierarchical emphasis has historically been most intense, but is no longer working as a single power system. Thanks

---

[24] For a more complete treatment of the Strategic Contingency Theory see:
Gerald R. Salancik & Jeffery Pfeffer. "Who Gets Power and How They Hold On To It: A Strategic Model of Power". Organizational Dynamics. 1977, 5:3-21, 3-20.

primarily to the efforts of Francis Asbury (1745 - 1816), the Methodist regional or state conference was vested by the members of the local church with sole authority. The book of discipline kept everything and everyone in line. The preacher was changed so often that he never outlasted his honeymoon or the welcome (and never became a threat to local power chieftains), and the funds of the local church had a primary mortgage on them (apportionments) by church law. The apportion levied by the conference had to be paid by the local church in order to remain in good standing with the conference.

Gradually, however, that too is going by the wayside. Due to the appearance of widespread financial abuse by the conferences and because conference politics became so out of touch with local needs, would-be members, old members and the young of the current members have abandoned the local church. Recently, as Bishop Richard Wilke penned his prophetic and now widely read book And Are We Yet Alive?, he asked Lyle Schaller, America's best known authority on congregational life, to comment on the United Methodist "system." Schaller's reply went as follows:

> 1. Currently "the system" rewards numerical decline and punishes growth. (Who receives the subsidies?)

2. The system encourages pastorates of two to five years rather than long pastorates. Longer pastorates stimulate growth.

3. The graduates of some seminaries are more likely to be pastors of numerically growing churches than are the graduates of other seminaries, but this is not a factor in advising people on which seminary to attend.

4. The first priority is to take care of pastors; taking care of churches is a lower priority.

5. Big congregations account for a disproportionately large share of new members received every year, but the number of large congregations has shrunk by one-third since the 1968 EUB/Methodist merger.

6. The capability to pastor a numerically growing church is not a factor in admitting ministers to conference membership.

7. The compensation system rewards pastors who leave the pastorate for a denominational position rather than rewarding ministers who remain in the pastorate. (Exceptions do exist.)

8. The new church development process now requires a series of permission-giving steps that discourage new church development.

9. Motion pictures are the most effective channel of communication to move a congregation from decline to growth, but the United Methodist Church chooses to emphasize the printed word and slides to change attitudes.

10. The women's organization (United Methodist Women and its antecedents) once was organized around principles that were inclusionary and now is organized around exclusionary principles.

11. The organizing principles advocated for youth ministries tend to result, ten years later, in those youth not being active members of any church, or at least not in a United Methodist congregation.

12. In a world that offers people choices, the UMC tends to offer two choices-take it or leave it-rather than three or four choices.

Schaller concluded:

I expect, Bishop, that you may find that the present United Methodist Church value system will make it impossible to change most of the present operational policies that appear to inhibit numerical growth. That may place your committee in the position advising pastors and congregations who want to see their congregation reach, serve, and include more people to ignore much of the present UMC value system and many of the current operational policies."[25]

Increasingly Methodists, like the Congregationalists, find many conferences bankrupt and unable to wield authority over the local church. Because of seriously declining memberships these two denominations, and most other mainliners, have authority systems that no longer work. Many conferences and denominational executives are out to "save their own necks," irrespective of who they harm. Pastors live in constant fear of losing not only their jobs, but more importantly their health insurance and pensions. Simultaneously, a myriad of local church leaders wield their power, which is based on the scarcity of resources and people, over the entire system. This local cadre rules over a local church which is growing ever smaller and that it desires to keep small and poor. The rationale of these local power brokers is simple: If their local churches were to grow and prosper, money and people would no longer be a Strategic Contingency, and subsequently they would lose their power edge. It is for this reason that the local church power core continues to "farm failure."

It should be noted again that all the charges levied above can be said of all mainline churches. I've chosen the United Church of Christ, the Roman Catholic Church, and the United Methodist Church because they represent a broad cross

---

[25] Wilke, 61-62.

section of the institutional power paradigms. For example, Leonard Sweet began writing Quantum Spirituality as a prophetic critique only to his own United Methodist denomination. However, he found a welcome audience in other church groups due to the profound truths he tells.

Power has indeed moved down, all the way down to the local church. As we have noted previously this local "tribal house," already in a retreat mode, thus becomes even more isolated. It seeks non-affiliation, smallness and is currently unaccountable to any higher authority (including God). Local leadership has become survival management. Resources, pastors, worship modes and goals are "selected" to encourage failure and the power struggles formerly unseen by the rank and file of the church are now a part of their lives seven days a week. Anarchy has replaced order just as surely as failure has replaced success.

This then leads to the second reason for our current awareness of political power being wielded in the "old church parlor." When one sees power plays up close on a day-to-day basis, especially in "God's house" where such things "don't take place," such awareness can become addictive and all enslaving. The human response to this atmosphere can lure others normally repulsed by such political maneuverings into the excitement of the action. Common sense and "The Cause" are soon forgotten and is replaced by the promise of winning.

Very Best Friends

In 1989, the cadre of the First Church was dissatisfied with its pastor. He was fresh from seminary and was highly idealistic. He loved to work with youth and was obsessed with working for God in his first parish. In the beginning the little church of ninety was impressed by his love and ambition, but the love soon turned to hate. The attendance on Sunday morning rose steadily from a low of 88 to 110 in eight months; within a year it topped at 209. The youth group grew from 4 to 63, the Sunday school grew by 800%. The weekly income of the church skyrocketed from $1100 to $2600. The power cadre became incensed. The reason? Their political power base, scarcity, was eroding. This coterie of long-term leaders had based their power on their control of scarce resources (people and money). Therefore, they needed the church to be in chronic failure in order to wield that power. When these conditions were no longer present, they felt the need to fight for survival.[26] They had become addicted to holding the power to such a degree that even church success could not replace its narcotic-like effect.

As scores of lay people (the energy factor - the people in the pew) watched helplessly and in disbelief, the cadre attacked the pastor. They used every committee opportunity to try to discredit his every movement. When he'd go on vacation for three or four days, new complaint venues would

---

[26]   Pfeffer, 69-70.

be drawn and redrawn. They enlisted a powerful denominational political player to see that the conference hierarchy received a constant flood of complaints which resulted in questioning his every move at the state level. Rather than standing up for right and efficacy, politically motivated conference officials were able to block his ordination effort. Finally the local leadership attacked the youth program, the new pastor's greatest success, openly ripping the young people of the church to shreds. Friends of the pastor were offered subtle rewards to become chameleons of the cadre, and unaligned satellites were pressured to align more strongly.[27]

Within months of the height of the two year success period the pastor left, the youth left, most of the newcomers left, the money left, the excitement left, and some long term leaders left. The reason for this great abandonment was that friends and relatives saw their lifelong acquaintances becoming evil, ugly people in an open war for power and control that obviously had no place in God's house. The church of Jesus Christ had become forever spoiled for over one hundred and fifty people, another generation had become aware of cliques and power struggles in the church and First Church returned to

---

[27] Pfeffer, 44. Note: "Chameleon" is a term used by group dynamics experts to describe persons whom "hang around the chief power players and try to imitate them, doing as they do. "Satellites" are those riding on the coattails of the main power actor. Satellites may be from other power clusters, but may align with a secondary power leader to achieve a particular goal. Most members of a group's cadre can be thus classified.

its former pattern of chronic failure, which has become worse over the years.

As power in the church increasingly vests at the local level, and as the provincial interest of local churches become the foundation of ministry worldwide, we can expect to see the outreach ministry of the entire church become more inwardly focused. Once an organism enters the stage of chronic failure (your church may already be there) any effort to save it by reversing the trend will be met by vicious reactions from friends on the church council or board. If a church is failing, it's failing because the members and the leaders want it to fail. If your church is not growing, it doesn't want to grow. The only hope is for the membership to redirect leaders or chose new leadership. The first task of the church member is to become aware of the way power is working (pejorative or productive) in his or her church. These lay people must be willing to ask questions and demand answers. Most of all, to save our local church and perhaps our faith tradition, we, both clergy and lay, must be willing to lose some "very best friends."

As a final note, First Church stabilized at 90 members after the pastor left. Four years from that date, however, the church split again over the issue of expected growth, and on Pentecost Sunday, 1993, forty-four long-term members left the church and joined another local Evangelical church. The power players are now alone numbering below forty persons as

Britt Minshall

active members. As I write, a motion to close the 200-year-old church is being considered.

TRIGGER POINTS

1. Name and discuss power plays you've witnessed at a denominational or state conference level.

2. Were there far reaching consequences of these actions? Were there victims?

3. How are "whistle blowers" or other persons who challenge the status quo treated in business? In government? In the church?

4. Are power struggles apparent where you work? List and compare power actors' personalities.

5. List five examples of power used *productively* in your church.

6. Do the same for *Pejorative* power.

7. Discuss Lyle Schaller's twelve observations on the Methodist system and relate these points to your denominational system.

8. What would be helpful for local church members to be aware of in their handling of power at the congregational level?

CHAPTER III

THE POWERS THAT BE

On a warm evening in May of 1993, Tom and Kathy announced that they were leaving their small California church in order to return to Texas to seek better jobs. The couple, a typical nuclear family (Mom, Dad, and three small children) had been one of the most popular families at St. Ives Church, and this news was devastating to many people who knew and loved them.

Typical of small church etiquette, the news went out through the congregation that someone ought to do something for the departing family. Also typical of small churches, there was no organization or structure to allow this to happen, so when Mary, an older woman in the church, said she'd do something, the matter was dropped as a job that was completed. Nothing was said until the last three days when, quite by accident, it was discovered that Mary had indeed planned a party - a private party. She and Tonya, one of the matriarchs and main power holders in the church, had joined forces and decided to give a farewell reception at Mary's home inviting a "chosen" cross-section of the church.

Those invited were from both of the power centers in the small church, but primarily from what I'll call the "Aristocracins"[1] (power force #1). Some of those invited had known Tom and Kathy for several years. Many, however, had known the couple for only a few months. These newcomers that were invited all had one thing in common: They were seen as the up-and-comers in both the church and the community. The active membership of the church was about 125; twenty percent of the church was invited. The other eighty percent, among them the majority of the people who had been long term friends of the couple, were heartbroken, angry, and hostile.

What you have just read wasn't an account of a going-away party, it was in reality a homecoming party, given by a center of power. The Aristocracins were using the departing event of one couple to demonstrate their political power, and to exhibit their powers to the rest of the church. By staging this event using the control of a strategic and scarce resource (the leaving, celebrity couple and the hostesses for this "in"

---

[1] I will use this term throughout the book. It is my term for modern day "Guardians" (Plato's Republic). These social Darwinists believe their high level of accomplishment in business and professional life makes them particularly suited for church and civic leadership. In most church settings only one family holds title to this patrician center of power. However, this family is quickly surrounded by "lesser" souls acting as chamelions or satellites. This power bloc is the Aristocracy of the church.

Renaissance or Ruin

event) the matriarch of power center number one was establishing the power base of the group. This was the place to be, there was no alternative, and to be invited said "you're in," to be excluded was to remind you that "you're out." This event also served as a recruiting event for the Aristocracins.

In 1944, C. S. Lewis delivered an address to the students of Kings College, London. He used the opportunity to warn the students of an undiscussed phenomenon that was the true driving force behind society. This force, that Tolstoi referred to as the second or "unwritten system" of society, is now called *power politics*. Lewis assured the students of its pervasive nature, telling them it was very present in their school as well as whatever hospital, court, business, or college they might frequent.[2] He said this force, which he appropriately named *the Inner Ring*, was present even in the diocese. He, coming from a different era, was referring to the professional clergy within the church. Today, however, this inner ring permeates the local church as well as the halls of government.

C. S. Lewis informed the student body that a major force in human life is "the desire to be inside the local ring and the terror of being left outside." Author Cheryl Forbes talks of this power center being the basic force under which all human organizational work and its operation is the common

---

[2] Cheryl Forbes, The Religion of Power, (Grand Rapids, Zondervan Publishing House, 1983), 12.

51

denominator linking most, if not all, human activity.[3] If one wants "in," for either *power* - need, *achievement* - need, or *affiliation* - need, one should play by the rules of Lewis' Inner Ring. Those wanting in will walk the walk, talk the talk, wear the proper dress.

The thing one learns from interposing C.S. Lewis with the Aristocracins' party held at Mary's house is how the power wielders (the leaders of the inner ring), use the affiliation desire of people or the fear of dis-affiliation, which is even more pervasive in our society of lonely people, to control the loyalty of those both inside and outside of their group. The need for satisfaction becomes the *strategic contingency*. If the power wielder purports to fill that need, the follower joins the ring.

Actually, the principle here is much like the principle involved in the judo lessons I received during my police training twenty years ago. If an assailant is coming at you, you control the situation by using the assailant's own body forces to put him/her in the position most advantageous to you. The power wielder is skillful at going along with the fears and desires of people to put them where the power-wielder wants them in order that these now controlled subjects do the power-holder's bidding. Often, those controlled do not realize they are being manipulated.

---

[3] Forbes, 22.

There are three basic things I should like to look at in this chapter:

- *The power personality*
- *The tools of power*
- *Power at work in the local church.*

The Power Personality

Let's go back to St. Ives and look at its political make-up. This exercise should make it easier for the reader to evaluate the power system in his or her church. At St. Ives there are two power centers. I have named these the "Aristocracins" and the "No Group." There are however, three charismatic personalities that govern, even overshadow, church life. The three are Thomas P., Nelson A., and Louise M. The three are notable because they embody the archetype of every personality seen in the social setting.[4] They also form the driving force in any organization, church, group, business or government body. These personality structures, or "complexes," have many sub-groupings and ways of acting out. From infancy, however, they are found in every person with respect to social interaction dynamics.

---

[4] Although St. Ives, the people, and the situation described is fictional, combinations of these personalities are typical of easily 70% of American churches. No value judgments are intended to be offered in any of the case studies in the book.

The first of these motivator complexes (the *need to achieve*) is exemplified by the behavior pattern of Thomas P., the titular head of the Aristocracins. Thomas is a business man of some success having over twenty employees and an excellent local reputation. He is ambitious, but exhibits a mild mannered personality. Thomas has served as an officer of the church for many years. His father is the founding patriarch of the church. Dad is a millionaire, rising from the California frontier business days; a self-made man of the first order.

The second of these complexes (the *need for power*) appears quintessentially in the life and actions of Nelson A. Nelson is an editor at a local publishing house and is the most educated man in the congregation. Nelson is seen as the leader of the "No group." He has served for years as the head of the Property Committee. Nelson is a very empirical person, he tends to think strictly in a conservation mode and possesses little ability or desire to stretch to achieve anything beyond present reality. In spite of the positive force of his graduate school education, his laid back personality has apparently kept him from acting on any dream of personal success he may have had in his youth.

Lastly, meet Louise M., who represents the third personality complex and motivator (the *need for affiliation*). Louise is a latent alcoholic and exhibits a high degree of "hyper-retensivity."[5] This fear of loss is common, especially

---

[5] Inordinent fear of change or letting go of things, including money.

among the post-Depression generation since many families experienced losses during the formative years of the children born from 1930 through 1940. This reality of loss, and perhaps shame, created in Louise a dread fear of parting with anything and an even greater fear of losing her affiliate relationship in the church. This relationships has replaced her nuclear family. There appear to be several other hidden fears that plague her family. All these factors combine to create a high level of paranoia that manifests itself in a combative behavior mode.

These three are rather typical of millions of other men and women of our communities. The needs that drive their social inter-action (*achievment-power-affiliation*) form the common basis of all human social engagements. Numerous combinations of these behavior complexes can be found in every church, business, and family. Also remember that while typical, the personalities of these three are not the only manner in which these needs manifest themselves. The reason is that in every person one of these three needs becomes primary; however, riding under the primary need in each person there are secondary and tertiary needs that interact with each of the primary ones. For example, while Thomas interacts socially mainly out of a need to achieve, he also has strong secondary needs of affiliation which mitigate the primary need. Further, he, like all of us, has a need for power which, to the extent it is present in a person's life, will alter that person's final public or political personality.

We develop our social power attitudes and political personality slowly. As we mature the ideas that will form our power posture impact our choice of the "inner rings" (power centers) to which we either affiliate or disassociate. This development process strongly mirrors Freud and later Erikson's models of our ever growing involvement with the world outside ourselves. When dealing with others in the church setting it helps to know something of this process that David McClelland calls "the classification of power orientation."[6]

Beginning at infancy, says McClelland, our power is seen as coming from others. If all goes well we develop an appreciation that power comes from outside ourselves like the milk from mother's breast. During this "*Stage I*" process of growth we realize that "it (power) strengthens me." Later in life, again if all goes well, we are able to draw strength from others. Our mates, our friends, our church family are seen as trustworthy to deliver to us the things we need. If the growing organism (person) is well served and finds trust enough to go on to the next stage, the child will prefer to internalize his/her knowledge and then move forward. If there is little trust, this person will stay where he/she is, and adopt a "clienthood

---

[6] David C. McClelland, Power: The Inner Experience, (New York, Irvington Publishers, 1975), 13.

Renaissance or Ruin

status" in life. These people are most happy serving other more powerful people.

In your church, a person "stuck" at this level will tend to practically "kill themselves working around the church." They will be very respectful of not only the "Reverend" but also tend to see the educated, accomplished leaders of the church as masters worthy of service. No matter how hard these *Stage I* people work in your church they will never be invited to be part of the "inner ring." The power-wielders "use" this type of person as a chameleon (one who imitates the power personality), especially at times when every vote counts. Most often they use the *Stage I* person's desperate desire to affiliate with such an educated or successful person. In one church, a lady named Barbara (*Stage I*, low self-image), a close friend and ally of the local pastor, was "wooed" over to go against her pastor and friend by a skilled power-wielder in the church. In this case a local manufacturing man sought to be the patriarch of the church and saw the opportunity to take that position by dethroning the popular pastor. Barbara's need to be appreciated by influential, successful people was enough to pull her temporarily into the rich man's "inner ring" for just long enough to get her to turn on the pastor. Once the pastor had left the church, the "chameleon"[7] Barbara was relegated to her "rightful" place as an outsider to the church's power center.

---

[7]   See Note 25, Chapter II.

As children grow, most move to *"Stage II,"* the "I strengthen myself" stage. This child soon resents having to depend on others for all its needs, so that she/he begins to exhibit rebellious behavior. Dynamic theorists have spoken for years of this phase, labeling it the anal stage of development during which the child begins willingly to control his or her bowel movements. If a child were to still be at *Stage I* behavior, the child would cry for a half an hour to get a wet diaper changed. At this later age this still might be necessary. However, once cleaned up and changed, *Stage II* is experimented with, and the child will force a pending defecation just to show he/she has control of the diaper and the changes. The by-word at this age is "No." The child cannot "do" (enact) many things, but the child can say, "No," when told to put away its toys or "No" to keeping a clean diaper.

Many people never get past this *Stage II* method of social acting. They are usually marked by many signs: Exaggerated involuntary outbursts, non-success in business life, inability to leave home, and/or a negative pessimistic personality. These persons often develop passive aggressive behavior patterns in order to strengthen themselves. "No" becomes their special symbol and translates into strength and power.

An example of *Stage II* power behavior exhibited in older teenage males follows:

> You are driving west on 76th Street in Miami, Florida (any large urban setting will do). The street is narrow, with cars parked on either side. You're driving in a new Oldsmobile. You're well-dressed and upper middle class and you obviously do not "belong" in this neighborhood. Streets here are lined with much older cars, many abandoned and graffiti-covered. You become aware of your strangeness to this place. All of a sudden, you are stopped in your tracks.
>
> A car with a load of single young men is stopped, blocking the street, while one of them is leaning on the outside of the driver's window talking to those inside. You pull up behind the older beat-up car, but it doesn't move. You can't drive around the blocking car, there isn't enough room. So you wait. After two or three minutes you honk your horn, but the kid outside only responds by giving you a vicious stare to let you know if you do that again "it's all over for you." So you wait, and you'll wait until the boys are good and ready for you to move. Usually they'll play with you, acting like they're moving, but then begin to talk again.

Guess who's got power for perhaps the first time in their lives? Their power over you is based on their ability to say "No, we won't move" and "No, you can't move either!"

This *Stage II* mode of social interaction may result in either or both of two phenomena:

1. Over cautiousness, fear to venture out, fear of letting go (especially of money), and a heavy dose of skepticism or pessimistic decision making, and/or

2. The passive-aggressive[8] failure identification exhibited above in the gang of boys in Miami. In the latter case one's vocational life is seen as so hopeless the only power one can ever hope to exert is to say, "No." This is exemplified by the three year old who continually says "No, I won't pick up my toys," or the teen saying, "No, I won't move my car." Compare this to the faction in a church which stands firm, saying, "No, I won't let the church buy hymnbooks;" or, "No, I vote against the membership drive," or, "No, I won't let the church spend the money on ministry, let's build our reserves."

Of the three dominant personalities at St. Ives, Thomas P. (the achiever) could not very well remain *Stage II* and emotionally survive. Nelson (the power seeker), however, is a *Stage II* person. His power drive combined with his *Stage II* passive-aggressive personality has held the church at a dead

---

[8]   Passive-aggressive is the better known terminology for the personality human resource experts often label passive defensive. Passive defensive more accurately describes this behavior complex.

standstill. The third player, Louise (the affiliator), needs desperately to belong, therefore she acts out a *Stage I* level of servitude, but her hyper-retensivity (don't spend, don't give away, don't change) indicates she is also at *Stage II* in development. In this case Nelson, the power-wielder, befriends Louise, the affiliate, and creates a "satellite" power center. Nelson plays on her fear of change and loss of money by promising to continue to be the "No" power. This appeals to Louise who wants "No" change, "No" new members, "No" spending.

A satellite, unlike a chameleon, usually has his/her own agenda which is adopted by a power player's trade-off and support. In the case of St. Ives you can begin to see a church paralyzed by a dominance of *Stage II* "No"-ism. Remember both Nelson and Louise are big wheels in the "No" party.

"Stage III" maturity levels boasts an "I can have an impact on others" feature. While our churches are replete with Stage I and II people, *Stage III* personalities are not as present unless they sublimate their power traits, which often is done by becoming a pastor or conference official. These folks are the active aggressives[9], the real competitors. They discover during childhood that they can strengthen themselves by controlling others. This "phallic stage" in men is most often apparent

---

[9] Aggressive personalities manifested in the negative are often labeled aggressive defensive. It is the defensive portion of this complex which accounts for the psychopathology.

during the younger years. If all else fails (i.e., control in one's business or vocational pursuits), this control can be directed towards one's spouse and/or children. As the *Stage III* personality gets older, a great number revert to *Stage II* or even *Stage I*, finding *Stage III* uncomfortable (some alternately go on to Stage IV). Those who remain *Stage III* social actors tend to be aggressive entrepreneurs, real operators, or strident failures of the "Archie Bunker"[10] type. *Stage III* people who exhibit pathological or defensive behavior include the mother who smothers her child with such "love" that the child is never permitted to mature or grow to adulthood. In a man, not properly socialized, the *Stage III* personality can revert to crime, particularly white collar crime, or to violence, rape, theft and murder. This person uses sex or property or both to control others. The United States government has often acted in a *Stage III* mode in its dealings with third world countries. We trade arms to tyrannical dictators allowing them to control the populace, reaping slave labor. In this case the resulting power is used to regulate the price of bananas, coffee, or sugar. We thereby steal their natural resources, rape their children's future and violently use troops or mercenaries (the

---

[10] For those too young to remember, Archie Bunker was the chief character in a 1970's sitcom popularized by the portrayal of the all too familiar boisterous, arrogant, controlling bigot Stage III personality.

Contras,[11] for example) when the oppressed peasants rebel. The country's dictator uses our weapons, bought with the blood of the people, to control their labor.

Most individuals with this very high power need orientation soon tire of the Stage I and II laid back, really regressive manner of church life. Mainline "church" people tend not to like *Stage III* folks because they're so "pushy, noisy, and action-oriented." However, a conversion experience to Christ makes the *Stage III* person much more acceptable. This gift of the Holy Spirit redirects the aggressive behavior, shifting the new believer away from alcohol, violence, wife-beating, and peripheral behavior toward a war with the devil. If this person's converted *Stage III* behavior is not properly dealt with during the faith journey, this go-getter will often migrate to higher positions in the church, not realizing that their aggressive behavior may impact on more than just Satan, but the people of the congregation as well.

While mainline denominations have done a "too good" job of weeding out this type from the ministry, thus losing

---

[11] During the decade of the 1980's, the lower and middle class people of Nicaragua rebelled against the oppressive tyranny of the Samosa dictatorship. This regime had acted as a pawn and agent for the interests of the large fruit packing houses of the United States. The Sandenistas (winners of the revolution and arm of the indigenous people) attempted to bring stability to the country. However, the former wealthy class hired an army to be outfitted and supplied by the Reagan administration, against the rules of the U. S. Congress, to overthrow the legitimate new government. This army of mercenaries called themselves the contras.

some badly needed sublimated aggressiveness, fundamentalist groups extol this type of behavior, resulting in churches that are literally one-man kingdoms. It should be remembered when dealing with *Stage III* personalities that God made them, too. When converted they work for the kingdom no less effectively than Stage II or IV personalities. Saul of Tarsus, heading out from Jerusalem, fresh from his stoning of Stephen the Christian, was most assuredly a *Stage III* active-aggressive personality. The same, but now converted, Paul of Tarsus was no less a *Stage III* personality, even after an encounter with Christ and a subsequent fifteen year nurturing in the church. When he finally "hit the road" for God, he fathered the Western church. Peter the Fisherman, Billy Sunday, R. W. Shambach, Francis of Assisi, Charles Finney, John Newton, and this writer are examples of the Stage III converts.

If the traditional church has made any serious mistakes during the past forty years, the determination that this aggressive personality type has no place in the denominational church is at the top of the list. The result has been the loss of a great reservoir of professional and lay leaders. Also this type behavior pattern, often resembling a salesperson with an exaggerated sense of immediacy, forms the nucleus of any evangelical force destined to replenish the church with persons outside its ranks.

Historically the American Church, which grew in leaps and bounds from 1750-1920, was replete with men and women "on fire for the Lord" -- now you would be hard-pressed to find any in a Mainline Church.

The "*Stage IV*" power matrix is signaled by the subject's belief that, "Power moves me way beyond myself to do my duty" - to do what's right is the thinking theme of this level of personality. It's a "super ego" level of action that nurtures the highest levels of social ideals. Jesus himself would be a great example of this level of being, but it goes beyond Him to be exemplified by the lives of certain people in every generation. Most churches do not have one of these people, so we won't spend much time on the study of this personality. These folks are truly slaves to the highest righteous calling of God. Abraham Lincoln, Ghandi, Martin Luther King Jr., President Jimmy Carter in his post-presidency ministry, and the apostle Paul in his later years, fit into this mold. The main thing to remember about a *Stage IV* personality is, if you do meet one, help him or her to feel loved and support his/her efforts. These "chosen ones" of our species engender the greatest hatred from the merchants of evil in our society. All too often these crusaders find themselves alone and unsupported, even by their closest friends. Also caution is suggested. *Stage IV* people can be drawn, by pejorative power forces, into a messianic relationship with others. The same personality that is willing to use productive power for a higher authority (Thomas Becket) may, likewise, surrender all to a lower pejorated power (Adolph Hitler).

Every other person who populates the church falls into one of these molds. There is inherently neither good nor bad in any type and yet the possibility exists in all of them for both good and evil. Each person's motives and desires then bend and twist his or her individual energy to interact with the community to form that person's collective social power structure which is then either *productive* or *pejorative*.

The Tools of Power

St. James Church had always been known to be one of the most progressive Baptist churches in the south. Yet on Sunday, June 2, 1978 the pastor stood in the pulpit with a 30.06 rifle on the podium, warning the leadership of the church not to go near the parsonage or someone would be hurt. The pastor's eighteen year old daughter was graduating from high school and had decided to host a graduation party for her close friends. "Great idea," had been the response of Deacon Jesse Jones, whose daughter was a friend of the graduate. Great, that is, until he found out that a black girl was also invited to the parsonage party. "Not in my church's parsonage," said Jesse.

During the next month deacons met and the voice of ministry was stifled as Raleigh watched the church eat itself alive with hate. At 11:00 A.M. the day before the party, a brick came flying through the window of the parsonage narrowly missing the pastor's two year old child asleep on the couch. His wife saw the car and realized three of the church's officers were involved. Thus, the Sunday following, the pastor appeared in the pulpit using the rifle and the microphone to inveigh against the racist attack on his home.

Samuel Wesley, father of the founder of Methodism, John Wesley, and his entire family barely missed death in 1706 as angry parishioners burned Samuel, their pastor, out of his vicarage. A century before this, Richard Topcliffe, who lived near Westminster Abby and was a champion of Protestantism, tortured Catholic priests in his own home and enjoyed every minute of it, once even admitting, "Yes, you are Christ's fellows," all the time laughing as the priests came near bleeding to death.

These are all examples of *pejorative power* at work in the church. One might hope that your church will suffer far less than the Wesleys or the pastor with the rifle. However, this same vicious force, manifested as infighting and factionalism, ruins church after church. While less spectacular or newsworthy than the medieval torture chambers of the Inquisition, nevertheless, it brings churches to failure - from which they cannot recover.

Power at Work in Local Church

The Church of the Samaritan had been a successful parish. Minor petty fighting had been abundant, but, in a single encounter in 1970 the church power structure went sour.

Many tend to date the church's destruction from that event, which is not completely true. A church develops its personality posture primarily from the combined ethos of its leaders or managers (power centers) and their primary motivators. A church does not "go bad" because of a single incident. We should also remember that the power players in each church serve at the behest of the people in the pews. Therefore, to say that the power core is completely responsible and the rank and file are "squeaky clean" would be fallacious.

    At Samaritan, while all appeared peaceful, during the golden era of its most revered pastor, a group dynamic was developing that was to eventually be its downfall. The choir director had a nasty way of rebelling against the pastor. If he didn't like the song he would stop singing in the middle of the song and change the selection. The pastor watched with chagrin, but did not dare challenge him. He had become closely attached to the family that was the nucleus of the power group. This "Aristocracin" family had the numbers and the money. Most of the rest of the people in the pews were either too elderly to know or care, or too busy with their own affairs to challenge the status quo. The patriarch's children grew up in the church and the beloved pastor did much to accomplish their rearing. All the while, a gradually growing acceptance of nasty tantrums (aggressive-defensive behavior) began to be accepted behavior among the core members of the congregation. Temper flashes began to be the way to do business (*Stage II*

Renaissance or Ruin

behavior). Even though issues would be resolved, a mistrust of each other developed and became psycho-pathological in the church.

Also during this period the chief patriarch of the family refused to submit to the lay authority and did as he pleased. He did not give regularly thus establishing a pattern of non-giving. Instead he would give to particular pet projects. Often these would be spectacular and otherwise unachievable by the poor small congregation. These gifts included a giant stained-glass window, two parking lots, an educational building and a twenty-passenger van.

Remember that every person in a social setting exhibits a power profile (Stage I, II, III, or IV), and that these profiles are attached to that person's needs in a social encounter (achievement-power-affiliation). With this in mind, let's analyze the personalities of Samaritan.

The family patriarch (raised in poverty, with an absentee father, a mother who kept things together by sheer luck, precociously sent to work to bring home the bacon) developed easily into a *Stage III* controller. His psychological need in the church setting was first for *power* (he needed that to control all encounters, thus avoiding another precarious childhood). Fulfillment of this need, however, took on an ironic twist, in that he acted out the image of the benevolent father he missed as a child. His secondary need was for *affiliation*. This replaced the sense of security he missed due to his loss of family stability. He met his *achievement* need by becoming a great business success, but in doing this no sense of belonging to a family had been realized (business relationships don't often supply this need). His resulting psychological profile follows:

- Heavy *Stage III* controller

- A high need for *power*

- Elevated need for *affiliation* which developed into a smothering love for the church.

The church became ever more oppressed under his "ownership." In part, the nasty behavior exhibited by the members toward each other was the congregation's way of venting anger, much as a frustrated toddler would do over the lack of self-determination in his/her own affairs. The congregation slowly became more and more inactive, more and more dependent.

The patriarch's son, Brett, had throughout the years built a personality antithetical to his father's. In most cases a domineering father will produce at least one son who is a "milque toast." Brett was the most quiet and unassuming of the patriarch's four sons, consequently, he continually received the patriarch's disdain. This has turned Brett into a vacillator between *Stage I* and *Stage III* power complexes. He wants to be a follower, he longs to be the low guy on the totem pole,

Renaissance or Ruin

thus fulfilling his dad's negative prophecy. However, his fear of emotional castration by his father, and fear of failure in life, leads him to try to be a power player. He has never, according to his father, succeeded in business "like his brothers did" (he has in fact done very well). Consequently, Brett became his father's underling and successor in the church (the church became the relational point for the two). Brett's social portrait looks like this:

- He is primarily a *Stage I* orientor

- Has a high need to *achieve*,

- with a secondary and elevated need to *affiliate* ("If I can only please Dad and be loved by someone").

I, and indeed many other men in our churches, can relate easily to Brett. While our backgrounds and parents may differ, the parental stimuli and relationship is so similar that we've ended up being about the same people, socially speaking. We are endlessly attempting to please our parents, having little success and, therefore, adopting the society around us to fulfill our need to belong.

Now into the church enters Robert and his wife Delores. When these folks joined the congregation in 1969 a great shift was about to take place. When environmental shifts take place within any group, company, nation, or church, the result is often war, and it was. Robert too had something to prove to his parents, to his wife Stephanie, and to himself. Robert is a *Stage II* power orientor, probably due to many disappointments in childhood and adult life that said, "Play it safe, don't rock the boat." Robert therefore, became an avowed pessimist and acts out as a passive-aggressive. His social need is *power*, as he tries to control a world he sees as unsafe. His secondary need is for *achievement;* he feels deprived because he is "stuck" in a career not of his choosing.

Robert's wife is also a *power* seeking person. Many writers discount this need in women and focus on men only; I believe this is a major mistake. The only difference between most men and women with regard to power profiles is that most men will issue power challenges openly (males are raised to be competitors, and this trait in males is valued), while females seek power through relationships. The church in America, with its lack of prohibition against females in leadership positions, is particularly prone to foster power complexes, often latent in women due to societal pressure. In 1970 it was not yet socially acceptable to be a female power seeker[12].

Delores, however, appears to also suffer from a genuine fear of life - paranoia even. She reports she was brought up in an abusive, alcoholic family. Persons reared in this environment often suffer from fear of abandonment which,

---

[12] McClelland, 91-93.

Renaissance or Ruin

in Delores' case developed into full-fledged paranoia. All of these circumstances worked together to harvest a real hatred of God and a mistrust of the male figure.

When these two strong, often negative personalities hit Samaritan Church, a shift occurred. A new power bloc was about to be born. An informal understanding developed between Robert and Delores and Brett and Stephanie. They were all about to get even with their dads and grab the power in the church from the hands of the patriarch and his generation.

The encounter you are about to witness is played out in hundreds of churches each year. I will label this method of church war "the gunfighter strategy," a familiar plot in movies of the old West. The new would-be champion in town would "draw down" on the most powerful gunfighter in the area. If the old gunfighter was killed, the challenger, no matter how young and inexperienced (many were mere children), became the new power holder.

The chosen victim in the case of Samaritan Church was not the town Marshall, but rather the venerable and popular pastor. Pastors make easy targets because they're not supposed to fight back. This new breed of power players (the coalition of the new-comers [Robert and Delores] and the young challengers of the Aristocracins [Brett and Stephanie]) were able to secure the pastor's resignation, thus satisfying their needs for *power, achievement,* and *affiliation* in one fell swoop. The coup d'état was accomplished and the people in the pew were blind to the proceedings.

This story is told in such depth in order to let the reader realize how involved church "powers that be" are in their makeup and involvement. Samaritan, even though fictious, is typical of the inter-generational, inter-cultural, and inter-personal group dynamics that power the engines of many small- or medium-sized church. For years clergy, and lay people alike have far over-simplified the political forces in the church. Most "churched" people have become aware of the "inner-ringism" present in the church (they call it the clique), but few people have any idea of how complex, organized, and often destructive these forces, unchallenged, can be.

Even more astonishing, few have realized that these forces may actually be the main culprit in the destruction of the American mainline church. Now that we find our churches in chronic failure we must take time to look carefully at our leaders and at ourselves, examining each of our motivators. We can ask,

- ✓ What's really going on here?
- ✓ What are we doing with this church?
- ✓ Are we building or destroying God's house?
- ✓ Do we all agree this is God's house?
- ✓ What is the center of our church, love or power?

Since the power of relationships was at the core of the building of our churches, then the power of relationships must be at the heart of its problem.

As it now stands, it would appear that the pejorative power of negative personalities in relationships will be the downfall of a once great church. Soon the "powers that be" in the church - may be the "powers that were" in the church that is no longer.

As a final note to Samaritan's story, the promising future and ongoing success at the Church of the Samaritan was stopped dead in 1970 with the pastor's resignation. Over fifty members left the church when they realized what had taken place. Several pastors have tried unsuccessfully to revive the church, but it has become hopelessly ensnared in a political war between Brett's family and Robert's family. This infighting between the once formidable allies has rendered the ministry of the church moot -- the church can no longer pay a pastor and faces probable closure.

TRIGGER POINTS

1. Have you ever been either ostracized from or invited into an "inner ring?" Where and When?

2. Have you or someone you've known drastically altered your life or beliefs in order to get into a special group, club, or clique? Why did you or your acquaintance make that sacrifice?

3. Did you get back from the belonging what you expected?

4. Based on your recollection of the three most influential people in your life, do you think they were a Stage I, II, III, or IV power personality?
   ○ Compare your choices and rating with the rest of the group.

5. Write a four paragraph story describing a major event in your church's history that involved prolonged and serious conflict.

6. Were there power factions at work?

7. If the group feels secure enough, share your stories in a non-blaming manner.

CHAPTER IV

POWER, POWER, WHO'S GOT THE POWER?

An argument was erupting in the council meeting at the Second United Church. The church had called one of those "newfangled Bible-believing word preachers" and the powers that be were in revolt against the change. Actually, Pastor Hill was very moderate theologically and liberal socially, which should have made for a good marriage with the Second Church, but it didn't. Every board or council meeting erupted into a confrontation.

On one occasion the pastor was trying to institute the smallest of changes, quite encouraged by the denomination, but as usual there was a vicious counter-attack being levied. The pastor quietly addressed the council and said, "Look, I'm sorry that this much hassle has occurred over this small issue, but please know it's a denominational item and its mandate is quite biblical." The response came quickly from one of the opposition. Dorothy spoke up, "We don't have to listen to the denomination; we never have and as to the Bible that means nothing to us." She was speaking honestly and openly, giving a truthful testimony that should be entered into the mission statements of ninety percent of the small, struggling, often failing mainline churches across the country. What she was reflecting is an attitude endemic in the church of the 1990's. Thousands of churches operate under the precept that, "We do not recognize any authority in this church except our own and that includes our denomination, fellow churches, and most especially the Word." The great theme of the seventies, eighties, and nineties, "We want it our way, we deserve it, we'll take it and that's our business," has become the watchword of the church of the 1990's. These adversarial relationship patterns, while particularly abundant and destructive in the church, are widespread across society[1]

In this chapter we will examine three things. First, we will examine power vs. authority. Following this I shall discuss the negative power complex as manifested in church leadership. Lastly, we will look at the unloving personality, the primary player in the negative use of power.

Power Versus Authority

These two words are inextricably intertwined in common usage, even analogous to one another. Dictionaries

---

[1] Lyle E. Schaller, Strategies for Change, (Nashville, Abingdon Press, 1993), 31-32.

have difficulty defining one without using the other. In truth, there is a world of difference between these concepts, if correctly used, and there is an immense difference in the personality of one community which bows to authority and another community which lives off rule by the powerful.

Simply put, "authority" is power which has become legitimated.[2] In its proper context this power being exerted is extrapolated from, accepted by, and evenly distributed over a broad portion of the society. One of the chief benchmarks in any group's maturation into a community or a society is its institutionalization of control upon itself.[3] A society which is greatest at peace is the community where this "legitimized power" is accepted and not resisted. I shall add to this commentary, however, that the degree to which this authority is then celebrated reflects the level of functionality that can be achieved in any given community setting, all of the above being applicable.

Every society since the beginning of time has developed its own, often unique, criterion of legitimizing power. Most empire builders assumed that in order to be accepted by the local inhabitants as the governing authority, one had only to be

---

[2] Pfeffer, 4.
[3] Control here refers to a community's ordering of its affairs and the actions of its people. Persons exercising authority give up personal control, operating authoritative leadership from the supreme level of "integrated authority." For an excellent treatment of Authority verses Control see Celia A. Hahn. Growing in Authority, Relinquishing Control. Washington, *Congregations: The Alban Journal*, vol. XX, no. 2.

the victor over the indigenous leaders and armies, and ascend the throne of the vanquished. Alexander the Great, Julius Caesar, Charles the Great, Napoleon, and Adolph Hitler all truly believed that you could rule with authority by the imposition of power. That is one of the fatal and false beliefs of the despot. These men all ruled by "power," but never gained authority. Their forces had to be ever-present. If their armies turned their backs, for even a second, the conquered would rebel and try to reestablish that which they formerly accepted as "real authority."

Marshall Tito of Yugoslavia was able to force a state union of several separate entities, including the warring tribe of the Serbs, the tribe of the Croatians, the Muslim peoples of Bosnia and others from Macedonia. The authority of the union was never accepted by any side. Each held tenaciously to its own symbols and myths of legitimized power (authority). Once Tito died and the first ill wind blew in any direction, the forced union came to an end. The sheer power of the Soviet bloc had kept Yugoslavia alive. With no national authority mutually agreed upon, there became "no nation" and a war of separation, a national divorce has resulted.[4]

---

[4] This is a great oversimplification of this exceedingly complex issue. For an excellent, but brief treatment of the historical - political forces at work in Bosnia-Herzegovina, taking note to the Serbian view as well as the other two camps, see Igor Lukes' "The Birth of Our Yugoslavian Tragedy. A Mirror for Our Times and Faces," Bostonia (Spring, 1994): 20-26.

Renaissance or Ruin

In the church of the 1990's the same type of uneasy union is governing our congregations. Factions vie for power, each seeking to control the church either by controlling a scarce resource such as money or by naming themselves as God's prophetic heirs and therefore the legitimate authority. For example, an ongoing power struggle within many religious bodies involves the liberals in opposition to the fundamentalists. In this struggle the symbols of authority and the caches of power would be knowledge/wisdom versus the mandate of God prophetically spoken. To either of the above parties, however, the source of legitimacy is not God, but the acquiescing of the people to a power center, here named liberal or fundamental. The power and authority of God therefore is transferred to political power, that is, the power of people over people.

The two denominations hardest hit by this struggle appear to be the Lutheran groups and the Southern Baptist Convention. In doing a sociological study of these conflicts one soon concludes that there always seems to be a hidden, unspoken agenda that lies at the root of the struggle.

In the case of the Southern Baptists it appears that traditional urban southerners, educated townsfolk, and successful classes of people who matured during the 1950's and '60's are seen as too "sophisticated, educated, and citified" by a large number of the rural undereducated, poorer southerners. This latter group, which includes immigrants and many of the young, felt left behind. These "left behinds" brandished their theological conservatism which is always inherent in rural culture. The resulting, more fundamental theology appeals particularly to new converts and people emerging from uncertainty and confusion. These groups gravitated together. By using their common culture (the feeling of being left behind) converted to a theological cause, they overtook positions held by the hitherto accepted authorities. As an end result there are now two groups, each holding to different authority bases. One, the Cooperative Fellowship, represents the urban, more well-educated group; the other, the Southern Baptist Convention is now peopled almost entirely by less cosmopolitan, more rural members, and persons with less education.[5]

The underlying force at work in these instances is individualization - "I want what I want and it will be as I want it." In this formula the "I" forms the central focus. The people of the congregation laboring under individualization will empower officials and pastors who deliver what "they" want. There will be no thought under this system as to what is right or productive. Therefore, authority has ceased to be something external to one's self or one's church, as is the case

---

[5] Several Black Christian groups have previously suffered from the same problem of cultural differences developing into theological authority issues. The National vs. the Progressive Baptist; the African Methodist Episcopal vs. the Colored (now Christian) Methodist Episcopal church. All of these stories boil down to a power/authority issue.

of a social ethic, religious tradition, denominational canon, or God's word. It has been replaced by an internalized source of power legitimation - a particular community's own desires.

Pillars of Authority

David C. McClelland, as part of his monumental book Power: The Inner Experience, explores the four traditional pillars of authority in the church. These four pillars of the Judeo-Christian concept of authority, you will note, are foreign to the prevailing individualistic ethic now reigning in much of the mainline church.[6] These pillars are:

- *Submission*
- *Control*
- *Sacrifice of Self-interest*
- *Justice*

First, *Submission*; in this case submission to the higher, all present, all knowing authority of the Creator, who is the Lord God Jehovah. We as humans can only gain legitimate authority and power in this world to the degree that we have surrendered to that God. Noah was chosen by God because he found grace in God's eyes and not because he was a great boat builder.[7] Mary was chosen by this God because she was the

---
[6] McClelland, 283.
[7] Genesis 6:8.

"highly favored one,"[8] not because she was the best achiever at motherhood.

Both the major and minor prophets are seen as people who were in submission to God. Few of them, except perhaps the first Isaiah, were men of high accomplishment who received authority from their earthly position or level of education.

The second pillar of authority in the church has traditionally been seen as *Control*. An examination of two millennia of Judeo-Christian root doctrines will reveal that selfishness is at the heart of the corrupted human condition. The middle class American of the twentieth century is seen, worldwide, as a self-centered, ravenous glutton, devouring all the cash, land, food, forests, fields, power and pleasure that he or she can buy, charge, or steal without being challenged. Take note of the busiest place in any shopping mall - it's the food garden. The average middle class child is the proud owner of all sorts of amenities and will refuse to own an "off brand" of clothing, stereo or car.

The average mainline church member is the best fed, best clothed and best traveled person on the face of the globe. That same typical church member does no personal service to the poor, gives far less than the tithe (if he/she gives at all) and responds to prophetic calls to share the secure world of the local church with others by making sure no one enters this

---

[8] Luke 1:28.

Renaissance or Ruin

homogeneous cocoon. Middle class white churches are created to remain middle class white churches.

The same exclusionary practice is true of African Methodist Episcopal, progressive Baptist, and other black middle class churches.[9] Poor uneducated blacks are no more welcome in these churches than they would be in a white church. The store front church is their allotted place. In summary, a huge percentage of mainline American churches are diametrically opposite to unselfish places of ministry where people are encouraged to sublimate their ravenous appetites to own and control all things. Our churches are exclusive - not inclusive, they hoard and do not share. They laud their own power and decry outside authority.

The third traditional pillar of the church can be labeled the *Sacrifice of Self-interest* for the good of all. Recall that the fourth and highest stage of maturity, (outlined in Chapter Three) is the advanced level of growth in a person. It is the time when one is moved to accomplish things, and act out of duty even if it means personal loss. At this level a person understands the collective good to be more important than his/her own happiness and is willing to encourage those of their immediate family or interest group to give up special privileges to see that the entire community of humanity can benefit. We make these people our heroes - Malcolm X, Ghandi, Moses,

---

[9] Dwayne E. Walls, The Chickenbone Special, (New York, Harcourt, Brace, Jovanovich, 1971), 135-139.

Martin Luther King, Jr., and, of course, Jesus. The "intelligentsia" of pre-Soviet Russia were children of the privileged class of 1917, yet they fought and organized to break the back of the imperial power of the Czar, even though it meant the end of their special privileges.

The above idealists hoped to see all people share in the quality of life. The early Christian martyrs from Stephen through Polycarp were of the same mold, they were willing to be stoned or burned to death so that The Faith could continue and grow to the good of all people.

Contrast this life ethic to Ananias and Sapphira's story[10] in the New Testament. While all the believers sold everything that they owned and surrendered it to the community as a whole, this couple came and lived in the community, eating the food bought by all for all, while keeping their fortune for themselves.

Compare this third pillar, "the sacrifice of self-interest," to a contemporary congregation which votes to do what it does using the mandate, "it's in our best self-interest." Today's churches seem to rush to reflect the prevailing political ethic which led our country not to join the rest of the nations of our hemisphere in signing the Global Environmental Treaty of 1992 because it could not "benefit" the United States (already the richest nation on the globe by 4 to 1). Our churches are attempting to pattern themselves after the business climate of

---
[10] Acts 5:1-11.

the 1980's and 1990's that glorifies the creed of "avoiding any expenditure that does not accrue to higher corporate profits." The church, instead of providing an antithesis to profiteering, individualism, selfish interest, enriching politics, and utilitarianism, has become another extension of these godless ethics.

The fourth and final pillar is *Justice*. Here two themes prevail. The first is that believers are required to "be just" in their personal endeavors. This is referred to as personal holiness. The second requires them to call for justice systemically - this we name social holiness. Working from the assumption that God has given the believer much, not even withholding the life of God's Son, that believer is asked to seek justice for all of creation. The scriptures clearly ask this of the Christian, "For everyone to whom much is given, from him (her) much will be required, and to whom much has been committed, of him (her) they will ask more."[11] According to Paul, the very promise of the Holy Spirit, available to all upon entrance into the Kingdom of God, was righteousness (justice), peace, and joy.[12] There can be no doubt that the God of the Hebrew scripture was about justice when the psalmist wrote "Righteousness and justice are the foundation of His (God's) throne."[13]

---

[11] Luke 12:48, NKJV.
[12] Romans 14:17.
[13] Psalms 97:2, NKJV.

From the beginning of the human journey, in virtually every monotheistic tradition and in all ecclesiastical institutions, no one, even the newest, youngest confirmand, could deny these all pervasive themes of our faith. Systemic justice and personal justice or holiness can be given a scriptural validation as we view Jesus' teaching, "I was naked and you clothed me, I was in prison and you came to me."[14] A hypothetical mainline church council may then respond :

But Lord, we took YOU in we didn't ignore YOU!

Jesus might challenge that church asking, "Did you not see the homeless, the thousands going to prison each day due to drug addiction, the hurting AIDS victims, and the naked children of Ethiopia and the Sudan?" Many in our make believe, food-filled, cash rich, pleasure bound congregation would retort - "Yes, we saw THEM, but that wasn't YOU. We ignored all these needs, but never our own or yours." Jesus' final reply:

When you ignored these you ignored me.

The authority of the scriptures is given for the church, and the body of believers has traditionally accepted this ruling ethos of the church of God. This universally accepted tradition of the worldwide church becomes an even greater discipline

---

[14] Matthew 25:36, NKJV.

upon the local church. There can be no question as to what the conduct of the church must be.

Why then, we ask, is the local church so different? The answer lies in the shift in direction power takes at the grass roots level. At the upper level where theological statements are birthed and where global pronouncements are made, power and authority comes from above and from without. They are strongly impacted by not only four thousand years of prophecy but also by a universal "Tao"[15] that continually pressures toward the achievement of the best, most righteous, least selfish that humankind has to offer. Also, at these upper levels idealism has a clearer voice because there is far less stress exerted from the strain of daily existence on those involved.

As one descends the ladder of the degree of worldwide institutional involvement, one sinks further and further into provincialism and an extremely parochial mindset. The local congregation accepts the power of the people's pleasure (political power) as its ruling force and far less the authority of God or pronouncements of the universal church. Authority from above, impacted by the world faith community, is seen here as suspect and foreign - something to be questioned and perhaps defied.

---

[15] The Tao is a basic set of principles that developed into the foundation of the Chinese religion of Taoism. The tao or "way of man" contains a rule of life so basic that it appears to be part of universally accepted principles.

Pejorative Power

In the current era this defiance of authority is manifested in our churches as "pejorative power," that is, *power that has gone sour* and negativism is the most noticeable ruling symptom of this kind of system.

We must not forget that the small or medium church is an organism based on interpersonal relationships and little else. Smaller churches have little to offer in physical facilities (gymnasiums, pools, better church schools), therefore people who join these smaller one- or two-celled units are doing so mainly to receive the benefits of small closely tied relationships. These churches are satisfied with their membership size and structure.[16] Therefore any appeal to be a "giving out from self" unit, a "ministering to another" unit, an "inviting of another" unit, or a "joining in with another" unit, will meet with the universally accepted symbol of pejorative power - "NO!"

Something here is strong enough to supersede God's call to us to "go out" and bring in the lost of the world or to bring the light of justice to a dark world.[17] This something is the very philosophy upon which the church operates. One writer recently divided churches into two types.[18] One, the "Covenant Community," is the "Yes" church. It says "yes" to

---

[16] Dudley, 48-52.
[17] Matthew 28:18-20.
[18] Schaller, Change, 18-21.

biblical mandates, to growth, to deep theological commitment, to the future, and to being productive.

The second, labeled the "Voluntary Association," becomes our "No" church. Both justice and evangelism are dead issues. Once a church has mustered the pejorative power to say "NO" to God's authority, and substitutes instead its own self-centered desires of exclusivity, isolation, and retention of self, its facilities and its fortunes are set aside for the use of "our people only." In cases like this, we have stolen and sealed up into a kind of "unholy of unholys" the entire Kingdom of God. Jesus alluded to this phenomenon in the Jewish "church" of His day. The Pharisees, the cadre of the local synagogue, were working from behind closed doors dealing in exclusivity and closeness exactly as our churches are doing today. Jesus warned them, "You shut up the Kingdom of Heaven against men for you neither go in yourselves, nor do you allow those who are entering to go in."[19]

To be self-centered, to desire to keep a good thing to oneself is a normal human trait. To exert one's power to perpetuate the status quo is equally normal, especially in the more immature organism. This systemic narcissism and immaturity seem to go hand in hand in our era. But to achieve a higher degree of maturity is to surrender to the leadership of authority, especially a higher authority who demands the

---

[19] Matthew 23:13.

ultimate - that we become better than we are capable of becoming.

Power versus authority in our churches is the real issue. The polemical questions are "Will our churches continue to perpetuate themselves by self serving political power" or "Will we demand of ourselves, our friends, and our leaders an acceptance of God's authority." Our leaders, if they are to lead, need to seek higher values than the perpetuation of their own power centers, and even more than the survival of their own local churches. God's authority demands more. James MacGregor Burns talks of leaders who accept this authority challenge:

> Given the right conditions of value conflict, leaders hold enhanced influence at the higher levels of the need and value hierarchies. They can appeal to the more widely and deeply held values, such as justice, liberty, and brotherhood. They can expose followers to the broader values that contradict narrower ones or inconsistent behavior. They can redefine aspirations and gratification's to help followers see their stake in new, program-oriented social movements. Most important, they can gratify lower needs so that higher motivations will arise to elevate the conscience of men and women.[20]

A final word to potential leaders who can no longer stand idly by while their churches sink into oblivion. God's

---

[20] Burns, 43.

authority is always more power filled than the self-centered political aspirations of those with whom you will deal. You will always prevail in the end if you will persevere and be persistent in a godly way. You, however, will be threatened by adversaries with the non-fulfillment of one of your three psychological needs *(achievement-power-affiliation)*. The major weapon the power politician has to use against a reformer is the threat of being ostracized (non-affiliated). For a brief time you may feel the only friend you have in the church is Jesus Himself. Those who wish to see changes made and growth occur are usually told that what they seek will be disruptive to the community. Thus the universal desire for affiliation is used against the reformer.[21]

Power and authority, therefore, especially in the church, are mutually dependent. The congregation can only have the power if it is willing to surrender all to the authority of God. This will mean a complete revision in the prevailing organizational structure and method of operation if Christian churches are to live and thrive. Power will no longer work - we must mature into authority.

---

[21] Codependents in an alcoholic relationship will identify with this phenomenon. Non-drinking partners are taught that their life will somehow be ruined if they do not continue to enable the drinker to drink. The desire to secure help is curtailed by threats of, "I'll leave you if you..." or "If my boss finds out I'll get fired and we'll starve."

Britt Minshall

The Power of "NO"

The most prevalent thrust of congregational political power in the dysfunctional or "No" church during the last third of the twentieth century has been to say, "No." This negative assertion of power has brought the mainline churches to a standstill and has recently powered wholesale regression.

The North Street Church formed a committee some years ago to study the need for a new organ. The old instrument was on its last legs and constantly in a state of disrepair. It couldn't last much longer. The nine member committee looked at all the alternatives, and after many months they presented their recommendations to the church; "We should purchase a new organ from the XYZ Company at a cost of $38,000." The committee's vote was unanimous.

The church's ruling council voted 29 to 17 to urge the congregation to buy the new organ, assuming that common sense, the proper use of political structures, and the love of all for the church would carry the day. The members were then obviously taken by surprise when, come the day of the churchwide vote, a heated discussion took place. The fighting was hot and loud. At last a vote was taken and the decision was applauded by the "Yes" group - 188 voted to buy the organ, 186 said "No."

Then came the crusher! Bill Adams, a powerful member of the church, stood and asked for another vote. He said, "While I favor replacing this old 'clunker' we call an organ and I voted to support the committee's recommendation, in a voluntary association such as a church, we cannot act favorably on such a costly venture without a much larger majority. Therefore I am asking for a reconsideration in order to cast my vote against the proposal." On the next vote two other members switched their votes in order to keep "harmony and peace" and this time the proposal was defeated.

The first impulse one has is to say, "Ah, wasn't that a kind, loving thing to do - giving up your organ for the harmony of the church." There is, however another consideration. Lyle Schaller comments on this story in his book Creative Church Administration:

> A more careful examination of this reveals that the decision making and voting process...in thousands of congregations has been "stacked" to reward negativism, perpetuate the status quo, block change, encourage apathy, stifle initiative, provoke discontent, and cause active leaders to drop into inactivity, because of discouragement, frustration, and irritation.[22]

At North Street Church and at many other churches (perhaps yours) the "No" votes carry more weight than the "Yes" votes. In order to keep the 186 "No's" happy the others were willing to make the 188 "Yes" voters unhappy.

---

[22]   Lyle E. Schaller and Charles A. Tidwell, Creative Church Administration, (Nashville, Abingdon Press, 1975), 39.

Another case in point. At Hyde Park Church, the pastor suggested changing the time of service to allow for a complete church school program. The church had grown substantially in the past eighteen months and younger people were bringing several children into the church. However, church school was after church services, hence the children and their parents wouldn't stay because it rendered the Sunday family time (12 noon and later) too short to enjoy.

The church school committee said, "Yes, let's do it." The worship committee said, "Yes, let's do it." An informal church poll recorded 121 potential "yes" votes and two "no's." The day of the meeting came and the "Yes" speakers praised the plan. Many new members (with families) informed the leadership that they had been seeking other churches due simply to the inconvenient church school hour and were now so glad that they could stay at the church. All appeared ecstatic at the new prospects.

However, just before the vote was taken, one man, Harry Wolf, took the floor. Harry was the wealthiest man in the church and one of the oldest members, truly its patriarch. He said thirty words:

> My wife and I are opposed to the change. Our granddaughter will be late for church school if it moves to 9:30 because she has a new job delivering papers.

Renaissance or Ruin

Everyone felt badly that Janene, Harry's granddaughter, would be late, but after all one child late beats twenty-eight not being able to attend at all; right? - WRONG!

The vote was 94 "No" and 36 "Yes." The church school hour stayed the same. Harry's one "No" carried so much weight that it outstripped all the good intentions of 121 original excited "Yes's." In order to keep Harry happy the church willingly sacrificed thirty-eight young adults who eventually left the church in disappointment. An entire generation was lost to one man's negative control.

The power of "No" is awesome. It is almost always destructive. The United States' "No" vote on joining the League of Nations contributed much to the beginning of World War II. The racism that gave birth to the "No" guilty verdict in the trial of the police officers accused of beating Rodney King came close to ruining a city, caused thirty-eight murders, and cost $150,000,000 in riot damages. Whenever people say, "No," based on fear and negative pressure, misery and failure usually follow.

"No" means NO-thing happens, NO progress is made, things are NOT made right, and change does NOT occur. The church is living constantly with this phenomenon of negativism and the world outside our doors knows it. In the taped series "Word Power 2" J. Ray Price, the well-known expert on grammar and vocabulary, found need to define the word "inveigh." The word means to protest or to complain loudly. She illustrated her definition by saying that

> Many religious people in particular protest against change, especially in their churches. They 'inveigh' change thus keeping the status quo."[23]

The movie <u>Sister Act</u> with Whoopi Goldberg has become so popular that people sit and applaud in the theater as they witness the forbidding doors of a stagnated inner city Catholic church being forced open. The audiences are heard cheering as the people of the neighborhood respond to the introduction of rock gospel music and new worship methods.[24] Such spontaneous applause by huge numbers of secular society, and the use of the church as a model for obnoxious stubborn regressive negative behavior by other disciplines should signal the church that everyone is aware of our prevailing psychopathology.

Our churches have become the laughing stock of the nation because of negative leadership yelling:

"No" -- to a world crying "Yes."

The world apparently recognizes that the church's "No" arises out of response to fear of change, fear of the unknown, even fear of the people that Christ came to save. In other words,

---

[23] Word Power II, Career Track Publications, 3085 Center Green Drive, Boulder, CO 80301.
[24] <u>Sister Act</u> (Burbank, Touchstone Pict, 1991), Motion picture.

while God promised that those who accept the Son's love would be free from the bondage of fear[25] (paralyzing paranoia or dread) the world sees a church powered by fear and populated by paranoia. Nothing but negativism can come out of a body which bases its structure on a power base generated by fear. "No" in this scenario is little more than power gone sour, pejorative power in the works.

Incidentally, Harry Wolfe's granddaughter quit her paper route four weeks after the ill-fated meeting to change the Sunday School hour. The following year she quit the church altogether and gave as her reason, "There are no kids here anymore." Within seven months she was a pregnant and unmarried fourteen year old.

The Unloving Personality

Paranoia in its simplest form is the delusion that others are hostile toward you. The paranoid personality is fearful of all others. This psychosis frequently leads to either a person becoming catatonic (withdrawing into a mental stupor such as is seen in chronic massive depression), or the victim will act out aggressively, driven by this state of fear to aggravated defensive behavior.

The most passive of personalities when brought to a high level of fear will appear hate-filled and act out in an aggressive and negative way. Beginning with this knowledge

---
[25] Romans 8:15.

we can analyze the pieces of the personality puzzle that constitutes today's mainline congregation as it works through failure. The congregation in Sister Act would typify this. A once large congregation that formerly served the center of a city neighborhood, but whose congregants are now gone, finds itself a stranger in its own world, surrounded by "foreign" combatants.

Consider the world in which the mainline church finds itself today. As thousands of people of every color and description cross the borders of the formerly almost all white United States, the Celts, the Anglo-Saxons, the sons and daughters of the European tribespeople retreat in fear from the onslaught. They have been withdrawing for 30 years, first to the suburbs, then to the far out suburbs and then to the perimeter cities of "exurbia." Many thousands are looking to the hinterland for future refuge. They see the Smoky Mountains and the Ozarks as paradise, with Branson, Missouri as their capital of destiny.

When flight is not possible, the remnant withdraws into their tribal house, the old mainline church. Here they feel safe and can calm their xenophobic fears[26]. As they defensively pull

---

[26] Xenophobia is the fear of foreigners. This psychopathology has become acute in a world of massive migrations of people. Because the "first world" societies, populated primarily by white people, are the richest societies, the migrations of third world people is the most feared by them. The people of the mainline church are these Caucasian people, therefore xenophobia pervades their congregations.

Renaissance or Ruin

more and more inside of themselves, they bring others to them, each wave feeling more threatened and more defensive. These increasingly bitter embattled people become an ever larger portion of the congregation. Their defensive dislike of outsiders surfaces as chronic negativism. The resulting inactivity, lethargic worship, and lack of commitment to the Gospel begins to force the mission minded, goal committed Christians out of the church.

- Down goes the membership

- Down goes the money.

The church is now a closed system and begins to enter failure.

Once the membership decreases and the financial reserves sink to a corresponding low level, money is seen as the most scarce resource. The "strategic contingency" model of power and control swings into full action. That is,

1. The people who control that scarce resource (offerings),

2. Take key positions in the church, and then,

3. They define all the policies and programs of the church in terms of the lack of that resource.

4. They report that - we can "Not" do this because we do "Not" have the money.

> 5. Therefore the church says, "No" to the campaign to add members because we do "Not" have the money, and "No" to any outside contact, because we do "Not" have resources.

Since there are no programs there will be no new members, consequently their power is never diluted.[27] If a cash surplus should begin to accrue, due to an increase in members or missions, the power bloc ceases giving or acts out hatefully, thus driving off the perceived threat. Again, no money means no programs; the result is no new members, consequently, the strategic contingencies (money/people) are kept under control. On and on continues this cycle of orchestrated failure.

We were first warned of the anticipated coming of these fear filled paranoid folks in 1954, by Bonaro W. Overstreet, who could never have presaged the current crises.[28] He wrote for the Pastoral Psychology Series an article entitled "The Unloving Personality and the Religion of Love." He never once uses the term paranoiac or paranoid, perhaps out of ignorance of the connection, perhaps out of reluctance.

In the article, Overstreet tells of people recognized as emotionally deficient, unresponsive, indifferent to the feelings of others. He labels these people as "unloving personalities."

---

[27] Gerald R. Salancik and Jeffrey Pfeffer, "Who Gets Power and How They Hold It: A Strategic-Contingency Model of Power," Organizational Dynamics, Winter 1977, 3-20.

[28] Bonaro W. Overstreet, "The Unloving Personality and the Religion of Power," Religion and Human Behavior, Simon Doniger, ed., (New York, Association Press, 1954), 73-87.

He describes the Stage II developed person who stifles others with his/her "love" of them; the generous person who is always ready to bail out the church when cash is needed; the humble person who wants nothing for himself/herself but is always the victim of life.

The unloving personality, suggests Overstreet:

> Is marked by anxious self-concern; an exaggerated sense of being different from others, a lack of imagination about how other people feel - and therefore an exploitative tendency to use them as a means to his (her) own ends; rigidity of behavior; and a pervasive, chronic hostility toward life.[29]

He goes on to say that this type of person puts a strain on every social institution, but especially wreaks havoc in the church where the fundamental message is love. These people, often weary of many failed relationships, gravitate to the church seeing it as a place where they can be loved. Having found a place of safety, secure from this unsafe world, they become the "pillars" or "watchdogs" of the institution (cadre or core church).

Once in the body, having "escaped from their fear and isolation," they cannot enjoy the spontaneous and joyful experience. They could never allow themselves that experience outside the church, why should they experience it inside the church? Therefore they must work openly and behind the

---

[29] Overstreet, 75.

scenes to put an end to the happiness. Since the church is the social place of sanctuary where everyone is welcome, not only can they work safely from the inside, forming political networks of those who agree with their morbid relational thesis (satellites and chameleons), but slowly they drive out those who came to find happiness. As the fear level in a dysfunctional society increases, more and more of their type gravitate to the church seeking to find love and caring, but not being able to accept it.

Here the paranoid *unloving personalities* can find God without the risk of rejection. They can find God and once they have this universal parent trapped, they can punish God as the Father or/and mother who denied them love in their childhood.

Look at the preference pattern of these folks and identify them in your congregation:

> 1. The unloving person prefers either other worldly religion (fundamental type religion that has little or nothing to say about the social holiness needs of this life), or talks strictly in terms of denominational affiliation. To this type person enemies are perceived as either not Godly enough for heaven or as not one of us, referring to the U.C.C. or Baptist or whatever group to which this person aligns.

> 2. This personality protests against any changes, particularly in the worship service. A new

program or a new hymnal would be seen as a threat.

3. The unloving person would be adamantly against ecumenical unions or joining church to church in union or shared programs. These folks usually talk in terms of, "We don't need this in our church," or better yet, "Why should we join with the others - what's in it for us?"

4. The unloving paranoiac does not wish substantial growth in church membership. The fear here is that more people and resources will render his or her person or contribution as less important.

Any church hosting a large number of these people in its cadre would quite naturally reflect their overall personal preferences and meet their needs. It therefore would become a closed community, reserved for people like "us" who do things in "our" way, not looking to learn new ways and most definitely not willing to share with others.

In looking at this personality complex individually, we can often see people we know and others with whom we deal on a daily basis. The real shock is in the discovery that many of these people have joined our churches and monopolize the leadership positions, often remaining in the church as membership declines. With an increasing percentage of church membership exhibiting this personality pattern, our churches have become, themselves, paranoid organisms - unloving personalities.

A more contemporary account of the activities of these persons (antagonists) is handled by Kenneth C. Haugk, Ph.D., founder of the Stephen Series of lay ministry. He writes:

> Antagonism can obliterate a sense of the presence of God's love in individuals and in the faith community. It is an affliction of the whole people of God. Perhaps antagonism most frequently tears into the lives of church staff members.[30]

Unlike Overstreet, who paints this personality complex with one brushstroke, Haugk divides antagonists into three categories:

- *Hard-core antagonists*
- *Major antagonists*
- *Moderate antagonists*

He labels the *hard-core antagonist* as psychotic and, as I have done, attributes their personality characteristics to extreme paranoia. These would be the most combative of the group that Overstreet calls the unloving personality. Their sole cause in life is the destruction of other people's lives. The problem in

---

[30] Kenneth C. Haugk, Antagonists in the Church: How to Identify and Deal With Destructive Conflict. (Minneapolis, Augsburg Press, 1988), 20.

many cases is that outside the church setting where close loving relationships are fewer and farther between, these folks often seem perfectly normal. Acutely paranoid persons respond abhorently when approached by a loving person. Therefore, being present in the church becomes the triggering mechanism for their attacks. The professional "loving" person of the congregation (pastor or associate pastor) will engender the greatest wrath of these folks. They, by the very nature of their calling, approach the combatant in kindness, love, and ministry, thus initiating the attack mechanism.

  The *major antagonist*, says Haugk, experiences less serious, but no less active personality problems. These especially manifest themselves in the "overwhelming drive for power." Since these folks appear normal in virtually all of life's efforts, they are extremely hard to diagnose apart from their church life. Often these persons are just dysfunctional enough so as to preclude them from leadership in business and secular society, but in the church they can thrive like bacteria do in a warm, moist environment. Because of their desire for power, they will gravitate to the core of church life and slowly, surreptitiously destroy a congregation. It will usually take the termination of two pastors, and the departure of half the congregation before anyone suspects what is happening. The pastors will often recognize what is taking place but, again, relationships are so intertwined that parishioners will avoid seeing the antagonist at work.

The final category, the *moderate antagonist*, usually belongs to the group I've previously labeled as satellites and chameleons. They are not self starters or originators of their attacks, rather, they attach themselves to the coattails of another stronger antagonist. Also Haugk relates that they will back off more quickly and stay submerged longer than will the stronger types.

Preceding Haugk by forty years, Bonaro Overstreet offered this warning to the church concerning the presence of this personality complex. He writes:

> Its (the church's) obligation, however, is definitely not that of allowing him (her) to remake the church in his (her) own unloving image. It is not that of encouraging him (her) into the ministry; nor of letting him (her) impose upon the church his (her) own fear-ridden, guilt-ridden, hostility-ridden stiffness and narrowness.[31]

We have evidently ignored Overstreet's warning, therefore, our only hope seems to be:

> 1. Identify persons with this psychopathology and churches exhibiting a related socio-pathology resulting from prolonged concentration of these types in leadership positions.
>
> 2. Admonish, counsel, love, and convert to a true faith in Christ, and appropriate person to person

---

[31] Overstreet, 86. Parentheses mine.

relationships these individuals and our churches that have been adversely affected.

3. Reinvent our churches. Begin all over again. Recommit to God and God's love, to salvation through belief in Jesus Christ, and to personal and corporate living in and through the caring power of the Holy Spirit.

The scary thing will be the diagnostic process as we examine our churches and their leadership. The sheer number of churches reeling from the effects of the unloving personality may be at the epidemic levels.

Equally astonishing is the fact that almost half a century elapsed between Overstreet's disclosure and any further discussion of this problem. These folks are truly People of the Lie[32] and are evil in their intent and their actions. They have no place in the leadership of the body of Christ. "Their behavior is not successful in many other areas of life because in those areas it is simply not tolerated."[33] Unfortunately, as our churches reduce in numbers, we who are left adopt the attitude that anybody is better than nobody. What a mistake that has been. Now it is up to us to muster the courage to solve the problem that our apathy and unbelief have caused. I wonder if we have the faith or the courage?

---

[32] M. Scott Peck, People of the Lie, (New York, Simon and Shuster, 1983)
[33] Haugk, 39.

TRIGGER POINTS

1. Discuss examples from contemporary news media of government and/or religious bodies acting in a power mode. In authority mode.

2. The four Pillars of Authority are *submission - control - sacrifice of self-interest* and *justice*. Examine these four pillars individually. Develop a list of traits that are opposite of these.

3. Of these two types of characteristics, which are apparent in the life of your church?

4. Examine the characteristics of a "Yes" church. Compare them to a "No" church. Determine which type church you are operating.

5. Look at the percentage your church grew last year. This year. Then examine what percentage of your budget goes toward church growth and outreach. How do the figures compare?

6. Has the issue of new hymnbooks, a new organ, a different style of worship, or a worship time change come to the surface in your church in the past 10 years? What was the outcome?

CHAPTER V

THE POWER OR THE GLORY

Things were looking worse than ever in the village of the ethnic peoples along the river. In an attempt to make the nation the most modern and advanced in all history, the ruler of the indigenous people had reduced the status of the minority peoples to that of slaves. Work quotas for the refugee "foreigners" had been established, food stuffs were heavily taxed and labor laws had been abandoned.

The members of these minority nationalities, now living in squalor, had given up the image of their hosts as benevolent despots. These once free people, now slaves, viewed the country of their refuge as a prison and saw themselves as living in a morass of hopelessness.

One major problem in the Hebrew slave community was the lack of leadership. The raw energy of the people was being usurped by their overlords, the Egyptian power structure, and it was being used by the ruler Pharaoh for the building of roads, pyramids, and temples. The chance for leadership development was further diminished when Pharaoh commanded every male child of these Hebrew slaves to be killed at birth.[1] While the effort was far from successful, it did enough damage to the ethnic infrastructure to render the tribe void of male leadership for over a generation. It also put fear, even dread, into the hearts of the people.

One of the male children survived and was hidden in the very palace of Pharaoh and raised as an Egyptian. When matured, he had the breeding, education, and stature of an Egyptian nobleman. Mysteriously however, he found himself drawn back to the Hebrew village, doubtless exhibiting a need for affiliation with people with blood ties. When this young explorer, Moses, began visiting the Hebrew village, the two basic parts of a new power system began to crystallize:

1. A community in need of a powerful leader

2. A man with a high power profile and a need to affiliate.

This call on Moses' life revealed itself quite spontaneously when he witnessed an Egyptian beating an unarmed Hebrew. Without thinking, Moses yielded to his rescue complex and

---

[1] The story of Pharaoh's attempt at genocide is carried in Exodus One. After one attempt at killing all male children is unsuccessful, he commands that each male child to be born should be killed by the soldiers. Moses survived this attempt on his life. We have no data telling us how many others also survived.

killed the Egyptian in defense of the Hebrew slave.[2] In this one act he acquiesced to leadership among the Hebrew people.

There are two basic forces that exist in a leader. Moses exhibited the first by attacking the Egyptian. He *took the lead* and did what was needed or what was perceived to be needed - he took action. The second, however, did not engage at this time. Leaders are those who *move people to follow them*.[3] In this case, the people were not yet ready.[4]

From this moment of shallow victory and hope for the oppressed people, there emerged a time of gloom as Moses hid in the desert land of Midian. Deliverance was needed by the Hebrews but it was not yet to come. It could not come without leadership. Moses was far too young and too much an outsider to lead the Hebrews. The people were so filled with despair they were unprepared to respond to one act of heroism. The raw materials were present for leadership to emerge, but the time was not right.

Moses lived and grew to mid-life in the desert. Here he also came to know God. He came to have a personal

---

[2] A Rescue Complex is a term used by psychologist to define otherwise separate personality traits that trigger in unison when the holder of this complex witnesses a weak person being abused by a stronger one. Persons with this complex are perennial helpers of the underdog and usually become pastors, nurses, paramedics and the like.

[3] Leighton Ford, Transforming Leadership: Jesus' Way of Creating Vision, Shaping Values and Empowering Change, (Douners Grove, Ill., Intervarsity Press, 1991), 25.

[4] Exodus 2:13-14

relationship with God and he learned to both speak to God and listen to God. By revelation he received a vision for the future of the Hebrews. He became a part of the Hebrew generations before him, doubtlessly from the teaching of his father-in-law, Jethro, on faith and law, and by accepting his relationship with God as the God of his forebears.[5]

Now the final ingredient in the leadership formula developed when Moses accepted God's call on his life to deliver the chosen people. Moses' inner needs were to be met as his need for affiliation and his need for achievement were satisfied by surrendering to God's call. His desire to lead the people of Israel (Hebrews) to freedom, intersected with the willingness to convert his power profile into leadership and authority in their cause. God then revealed the mandate, the warrant, the blessing, the plan of action and the promise of achieving the goal. With all of these in his sheath, Moses returned to Egypt to secure the final ingredient necessary for success - the people's acquiescence to his leadership.

Millions of willing leaders dot the landscape of every generation; most disappear from the scene because people must accept a leader as their bellwether or nothing can happen. These leader/people pacts are always tenuous at best. With God's blessing and God's plan in hand, Moses journeyed to Egypt, risking all he had ever achieved in life in order to deliver the Hebrew people out of slavery.

---
[5] Exodus 3:6.

One would expect Moses to be joyfully received and proclaimed leader at once, but the reaction was quite the contrary. The response of the enslaved was: "Get lost." They would not heed Moses. It would appear that in 1200 BC, like today, more people would settle for present conditions - even if horrible - rather than accept change if offered. The leader's primary responsibility through the ages has not varied, that is to help people adapt and do something new. "Life is constantly changing, but most people fear change."[6] Moses, not unlike a contemporary pastor, arrived at his field of ministry thinking of Pharaoh as the only threat to the people. Moses soon discovered that Pharaoh was not the major enemy. The great threat to alleviating the oppressive situation was found then, as now, within the victim population itself.

Metaphorically speaking, Moses' situation is analogous to today's pastors who leave a place they call home (Midian), to go to a strange new place (the valley of the Nile), to deliver the people of the community and the church from the power of Satan (Pharaoh). Today's pastor, like Moses, soon finds out that the enemy without is easy pickings compared to the enemy that lurks within. The reluctance of the modern congregation to move forward is akin to the skepticism and fear found among the Hebrews.

The new national average of pastorates within the Southern Baptist Convention is 2.2 years. First pastorates in

---

[6] Ford, 42.

all denominations usually end within the first two to four years. One major reason can be found in that pastors are unprepared for the rejection of their pastoral leadership, particularly in small churches which are the usual call for novice pastors. Once encountering this complex fear of change, suspicion of leadership and personal rejection, many new candidates return to seminary. Many others opt out of the system entirely. Moses might have done the same, but God forbade it. God put Moses to the task and said, "Keep going, go speak to Pharaoh. Don't lose sight of the goal."

Moses was more fortunate than many local pastors. He soon had the opportunity to show his power and the power of God he proclaimed. God not only did miracles in the presence of Pharaoh, but also in the presence of the Hebrews. Thus Moses became a real power player as far as Pharaoh was concerned. Pharaoh, the external enemy, reeled back in defeat from the onslaught of Moses' staff and the power of this strange new God. In the eyes of the people however, Moses was not fully accepted in spite of the personal validation of God.[7] He became just enough of a hero figure and charismatic

---

[7] In all fairness to the people, it should be noted here that many current scholars would agree that at this point in Hebrew history there was little or no knowledge of the God of Abraham and the ancestors. Most of this faith tradition had been lost over the centuries in bondage. Therefore, the authority of Moses Yahweh would have been a moot point with the slaves.

personality to encourage the people to follow, at least on a trial basis.

At this level of interaction one must be careful not to view Moses' position as the leader with authority. At best we see him as a power by which the people were awed. Many pastors achieve this level of leadership in their ministry and never move beyond it. This occurs primarily in the pastoral centered church of 100 or 200 people. Many church lay leaders in this medium size church, searching for a miracle-worker pastor, never attempt this level of leadership for themselves, not wishing to seem haughty. Conversely, in the small patriarchal/matriarchal church (under 100) the pastor is never allowed to achieve even this level of leadership unless the pastor surrenders the pastoral authority and literally "locates,"[8] becoming a part of the local church community permanently. Modern congregations often evolve to a Moses-and-the-people type stand-off, gridlocked at the gates to an Egyptian city. A common picture involves a congregation poised to journey forward with a charismatic pastor/leader, while the supposed leaders hide, suspicious of the new pastor/leader and yet unwilling to assume leadership themselves.

---

[8] A now archaic term once used by Methodists to denote a circuit riding preacher who petitions the conference to be relieved of the responsibility of traveling. This state of non-transfering was frowned on most severely by early Methodists. The located pastor became a second class member of the conference.

Faith or Fear

The fragile relationship between Moses and the people can be seen as the Hebrews reached the Red Sea only to discover the enemy, Pharaoh, had recanted of his promise to "let the people go" and was now in hot pursuit. Little confidence in Moses is found in the railing of the people as they yelled in fear:

> Have you taken us away to die in the wilderness? Why have you so dealt with us to bring us up out of Egypt? We told you to leave us alone in Egypt. Oh, my, we're going to die in the wilderness.[9]

Any person who has been in leadership will empathize with Moses. While victories were the order of the day he was a hero, but given the prospect of loss, the followers turned on the leader. Note in Exodus 13:6-12, from which the above incident is taken, that the driving force of the rebellion against leadership was fear.

The first word from Moses in response to this threat is offered here as a pattern for the contemporary church leader in responding to congregational fear of change. Moses said,

> Do not be afraid. Stand still and see the salvation of the Lord, which He (God) will accomplish for you today."[10]

---

[9] Exodus 13:11-12, paraphrase
[10] Exodus 14:13, NKJV.

Renaissance or Ruin

Potential leaders in the contemporary church need above all things to be aware of the high fear levels of their congregation. While the situation is far different from that of the Hebrew congregation they should be prepared to say the same four things to their followers.

- Don't be afraid
- Stand still
- See the salvation of the Lord
- God will accomplish for you

First, *Don't be afraid*. We must be willing to openly acknowledge the paranoia that is endemic throughout our church and society. The potential leader must be able to risk retaliation from his or her colleagues in laying the blame for our community's problems squarely on ourselves. Identify the chief problem - *fear*.

Secondly, the leader must offer calmness. He or she must be willing to *stand still*, sort out the situation rationally, address individual persons and their problems, and be patient.

Thirdly, and I can not stress this too much, leaders in a Christian community must be willing, even eager, to call out the name of Jesus as the *salvation of the Lord*. Leaders in our mainline churches will spend hours talking of money, offerings, leaky roofs, clogged toilets, and unsuccessful membership drives, but will <u>never</u> call on the name of Jesus.

A church to which I once belonged had approximately 120 active members. It boasted 32 church officials and six congregationally proclaimed leaders. Of all these regulars only two were willing to say openly that Jesus Christ was their Lord and Savior, or any variation of that idea. If the words of the song "The Church's one foundation is Jesus Christ her Lord," are taken as true, then it would be impossible to be a leader in the church without being able to proclaim, accept and live by that fundamental statement.

Fourth and finally, *God will accomplish for you.* If church officers are not fully trusting God in their lives, then the tendency will be to take the reins and do anything and everything possible to accomplish the goal. The idea of servanthood under God is replaced by, "This is our show and we'll work it out." Some of the widespread acceptance of this utilitarian individualistic value statement comes from our Puritan roots. The stoic self-centered personality of the early American Congregationalist firmly established two basic premises of the American Christian ethic. One was the embryonic concept of being self-reliant, the root of modern individualism, and the other was that one's faithfulness could be measured by one's prosperity and achievements.[11] Therefore, the belief arises that the more you do yourself, the more you

---
[11] Forbes, 43.

accomplish without help from anyone, the closer to God's heart you are. America was built on the adage that "God helps those who help themselves." No, this is not a biblical quote, but most American Christians swear it is or ought to be. This ethic comes equally into conflict with Moses' posture of a leader's relationship with God - sit still and God will accomplish.

One would assume that the events that took place as the Hebrew exodus began would endear Moses to the people and establish forever a one-man, universally accepted leadership by all the people. After all, God did open the Red Sea, let the Hebrews through and then drown Pharaoh's hordes. The number one hit song of the day was penned by Moses' sister Miriam, which spoke of the glorious strength of the God of Moses.[12] Even in light of this obviously miraculous act, Moses was still not able to ascend to fully unchallenged leadership. How much more difficult it is then for the average local church leader of today to receive the mantle of effective leadership.

Few lay people or pastors live to see the waters part before them, rendering the job of leadership development in today's church a different and more difficult task than it was for your everyday prophet of the Old Testament era. But even for Moses more miracles were necessary. Just three days from the shores of the Red Sea the water ran low and the springs at

---

[12] Exodus 15.

Marah were found undrinkable. The people began to murmur. And they continued to murmur for weeks.

Each time things ran well Moses was a hero, and every time things went badly he became the enemy within. The problem (ever less as the journey progressed) was the same as the problem that faces a congregation today that wishes to cross Sinai or any other difficult passage to save itself. The Hebrews then, and our churches now need leaders. The Hebrews had one leader - that never works. Our congregations search for months for the "right" pastor; many seeking another O. S. Hawkins, or Jim Forbes, or Henry Ward Beecher for that matter. Some churches may be fortunate and actually hire great pulpiteers or charismatic leaders, only to discover they have accomplished little or nothing. The reason for the disappointment is that as soon as things aren't going right or "the leader" gets sick, leaves or dies, the party is over. The people will murmur and the congregation will go into failure just as the Israelites did.

Moses, a talented, God-inspired, God-connected, brave, sacrificing, caring, never-sleeping leader could not single-handedly pull off a leadership miracle, yet we expect our pastors to do it? After a long series of crises - complaints, miracles, restoration of order, and yet another crisis - the only thing Moses could boast was the power necessary to hold the line. Realistic broad-based leadership did not emerge and socialized authority was not accepted.

Leadership Not Power

In the darkness of this endless cycle of disappointments it became indeed the darkness before the dawn. It was then that God sent to Moses a visit from his wisdom-charged father-in-law Jethro. This became more than a family visit, however. Jethro had been sent to the beleaguered camp with a special ministry - that of *intentional outsider*.[13] Jethro, the outsider, could see at once the problem facing Moses. The day after his arrival at the camp of Moses, Jethro looked on as:

> Moses sat to judge the people; and the people stood before Moses from morning until evening.
>
> So when Moses' father-in-law saw all that he did for the people, he said, "What is this thing that you are doing for the people? Why do you alone sit, and all the people stand before you from morning until evening?"[14]

---

[13] Earlier we made reference to the concept of the "intentional outsider" having come across this term in Lyle Schaller's 1966 book <u>Community Organization, Conflict, and Reconciliation</u>. The origin of the term, however, seems to rest with the National Training Laboratory. The term is used to identify any outside person who enters an existing group with outside data and concepts. For a short period of a pastor's term of service he/she can qualify for this title. However, pressures to assimilate quickly render this pastoral gift void. In medieval times the Bishop of Rome would send a foreign born Archbishop into a strange country with this intentional outsider concept in mind. In more recent history the American church vested this office in the visiting revivalist or evangelist. This office now lays vacant in the modern church except in the case of outside consultants.

[14] Exodus 18:13.

Jethro's wisdom and years of observation immediately diagnosed a serious flaw (dysfunction) in the social make-up of the Hebrew community. One person was "the leader" and everyone else was "a follower." He realized that there were many potential leaders in the group, but that there was no institutionalized method of ascendance to leadership roles.

The churches today mirror the "Sinai situation." Some, usually in the more fundamentalist camp, have strong ruler pastors in an authoritarian role, speaking for God as Moses attempted. In this scenario, the energy of the church accrues toward pleasing the pastor.

Other churches, usually small or medium sized of the old line denominations, feature a strong lay figure or figures, herein referred to as Patriarchs or Matriarchs[15] who rule their domains with a cliquish, closed groups of satellites. In this situation, the main thrust leadership energy is devoted to keeping the pastor powerless and the membership as drones. In neither of the above cases, which easily represent 90% of America's Protestant churches, is there a truly non-biased, open mechanism for broad-based leadership development. In this circumstance power, not leadership, rules, and as long as power is the primary force, forward movement of the community is limited or impossible.

---

[15] A good treatment of Patriarchal and Matriarchal churches can be found along with other church types in Arlin J. Rothange's Sizing Up A Congregation available from the Episcopal Church Center, 815 2nd Ave., New York, N.Y. 10017

Institutionalized *leadership* is always open to change, new blood and growth. Institutionalized *power* is never open to change and it is never participatory. All organizations (churches included) that function on the power model have certain things in common. Three of these are:

1. There is commitment to decisions and strategies previously adopted, making it difficult or impossible for a change in course

2. Beliefs, practices, and rules take precedence over rational inquiry and deliberation of current situations

3. There is a perpetuation of co-power holders and their dependents in the ruling structure by their ability to control entrance into the structure and their ability to "obtain additional determinants of power." In other words, once power is in place it perpetuates itself, its holders, beliefs, and its management of the institution by allowing little or no changes.[16]

Jethro instructed Moses that leadership and not power was to be the authority in God's family. He tells Moses:

> The thing that you do is not good. Both you and these people who are with you will surely wear yourselves out. For this thing is too much

---

[16] Pfeffer, 289-290.

> for you; you are not able to perform it by yourself.[17]

The words of Jethro ring as true today as they did 3400 years ago. He goes on, however, and moves from admonition to solution - from power to glory. He offered Moses a plan for leadership development that was authored by God to guarantee the success of God's people. Jethro teaches:

> Listen now to my voice; I will give you counsel, and God will be with you. Stand before God for the people so that you may bring the difficulties to God.
>
> And you shall teach the statutes and the laws, and show them the way in which they must walk and the work they must do.
>
> Moreover you shall select from all the people able men, such as fear God, men of truth, hating covetousness; and such place over them to be rulers of thousands, rulers of hundreds, rulers of fifties, and rulers of tens.
>
> And let them judge the people at all times. Then it will be that every great matter that they shall bring to you...
>
> If you do this thing, and God so commands you,

---

[17] Exodus 18:14-18.

then you will be able to endure, and all this people will also go to the place in peace.[18]

In this one text, speaking the wisdom of God, Jethro laid the basic foundation for any attempt to lead a lost community out of failure and into the promised land. He elucidated every principle of leadership that any church, synagogue, mission society, or other organism of God's kingdom would ever need to know. This became the turning point in the forty year journey from Egypt to the promised land. Remember, however, the Hebrews had been a non-entity for almost five centuries; forty years, therefore, seems reasonable to form a cohesive community of self-leading people.

With the reading of this scripture we have reached the turning point in our journey as well. Most congregations that are:

- Willing to self-examine

- To confess their presence in a metaphorical Egypt - *the place of loss and lostness*

- To make the changes necessary, leaving behind the plague ridden Valley of the Nile, and/or other *practices and habits that no longer work,*

will find a God willing to lead them "to the place of peace."

---

[18] Exodus 18:19-23.

It is, therefore, time that we turned to view the promised land. We shall see the *principles of leadership* replace the *practices of power*, and we will see the creation of successful community out of the wreckage of group failure.

We have ventured, with Moses, from a place of power; now together, with him and his people, we shall view the glory that comes with leadership.

TRIGGER POINTS

1. Do you find it difficult or easy to equate the situation of your congregation to that of the Hebrews in Egypt? Explain.

2. Were you ever the prime mover in any group with the responsibility for making changes?

3. Was there opposition? How did you handle it?

4. Compare the roll of the modern day pastor to Moses in the realm of people management, and forward movement.

5. Compare your church or organization to the three common characteristics of a power centered group (page 125). Where do you stand?

CHAPTER VI

WHAT IS THIS THING YOU ARE DOING?

The Change Agent

Rev. John Harris accepted his first full charge parish after three years in seminary and three years as an associate. The church to which he was assigned was a high Anglican parish, St. John's at Broad Creek, Maryland. The church had been built in the eighteenth century and had changed little since that time. Like churches described earlier in this work, urban sprawl came to Broad Creek uninvited. Along with the sprawl came thousands of new residents to the area served by the parish. John was instructed by his Bishop to reach these new people, "That's your job. Build a different style - a bit more loose, less ceremonial, open it up to young families." With typical youthful exuberance John tackled the task.

The church was looking forward to his arrival, coming as their first full-time rector in many years. John reports that even before he arrived, however, many questions had been voiced. Most of these inquiries were really asking in several different ways, "If you come, what will you change?" Notice, the first concern was not over what could be accomplished but what would change.

John did make changes. He tried to get the church to support itself instead of living off Bingo. He lightened the medieval style altar area making it more open and inviting. He also replaced old, no longer relevant church school material with newer, more modern curriculum, and generally tried to bring the church into the mid-twentieth century.

"Looking back," writes Harris, "I am impressed by the naive presumption with which I did it. As anyone can imagine, these changes were negative to most of the congregation." However, not understanding this at the time, he pressed harder for change, but the congregation stood more firmly in place. He and the cadre (the core of the church) became stagnated in a struggle for control. In less than six months he had alienated most of the people. In a more congregational system (Baptist or UCC) with little or no denominational control, he would have been dismissed. In a connectional system (Episcopal, United Methodist, Presbyterian), two warring bodies (pastor vs. people) are often just stuck with each other until someone gives in.[1]

John Harris' story is familiar; it's played out thousands of times each year in church after church. I read John's account of his first pastoral experience just one month after walking away from my first pulpit after two years of exactly the same conditions and results. This situation is all too familiar to God's prophets and God's people.

If we look to Bible history we witness Moses, an archetypical John Harris, sitting in the same seat three thousand years before Broad Creek Church was founded. Moses had become entangled in the same kind of power struggle facing Harris, struggling with ever increasing effort to

---

[1] John C. Harris, Stress, Power and Ministry: An Approach to the Current Dilemmas of Pastors and Congregations, (Washington, Alban Institute, 1977), 13-15.

make the pastorate to which he had been assigned an effective one. God saw the pain in Moses' heart and sent a "change agent"[2] into the life of the congregation of Israel. This "intentional outsider" Jethro, the father-in-law of Moses, observed the power struggle and confronted Moses. He spoke out:

> What is this thing that you are doing for the people?...the thing is not good. Both you and these people who are with you will surely wear yourselves out."[3]

Jethro had witnessed a timeless super dynamic of the human experience unfolding before his eyes - the attempt of a leader to single-handedly introduce the one thing into a closed system that is needed most, but is wanted least - *CHANGE.*

John Harris looks back on his experience at attempting innovation at St. John's, and fifteen years later he writes:

> We are in a dilemma which we (the church) often do not even grasp; it irritates both clergy and lay leadership. It is, I believe, the core difficulty in our church life, and it springs from our unwillingness to face up to the need for change in a rapidly changing society.[4]

Unwillingness to face change so permeates the society of the late twentieth century that one business author alleges that even corporate America has begun to treat the innovator "like a one-dimensional (and weird) being with no interest in the

---

[2]   *Change agents* are, as often as not, also *intentional outsiders*. See Chapter V, note 8.
[3]   Exodus 18:14, 17-18, NKJV.
[4]   Harris, 23.

world out there."[5]

In government service anyone pointing out faults in the system and suggesting alternatives to the status quo is labeled a "whistle-blower" or is suspected of being a profiteer. In the church our response has been to label the lay person crying for change as a religious "fanatic" (liberal church title), or as a "commie or pinko" (conservative church title). As a student pastor in the United Methodist Church, when I sought to do new things, I was described as not being a "real United Methodist."

Later, when I attempted innovation as an ordained minister in the United Church of Christ, I was told I wasn't "really a Congregationalist and just didn't understand our ways." Pastors who seek to bring local churches into the current era are always met with opposition and are usually accused of being different - "not one of us." In other cases, attempts are made to discredit them, intimating they are liars or worse.

One of the first things a potential leader should realize is that leaders are called and appointed to face, introduce, and effect *change*. Long-term studies of a wide variety of companies show that the "most successful firms" not only maintain workable equilibrium for several years (church leaders are good at this), but "are also able to initiate and carry out sharp, widespread changes...when their environment shifts."[6] Churches traditionally do poorly in this area. The second thing

---

[5]   Tom Peters and Nancy Austin, A Passion for Excellence: The Leadership Difference, (New York, Random House, 1985), 28.

[6]   Jeffery Pfeffer, Managing With Power. Boston, Harvard Business School Press, 71. As quoted from Michael L. Tushman, William H. Newman and Elaine Romanelli "Convergence and Upheaval: Managing the Unsteady Pace of Organizational Evolution," California Management Review 29 (1986), 29-44.

those contemplating accepting leadership roles should realize is the loneliness that will be encountered. In many cases potential leaders in the church (clergy and lay) view the risks and trials of leadership, choosing a ministry of management instead. In these terms - *leadership* vs. *management* - lie the pivotal choice in the decade before us. Stated in real terms, this choice reflects *life or death for the church*. The question each person in a primary church position must ask of themselves is "Am I going to settle for maintenance management or shall I move on to creative leadership?"

Managers from Hell

For decades the terms manager and leader have been used interchangeably. For this reason, and because we've trained our minds to glorify management (administration) and suspect leadership (innovation), the church in particular and American society in general, are in serious trouble. Warren Bennis has coined the most widely accepted axiom concerning this misdirection of energy. He says:

> I was finally able to come to some conclusions of which perhaps the most important is the distinction between leaders and managers. Leaders are people who do the right thing; managers are people who do things right.[7]

He goes on to say that "American society... is underled and overmanaged." This same condition represents the most concise diagnosis of the cause of failure in the American church - *underled and overmanaged.*

---

[7] Warren Bennis, Why Leaders Can't Lead: The Unconscious Conspiracy Continues, (San Francisco, Jossey-Bass Publishers, 1989), 18.

In the church there are several factors that encourage members to choose management over leadership. First, the status quo is tremendously attractive, especially when it comes to existing friendships and relationships. Experts tell us most people choose a church for its value as a community offering needed sanctuary. If we are accepted and become accustomed to receiving the accolades, security, and the pleasurable feeling received from safe relationships, we are not going to endanger those relationships. If change occurs, we become aware that it could cost "my friends and myself more money and it could force me to interact with new, strange, and different people."

To illustrate just how addictive security and familiarity can be, let me share the following from my memories. Several years ago, before the interstate highway system was finished, I remember driving through the South on old US 301. There was only one national chain of restaurants at the time and they were few and far between. The quality of food they served was mediocre, the service terrible, and the prices excessive. In spite of this, my family passed by hundreds of other local establishments, not willing to try anything unknown for fear of the outcome. We often drove for hours, to find the warm sense of security found under the familiar "orange roof." The status quo for us was terrible, but we still chose it over the unknown.

Secondly, many people in the church are uninvolved and often unaware of global forces impacting on the church. Many members called to official status in the church are unenlightened as to the system-wide failure the church is facing. Observation from the inside can be a real shock. Because lay persons are unpaid and have other priorities, it is a real sacrifice to give the time and effort necessary to productively respond to the need for change and leadership.

The temptation is to enjoy the status quo and ignore the dynamic issues facing the leaders. Conversely a manager can simply sit back and keep the "old girl afloat" during his or her term of office and let the "next guy handle the problem."

Thirdly, and this is a relational matter again, we have been taught to "work through the system and not to challenge it, we are taught not to be a maverick."[8] A lay person anticipating leadership is often overwhelmed by:

- ✓ at least 2000 years of tradition

- ✓ dedicated experts who are well-trained

- ✓ "It's always worked before, why change it?" logic

- ✓ the fear of being chastised and embarrassed by others.

I have seen marriages threatened and families go to war over a church relational issue. It takes a lot of dedication to challenge an embedded custom, even if everyone knows the practice is counterproductive. It takes even more courage to introduce a vision for the future, especially when doing so may mean Christmas dinner alone or a locked bedroom door.

All of these factors impact upon and are impacted by the specter of a church stuck in a "monochronological"[9] time warp. This time warp is reinforced by the symbols, ideas, and need satisfaction structures of a "world gone by." The operational philosophy of the mainline church is being held

---

[8] Lyle E. Schaller, Create Your Own Future!, (Nashville, Abingdon Press, 1991), 19-20.

[9] Leonard I. Sweet, Quantum Spiritually: A Postmodern Apologetic, (Dayton OH, Whaleprints, 1991), 2.

firmly intransigent by the generational ethic of those who experienced the "religious boom of the 1950's." The officials, administrators, core members and membership at large in the mainline church were born well before World War II and matured in the period from 1940 through 1960.

An unexpected development from this "era lock" is "the inability of the mainline Protestant and Catholic denominations (and churches) to attract and retain adults who were born during the baby boom following World War II."[10] To compound the problem, the children born of the 1950's, 60's, and 70's, following on the heels of their parents triumphant and prosperous generation, have acquiesced to a kind of "hold the fort" - "conserve your assets" mentality. These children have not found the strength to venture forth with their own vision. It's as if the anomalous growth and innovations of the first half of the century have left those of the second half destitute of ideas or purpose of their own.

While in theology school at Emory University in the early 1980's, I can remember much talk about "the age of apathy." This reference was being made about the people of congregations contemporary to that time who were being expected to assume leadership roles in their churches, but were declining Instead, they were opting to become managers of the status quo.

In his book <u>Transforming Leadership</u>, Leighton Ford focuses on this situation:

> There seems to be an adequate supply of leaders aged over fifty-five, with many emerging under forty, but there are not so many in between.[11]

---

[10] Lyle E. Schaller, <u>It's A Different World! The Challenge For Today's Pastor</u>, (Nashville, Abingdon Press, 1987), 84.
[11] Leighton Ford, 24.

Renaissance or Ruin

He goes on to list the six factors on which this deficiency in the social personality of America can be blamed, and the reader will recognize many of these from other observations in this book. The six factors are:

1. Cogent parents / Docile child

2. Instant gratification

3. The breakdown of extended families

4. Over-specialization

5. Individual powerlessness

6. Skepticism of authority

First, the *strong father - weak son* theory. Typically cogent parental personalities with laudable, accomplishing lives, foster offspring, the greater number of whom are docile and apathetic. It may be that these children see any attempt at accomplishment as useless or as being dwarfed by the overly successful parent. An old Indian proverb states that "nothing can grow under a banyan tree," said tree being symbolic of a large all-encompassing powerful personality.

Secondly, and partly as a result of the parental personalities above, is the fact that those born in the 1940's and 1950's grew-up accustomed to a life of *instant gratification*. Their parents were so successful partly due to a driving fear of failure that came from childhood memories of the great

Depression. As a result, this W.W.II generation worked hard, saved hard, and accomplished great things to insure that they and their children would never want again. They achieved their goal. That generation, now the senior citizens of the 80's and 90's, have more money and power than any other generation of older people in history. Their children have, therefore, been reared on a fertile diet of money, pleasure, and an abundance of goods. These children are now the 40 to 55 age group who have become accustomed to getting what they want, when they want it. There is little basis for leadership here.

Third, we must consider the *breakdown of family* ties. Because of divorce, parental separation, and massive movements of populations away from nuclear families, there has been little or no modeling for this leaderless generation. These cultural components continue to wield ominous influence even over the lives of the currently maturing generation. Those reared during the 1940's through 1960's grew up in a time when divorce proliferated. Combine this with the wider acceptance of absentee parenting, and a picture of gradually fraying connections to traditional values begins to emerge.[12]

The strong connection to things like church and faith were put aside in lieu of greater mobility. Fifty percent of the people in their forties live hundreds, even thousands of miles away from their ancestral family birth place. The strong devotion toward, and desire to serve and preserve, the "old church house" is no longer prevalent. Also, with no older

---

[12] I do not use the term "traditional values" in the political or narrow context that has come out of the conservative right during the election campaign of 1992. Here I refer simply to cultural customs attached to the family church house, and reinforced in the operations of rights (rites) of passage, that formerly were embedded in, and easily transferred to, each succeeding generation.

relatives in close proximity, doing the work of the deacon or agonizing over the church's plight, no model exists to whom the younger generation can turn to learn how to live the life of an active church member and leader.

The fourth factor shared by the business world and the church is *over-specialization*. The potential leader of the contemporary era is reared and labors daily in a world that has become divided and subdivided into areas of endeavor and discipline. Under these circumstances, it is hard to develop institutional leadership in people. A true leader with a wide enough power base to effect broad institutional change must be able to see the overall situation.

Managers and workers today are indoctrinated to become absolute experts on one small specialized function, to turn inward "onto" their specialty. The long held practice of looking over the wall to see what is taking place in reference to the whole is now discouraged. No church leader can expect to be effective while being exclusively focused on one area of endeavor to the exclusion of others. The church may be one organism, but it's made-up of many interdependent functionaries. The spiritual - the practical, the past - the future, the traditional - the innovative, the earthly - the heavenly, even the human and the Godly, ALL must be in focus. Church leadership must be broad-based, eclectic, and altruistic even while retaining the self.

Fifth, there appears to be an over-riding sense of *powerlessness* to inaugurate change in society as a whole. Earlier I addressed the issue of power in the church, of how power and lusting after it seems to have invaded the church. Remember also that there were two kinds of power. Pejorative power which only serves to inhibit change and satisfy self, while its antithesis, productive power, helps to create, change, and do good work. The sense of powerlessness felt in contemporary society comes from daily encounters in a world system which runs mainly on pejorative self-serving power. Young idealists are recruited into the secular system often desiring to create new and better systems to benefit larger numbers of people. These young dreamers desire to wield productive power, but become discouraged as controlling self-gratifing power interests thwarts their every plan.

Jack Welsh, the ambitious and effective new CEO of General Electric recently discussed the tenacity of this force and its effect on a multi-national corporation. After rising to the company's chief post, Jack was left the job of turning around the unproductive, unprofitable manufacturing giant. Like any good executive, he did the painful task of cutting payroll. Next, Welsh instituted new programs of employee involvement, quality control and innovation. His plan worked. By 1988 the company was in the 4% to 5% growth area and was seemingly on its way to Twenty-first century expansion and profitability.

Then it happened! A small core of old-liners at the center - Welsh calls them "bureaucratic bosses from Hell" - began to use pejorative power to unravel the work force. Their tactics so demoralized the new, young, bright executives that Jack has had to spend the last three years in re-training the embedded power core. He had to convince them that we as people are not powerless to change the world in which we live. If helping these old-line managers see that there was a broader, wider vision had not been accomplished, the G.E. Company, built over a century of hard work, could have disappeared in 24 months.[13]

---

[13]   Noel M. Tichy & Stratford Sherman, "Walking the Talk at GE", Training and Development, June 1993, 26-35.

Many people today work not only in cubicles, managing a small specialty, but are also controlled and isolated by the cubicle. We have been taught to work through the system, but the systems in our society are so large and complex that most perceive it as useless to attempt to carry a visionary idea or a corrective concept through such a maze. Even Jack Welsh CEO, with seemingly unlimited power, had extreme difficulty pulling it off. The result is a forced apathy or a sense of powerlessness. "Why," asks the idealist, "should I attempt change or exert leadership when such a maze of obstacles stands in my way."

By Whose Authority?

The sixth and final contribution to the overmanaged, underled society is the modern *skepticism of authority*. Ironically this attitude began in a time of change and in an era of vibrant leadership.

The 1960's brought a time when the very non-leaders of today were playing their one-and-only leadership card. A great assessment took place during those years of upheaval when all of the traditional standards of authority were called into question. Governmental authority was being misused, killing thousands in Vietnam. Racial, political and ecclesiastical authority was found to be the chief force in perpetuating racism. Business and labor's authority was also exposed in that they practiced excluding millions from the work force while paying high premiums to others. The flag was burned, the politics of the country challenged and a general discrediting of traditional authority was shared by an entire generation.

Parental authority, seen as the basis of all socialization, was called into question for the first time. Millions of people came forward to tell of physical, verbal, and sexual abuse they had suffered as children. Fatherhood and motherhood went down the tubes. To these revelations we've added Watergate, "Irangate," Jim Bakker, Jimmy Swaggart, and the many priests and ministers arrested for acts of sexual immorality against parishioners and staff members. Scandal after scandal has left this generation of emerging leaders bereft of any trust of authority.

A two-fold problem emerges from this situation. In order to wield the authority and to be a leader, especially in the church, one must be first willing to surrender to authority, and to do so in two ways. Every leader in every church needs to surrender to God's authority. Those serving in the more conservative churches would more readily admit they have done this than would their counterparts in the typical mainline church. These mainline congregations with a liberal humanistic slant in theology would almost defy one of its core members to surrender to God's authority.

The second basis of authority that needs to be recognized and accepted by every church leader is the authority of the congregation. Here the conservative would perhaps have greater problems then the mainliner. Some individuals would find it easier to surrender to God, who cannot be seen, than to the board of deacons, some of whom may not have the follower's respect to begin with. Each member of that same deacon board must, in turn, be willing to then surrender to the will of the congregation. For the power personality, this is often an even harder pill to swallow. The successful church leader accepts both of these authority foundations.

When Jesus was asked to define the bottom line of all religion and relationships of the church, He said

> to love God with all your heart, soul, and mind (this includes submitting to God's authority),

and love your neighbor as yourself", (submitting to the authority of your fellow believers).

The plaguing question for the generation of the *fin de' siecle*[14] remains, "can we produce leaders from a generation of people who will not accept authority?" The answer of course is No.

Thus we find ourselves embedded in an age of pernicious apathy. An in-between age which follows a generation of great movers and shakers, living, as it were, under a banyan tree where nothing is able to grow.

In this world of specialization, individual powerlessness, skepticism, and apathy, the church has often - no usually - opted to hire its leader. Immature, dependent, narcissistic, and therefore failing groups, often give-up internal leadership and turn to one strong leader. This is what the Israelites did with Moses. This return to a childlike method of carrying out business is a regression to a time when we had a strong Mom or Dad to follow. The result is a leadership void among the greater portion of the laity and clergy. This is accompanied by an over dependence on one or two leaders; a condition, as we have seen, which soon degenerates into despotic rule.

This unacceptable situation of hired or self-appointed rulers can occur quite naturally because some individuals seem more fit for the job of leading. Also some desire, often selfishly, to lead more than others. Finally, most people would rather be followers, willingly following other individuals - it's less risky.[15] That is one of the beauties of hiring your leader - he or she can do all of the innovating and the congregation can do all the complaining. Then when thing get too touchy, you

---

[14] *French*, Turn of the Century.
[15] M. Scott Peck, M.D., <u>People of the Lie: The Hope for Healing Human Evil</u>, (New York, Simon and Schuster, 1983), 223.

can fire the leader. A similar condition prevailed in the time of the Exodus. Moses had some that challenged his authority but few that would be willing to share leadership. Some chronic complainers wanted to "manage" the situation by returning to Egypt, but no one volunteered to help "lead" forward into Canaan. Many were willing to inveigh to maintain the status quo, but few stood in public to acclaim God's promise of a change - from slavery in the desert to freedom in a land flowing with opportunity. That was too risky.

In a recent article in <u>Training and Development</u> magazine, chief executives from many leading firms were polled to find which of 31 educational and developmental topics they thought to be vital for the decades of the 1990's. Eighty-nine percent saw leadership training as vital; this figure was up a smashing fifty-one percent from just a few years earlier.[16] Many chief executives are encouraging employees to challenge their own systems, promising immunity from retribution and asking executives to become risk takers.

Many progressive firms are using their authority to reinvigorate leadership by introducing Tom Peters' concept of "MBWA" (management by walking around).[17] This encourages the manager to get out of the office thus confronting the world, bringing it and customers, as well as the demands of the society they serve, into the operating philosophy of the company. This process opens a closed system to innovation, welcomes in the outsider, and encourages changes to reflect the environment. By meeting the needs of the society in which the company resides, success is assured.

Contrast this to the contemporary Christian church. The house of God built upon the innovative, revolutionary idea

---

[16] Robert W. Mann and Julie M. Staudenmier, "Strategic Shifts in Executive Development," <u>Training and Development</u>, July 1991, 37-39.
[17] Tom Peters and Nancy Austin, 6.

that God wanted to know humans and have humans know God. God was willing to risk everything, giving up the safety of heaven to literally "Manage By Walking Around." Jesus was God involved in MBWA.

- Jesus came as an *intentional outsider*

- He lived as an *agent of change*

- His preaching and teaching was filled with *openness*

- Jesus finally died to gather *every person* from every age *into the kingdom of love*.

The current practice of the mainline church, that of doing things right - rather than doing the "right" thing, of management over leadership, has proven disastrous. We have left His church hiding in fear of change, a closed system rather than an open community, and the least inclusive, most isolated, most racist, and most divided institution on the face of the globe.

In desperation, one can almost hope that Jethro, God's change agent from a bygone era, would come again, this time to prophesy to the church of Jesus as he did to Moses 3,000 years ago, saying:

> What is this thing you are doing...the thing that you are doing is not good.

Britt Minshall

TRIGGER POINTS

1. Draw a small circle (dime size) in the center of an 8 1/2" x 11" piece of paper. Place your initials in the circle. Draw other like circles on all sides of the first, each one representing your closest friends and relatives Next, out from these but touching the second group draw still more circles, each one standing for other less close friends and acquaintances. Finally, draw an outer layer of circles to represent the number of church members you know well and others in your sphere of activities. In conclusion, draw straight lines between your circle and all of the others. Also draw lines connecting each of the other circles.   Now using this tangled mess:

2. What considerations arise in trying to introduce change into any such model?

3. How many people in your discussion group are represented in each other's drawing?

4. When considering making a suggestion involving a change, which of these factors would deter you most often: 1) Church tradition. 2) Lack of knowledge. 3) Fear of making thing worse. 4) Fear of being embarrassed or rejected.

CHAPTER VII

GOD WILL BE WITH YOU

In the midst of the darkest years of the struggle for religious toleration in Poland, Cardinal Stefan Wyszynski, the prelate of Poland, had a dream. On the night of March 13, 1956, as he slept in his bed, during the small hours of the morning, a vision so clear and so intense that it wakened him, befell the Cardinal.

He dreamed that he and his arch-adversary, President Boleslaw Bierut, the number one man in Polish Communist politics, were walking together on the streets of Lubin conversing as they had many times in the Belvedere Palace. Just then the Cardinal dreamed that he wished to interject an important thought on church-state affairs, but as they reached an important intersection, the Polish President just disappeared. The Prelate struggled to find his adversary as he proceeded to cross the street obeying the rules of the road, crossing in the crosswalk and obeying the signal. He looked up to see Bierut jaywalking and wandering aimlessly ahead of him. He apparently thought of warning him of the danger in that style of action but just then the President disappeared from view again. The Cardinal could not find his political enemy, so he woke up from the dream with a start and proceeded to begin his daily routine.

A few hours later after morning mass the Cardinal turned on the radio to learn that late on the previous evening President Boleslaw Bierut of Poland had died a thousand miles away in Moscow. He had not been sick, there had been no warning and the radio announcement was the first to be made. Andrzej Micewski, Wyszynski's biographer, admits "The dream must mean more to parapsychologists than to historians,"[1] and I postulate many will share the same idea in reading of this book. Many wishing to "get a handle" on leadership/power issues in the church, ascribe little value to religious forces or God's supernatural workings occurring within our modern age. They see these events as idle superstitions.

Cardinal Wyszynski, however, was an empirical personality and not given to spiritual visions. He had been born and educated in Poland and attended college later in Rome. He was a good "team player" displaying tenacious obedience to the church and worked long and hard in the parish. In 1946, at the age of forty-four, he became the youngest Bishop in Poland. He continued to be promoted

---

[1] Andrzej Micewski, <u>Cardinal Wyszynski</u>, (New York, Harcourt, Brace, Jovanovich Publishers, 1984), 151.

because of his persistent work of negotiation between the church and the communist state. He was imprisoned for his "hard line stand concerning the church" and became a hero of the church. Between 1957 and 1970, while he served as head of the Polish church he won every round in the perpetual conflict with the state, and is seen today as a martyr of the church and a hero of his nation. He worked diligently within the system, from his youth until six days before his eightieth birthday, finally succumbing to cancer of the lymphatic system.

When investigating the church, one must be aware that this earthly institution, more than any other enterprise of humankind, is subject to continual contact with God and consequently the mysteries surrounding creation and its creator. Therefore, the inexplicable, the not wholly scientific, and the not always rational must be expected. The Cardinal, a career church politician and statesman, was not the type to extol mystical encounters with God, nevertheless his dream was far from explainable.

Every organization that is contrived by the human race must receive authority for existence and its mandate to operate from some source greater than itself. This mandate then becomes both its warrant and its reason for existence. In the natural scheme of things any enterprise that deviates far beyond that warrant, without specific and agreed amendment by the authorizing body, cannot long endure. In most instances, organizations which last the longest are those who constantly maintain a close dialogue with both the authorizing body and the ever changing needs of the social environment in which they exist. In this balanced state there is created an ever changing dialogue, forcing continual realignment between these the two polemical entities (authority and environment). This constant tension results in an ever changing mandate and the perpetual issuance of amended warrants.[2]

By way of example, W. T. Grant and Company received its license to operate a retail store from the states in which it operated. It received its mandate to operate from its board of directors and stockholders which gave it birth. The company was able to offer a product that was highly acceptable to the people of the communities which it served. Therefore a relationship based on service was inaugurated. The needs of the post World War II community changed drastically, but the company kept the dialogue open and thereby changed its marketing strategy to meet those needs. This market force for change operated as follows:

- People rated the company by their patronage.

- The company realized the rating in profits.

---

[2] The Constitution of the United States is so successful for this same reason. Factional interests ever placing pressure at the extremes continually creates an amended document. If the Constitution were static it would break, figuratively speaking, its fluidity keeps it ever a living organ.

- W. T. Grant revised their mandate to reflect these demands.

- The people accepted the revision and increased their purchases.

During the late 1950's, the needs changed again and the company responded with yet another new mandate. This gave its stores a revised warrant. The result was unheard of expansion. As long as the W. T. Grant Stores were permitted to keep this interaction going between the people (environment), and the authorizing authority (its owners), the company thrived.

But then something happened!

Middle management began to operate the stores for their own benefit. Many district managers, merchandise managers, and store executives, in concert with some upper level executives, isolated the company from the people of the community. They ignored and outright denied the authority of the stockholders and the board. Because little upper level leadership was being exerted on middle management, the open relationship between the server and the served gradually closed. Necessary change did not occur and the company began to die. By 1979, the once great retail giant was gone. The cadre (middle management), those that Jack Welsh of General Electric would later call the "bureaucrats from hell," had not stood before the owners reflecting the needs of the buying public, therefore the organism ceased to function.

In this respect the church is little different from W. T. Grant or the Great Atlantic & Pacific Tea Company (A & P), also dead for lack of leadership. The church exists by nature of a mandate from its birthing authority (God), for the purpose of serving its community (the people of creation). The cadre of the church is comparable to the leaders/workers who receive the operating warrant of service. Throughout the history of the Christian church, this tension between the natural and the supernatural, *humanity* - (the explicable), and *God* - (the miraculous), has energized the church. If the church denies either the continual influx of people or the active miraculous power of God, it disallows God's intervention in human life. In this case the flow of righteous force, literally the dialogue between God and the world, ceases to pour forth and the life-giving stream will stagnate.

Sociologists, anthropologists, and psychologists have begun to see life force as a series of "deep-flow, micro-flow, and non-flow modes." Every experience of our being can be categorized as one of these states. If a person spends too much time in a state of micro-flow (coffee breaks, television watching, etc.), that person's mind and life flow begins to dwindle to a trickle; in contemporary popular language the person becomes a "couch potato." In this state the person's life trickles by in a state of "existence" moving toward a non-flow state. This state of mentality can be likened unto the physical state of a person in a coma, the veins and arteries of the body, deprived of the effect of exercise upon the blood flow rate, may soon be subject to blockage and eventual death.

When the church, which is designated by God to be a very deep-flowing experience, begins to deny its interaction with God and further isolates itself from the community outside its walls, it suffers from "flow deprivation." It begins to exhibit "tiredness, sheepishness, and decline in creativity."[3] Instead of existing in the world as the purveyor of the "rushing mighty wind" described in Acts, Chapter Two, it becomes an indolent, languid flow not unlike a stream of molasses.

- Premature death always results.

This is equally true of a retail corporation, or an organization birthed by God. During our generation, God's great mover and shaker, the church, has become the world's largest couch potato.

Leadership is the only force that can sustain victory over such a chronic social situation. W. T. Grant Company could not muster the required leadership. Neither could the once great A&P Company.

---

[3] Leonard Sweet, 71.

The bottom line issue we must address here is really two-fold:

1. Can the church formulate godly leadership amongst its ranks?

2. What does Christian leadership entail?

Defining Leadership

The modern word *leadership* is a term derived from two ancient words - 𝔏𝔢𝔞𝔡𝔢𝔫 and 𝔖𝔠𝔥𝔦𝔭. *Leaden* was an Anglo-Saxon word which meant *to move an object by pushing from behind, pulling from in front, or prodding by walking alongside.*

By the period of the Middle English the word had come to include the moving of people as well as objects. Shortly thereafter it began to mean moving only people and not objects.

The suffix "ship" or *schip* comes from the Old English evolving through middle English. It was used to denote the *ability of creating a new thing out of an existing thing - a skill to form a new thing.* The word "Shape" has the same root.

When we place these two parts together, as we do to form the modern word leadership, the amplified, contemporary word leadership literally means:

> The ability to move a person or a group of persons to create or shape something new out of something old. To change the position of said person or persons by pushing from the rear, pulling from the front, or walking beside. The ability of one person to direct, encourage, and guide other persons to grow and achieve a better, stronger position by altering, changing, or introducing new ideas or visions.[4]

It should be noted that throughout the above definition there are references to leaders being able to introduce change, growth, and movement.

During the early part of the nineteenth century, America became a nation that extolled management and discouraged leadership. A *manager*, according to the dictionary definition, is one "who dominates or influences, one who has charge of or the responsibility for..." The question is left - for what? In this definition there is no imperative for movement or growth - for change or creation. Management then is maintaining, not moving forward. It is easy to see in this definition, and in the practices of American business of the past seventy years, the source of Warren Bennis' axiomatic

---

[4] Brinton P. Minshall, "The Leader's Ship: The Development of a Model and Curriculum Leading to Proactive Lay Leadership in the Local Church," D. Min. dissertation., Boston University, 1992, 33.

statement:[5]

> ***Leaders*** *do the right things;*
> ***managers*** *do things right.*

Subsequent to reading this clarification of these two terms, the reader may be able to recognize the major problem of the church, bred in a society that is *management oriented* and *leadership excluding*.

A ***manager***, as here defined, may be committing a great evil, all the while doing things "just right." If, for example, a Mafia chieftain were to be deported, he might leave his drug empire in the hands of an able manager. By using the right (correct) techniques of production, distribution, and collection including murder, coercion, or blackmail, the manager may be able to maintain the drug business indefinitely. No matter how well-dressed, articulate, or educated this "manager" might become, his actions could never be defined as "leadership." He's a manager because he's upholding his boss' orders and he's *doing things right*.

A ***leader***, on the other hand, is mandated to always do "the right (good, proper, just) thing." A leader would never be found in the illicit drug trade because it is illicit. A leader could never become the head of the Nazi party because it's not just. A leader would not consider getting his or her own way by manipulation or political force, because it's not proper.

---

[5] Warren Bennis, 18.

By using the same analogy and working definitions, traditional management can be of little use in the church because the people who hold responsibility in the church are ALWAYS charged with the creation of that which is good, proper, and just. A manager is of little help to a stagnated church because managers only maintain and keep things going as they are.

The leader in the church, on the other hand, responds by working to create better out of lessor, by moving people to a greater place. The leader accepts the ultimate challenge of breaking the status quo by introducing change and movement where little flow now exists and stagnation has set in.

When I first began to develop a model for leadership workshops I thought much of the above was a play on words, but I've begun to see it is much more. When Bennis says "Leaders do the right thing and managers do things right," he has created a viable working polemic (two opposite extremes) defining the area of responsibility in the human community. Leaders and managers are no more closely related than are architects and demolition engineers. They may have gone to the same school and read the same books, but outside the doors of the University they took two completely separate roads that never intersect in concept, methods or results.

Requirements For Church Leadership

Leadership in any setting requires many traits and disciplines, and in most settings these requirements are very similar. We will review these standard requisites for leadership later, but first we must look at the church, the field of our study, to establish the warrant or basis for leadership in that setting.

W. T. Grant Company, AT&T, and the church are, and/or were, well vested with leaders, managers and followers at the time of their greatest successes. In failure leaders either disappear or are shut out, and they are always silenced. Managers take over the helm and the followers are manipulated into accepting the status quo. As often as not, one of the first acts of the manager in taking control or becoming the ruler is to cut ties to any authority outside of the group.

In the case of Grant's, the runaway management circumvented and shut out the stockholders and directors who then refused to take leadership. In the case of mutiny in the military, rebellious officers shut out or cut off the rank and file soldiers from the General Headquarters and the government. When incest occurs, the controlling abuser shuts out all other authority in the child's life with threats and innuendoes, thus isolating the child. In a clique-controlled church, the pastor's pay is kept so low that he/she becomes dependent on the local hierarchy for "hand-outs," thus shutting out the authority of the congregation and the denomination. Also in this situation, the power core usually keeps the conference and the denomination at bay by not participating in inter-church programs. You will note that in each of these cases, the dialogue that keeps systems open, that flowing between authority and the subject or the people at large, is closed and therefore killed.

The first thing the would-be church leaders must do is to re-open the closed system. There must be openings at either end of the system to allow communication and communion to be reestablished. In this way, things begin to move first at a trickle, later at a gush. The molasses of apathy, like clots in the circulation, must be dissolved and replaced by the rush of the Spirit and the hopes of creation.

A chronic situation that has always affected the Christian church, whether hiding in the catacombs from the Roman government or in the European forests from the invading Vandals, Ostrogoths or Vikings, is the propensity of the congregation to evolve into a *closed system.* Perhaps Christianity inherited this tendency toward being a closed system from Judaism. The ancient Jews[6] saw creation as a "done deal." God began to act, and in seven *epochs* (days) it was finished, and that is that. They theorized that Abraham

---

[6] The general text and popular interpretation of Hebrew Scripture forms a model of closed community, eventually leading to a theme of racial, religious, and cultural purity. Ironically, it appears that throughout the early centuries, even to and through the Exodus, Israel was anything but one cohesive people, racially or culturally. For a complete treatment of this see John Bright, A History of Israel, Phila., (Westminister Press, 1981), 133 - 143.

was their biological father, followed by Isaac, Jacob...and so goes the lineage to the current race. According to Jewish thought, the blessing to all people (all Israelites) that Abraham's relationship with God was to bring, was closed to outsiders. Old Testament scriptures are replete with injunctions against, and instances of, punishment for interpersonal relations with peoples outside the race and the faith of the Jews.

The events of the first one thousand years of Christian history served to ensconce that closed system paradigm upon the theology of our churches. As the invaders from the north and east swept across Roman and post Roman Europe, the ever-present fear of loss eventually embedded deep into the European psyche a fear of change and the outsider (xenophobia). The church was the sole stabilizing force during this era. It was the one allegiance that was constant. It could be carried in the hearts and minds of fleeing refugees and recreated anywhere. Furthermore, entry into the church could be defined by submission to a belief in Christ. Not just a belief in any Christ, mind you, but in "Our" Christ. This was given to mean the Christ that "We" defined in "our" culture.

Through the ages, there have been many attempts at the formation of a Common Catechism. However, the initial splintering of our faith system between Eastern Orthodoxy and Western Catholicism has ever grown, dividing and subdividing. Early on, the church of the Celts in Britain evolved differently

Renaissance or Ruin

than the church of the Romans on the same island. Celtic missionaries to Germany carried that division which became sharper in the Northern European culture as time passed. In all these cases there appears to be over a 90% agreement on a Christian common catechism. Ironically, the remaining minuscule portion, perhaps arising out of the human need to own an exclusive deity, or to feel a one-ups-men-ship over others, tends to become the main focus of different ethnic and cultural groups. While somewhat simplistic, out of this historical development came the fear that creates the basis for the closed system of today - a *church of xenophobic isolation*.

The difficulty here is that the church does not have the option of being a closed system. Creation can never be closed. As long as time and the universe lasts, as long as there is a God, all creation is a continuing and *open system*.

Jurgen Moltmann attacked the closed system church in his writings. He even defines sin in these terms.

> Having called creation in the beginning a system open for time and potentiality, we can understand sin and slavery as the self-closing of open systems against their own time and their own potentialities. If a person (or a church) closes himself against his potentialities, then he is fixing himself on his present reality and trying to uphold what is present, and to maintain the present against possible changes...Closed systems bar themselves against suffering and

self-transformation. They grow rigid and condemn themselves to death.[7]

Moltmann alludes here to the deleterious result of a church maintained by status quo management and offers church leaders their needed mandate.

If we are then to save the church, we must support leaders who will challenge the status quo, open the system and risk two things:

- *Risk opening the system to God.* Reintroduce the concept that we are the church of the Firstborn of God. We, individually and collectively, belong to Jesus Christ.

- *Risk opening the system to all people.* Invite, even cajole, all persons into the house of God. Adopt an attitude of giving the church away and trusting God for the outcome.

These leadership praxis will create an invigorated, truly open system, free from the great sin of "closedness."

Methods and Means

Lyle Schaller offers some concrete advice to the many churches suffering from *closed system syndrome*, suggestions for neutralizing the status quo mentality.[8] First there is the

---

[7] Jurgen Moltmann, The Future of Creation, (Philadelphia, Fortress Press, 1977), 122-123.
[8] Lyle E. Schaller, Create Your Future, 25-26.

Renaissance or Ruin

"Crisis Method." He postulates that concerned parishioners can simply wait for the arrival of the long denied but long overdue crisis.

St. Charles was one church that chose this way of coping with change. For years the leaders had refused to change or to innovate. Absolutely no leadership was exhibited and a maintenance mentality had been in place for at least a decade. The leaders continually avoided any futuristic planning or challenges. The church officers did everything possible to appear forward moving, but were in reality forward facing only, but non-moving in position. The forces of the universe, however, will not stand still for long. Rust soon attacked a major air conditioner, then another, and then another. Electrical problems reared their ugly heads in one building. The drapes began to literally fall in decay from the windows. The heater in the sanctuary was condemned just as aged telephone equipment drew its final breath. St. Charles found itself in crisis. Unfortunately for the congregation, the pastor who had forecast these events, asking them to "stretch and be proactive," had, in frustration, moved on. The church continues to head toward failure as membership declines while its cost of operating increases.

St. Charles and thousands of other churches employ this reactive method of operation. These leaderless institutions do not exist to plan and work to meet visionary goals, but rather, tread water waiting to react if a crisis occurs. One diagnostic tool to use in examining a church to find out if it is reactive, is to note whether it is in perpetual debt, always feigning poverty, yet can rally to buy items for the self enrichment and pleasure of its membership.

Another term used widely for this type of operating philosophy is *reactive management*. Many businesses at the brink of bankruptcy have traditionally operated in this mode, and all parties involved know how exhausting and haphazard this method of operating can be. Crisis is a sure way to break the status quo; unfortunately, it is often too late to help the church rebound.

Another method, often proposed to break the status quo, is to involve the persons handling the budget process. Goals agreed upon by the church can be converted into budget items. In this way the program and the funding can be promoted simultaneously; thus each supports the other. Schaller cautions:

> This usually fails. One reason is the power of yesterday in preparing budgets. A second is that a crisis in budget preparation usually fosters creativity for cutting back, not for expanding ministry. A third is represented by that budget officer's admonition, "It is extremely difficult to introduce anything new in next year's budget. It is even more difficult to delete anything that has been in the budget for three or more years."[9]

---

[9] Lyle E. Schaller, Create Your Future, 26.

Another reason for almost certain failure in this area is the fact that the status quo proponents can simply work privately not to meet the budget. A big part of the shutdown of St. Charles' core membership was financed in this way. Therefore, even if funding changes are approved in any given year, mid-year revisions can cancel any progress.[10]

The third, and in the past most accepted way to introduce change, is to bring in a change agent in the form of a new pastor. Schaller feels that this is still "the most effective means of challenging the status quo." As a pastor, I strongly disagree. I concede that this continues to be marginally effective. However, while it may bring short term gain, it also fosters the formation of a strong block against change. The change agent pastor then becomes "the" party on which to focus. Consequently, the changes are "his fault." It was good until "she" came. The mentality develops that all will be well when "this pastor" leaves.

John Harris, cited earlier in this work, myself, and countless other men and women who have been used as intentional outsiders (change agents) can attest to the traumatic situation this places our families in. Our denominations cannot continue to spend seven or eight years, and twenty or thirty thousand dollars to train pastors, simply to feed them to closed

---

[10] A major factor in the Strategic Planning Process, to be covered later in this volume, will call for the budgeting of items proposed by the planning committee. This is a far cry from ad hoc use of the budget process for the creation of new programs to invoke change.

system churches who stand rigid, "daring" the conference or denomination to "make them" grow and be productive. It is not only bad management, it is cruel to destroy the hopes and dreams of these idealistic new missionaries.

Those that survive this ordeal became cynics who now know how to "milk" or "work" the system, surviving with as few scars as possible. How does one survive?

> Don't try to change things Exert your effort in becoming a denominational systems person, and be a non-threatening, non-innovating local pastor.

In other words, one soon learns to give the power center exactly what it wants. Our culture does not allocate deference to the pastor as a special and noble icon of the Godhead. This renders these servants helpless against the onslaught of a determined adversary.

Many of these same young idealists give up on the church completely and go into social work, teaching, or the chaplaincy. Therefore, I disagree with Dr. Schaller on both the advisability and effectiveness of this method in today's society. The days are long past when pastoral privilege allowed for him or her to be an effective agent for change.

We are left with only two ways in which a leader who wishes to "stand before God" can do so effectively, proactively, and with reasonable hope of beating the status quo and reopening the closed system entrenched in our local churches:

- *Intervenor as Change Agent*

- *Internal Leadership Factor*

The first of these remaining two options offers the intervention of an intentional outsider, a third party change agent who can be touted as an expert, holding authority from a source not easily impeached.

The second is to introduce an internal leadership factor, a new task force with great power and broad core church representation. The task of this team is specifically defined as a long range planning group. While this Strategic Planning group must represent the cadre, many of whom serve on the church's governing board, under no circumstance can an existing committee be used for this purpose. Also, volunteers can be invited, but the group must be intentionally selected from all strata of the church in order to guarantee full participation. Let us examine these two methods of effectively introducing change into a closed status system.

Intervenor As Change Agent

It is plausible to believe that if God had not delivered an intentional outsider into the midst of the Hebrew community along the Nile, the nation of Israel would never have been founded. Judaism, the religious outcome of this event, would have existed as a minor Egyptian sect, if it developed at all, and Jesus would have been born in Thebes, not Bethlehem. The person of Moses was essential as an agent for change in the furthering of God's historical goal.

Within two years, however, everything came to a standstill. The Israeli camp was in "gridlock" and the people had ceased to move. Why? Because Moses, the change agent, had ceased to be that intentional outsider and was now very much an insider and part of the problem. His ability to keep the system open and moving had been neutralized.

God, however, in infinite wisdom, had seen fit to deliver another Intervenor as Change Agent. Enter Jethro, with whose story we are now familiar, asking as he arrived, "What are you doing with these people, you and they will wear yourselves out." This intervention shifted attitudes and the working order of the community, the system was re-opened and progress was made.

Six hundred years after the Hebrews had come into the promised land of Israel, initially prospering, then conquered, exiled and returned, Nehemiah came upon the scene. As the newly appointed governor of the re-settled City of Jerusalem (444-432 B.C.) he discovered his people had settled into a period of apathy. They had lost pride in their Jewishness, their city, and saw little in their future. The city walls had lain in disrepair for over one hundred years, and in that age this indicated a total lack of self confidence and a civic identity crisis. The new governor, fresh from Babylon, became the change agent. Over great opposition he challenged the people to rebuild the breached wall. The community on the whole acquiesced to his leadership and answered the call. In fifty-two days the wall was rebuilt. More importantly, the closed system of the status quo was opened and a nation began to rise from the ashes of defeat.

Historically there are three methods of change agent introduction in the American church experience:

1. *The Pastor*

2. *The Evangelist*

3. *The Parish Consultant*

The first we have already discounted as having less effect in contemporary society than in our grandparents' era. The *pastor*, the *priest* and the *preacher* is seen now as an employee. He/She can be "gotten to" and more easily controlled than in former ages. Reliance on employer group insurance, denominational pension programs, spouse career location considerations, and the high cost of relocation all join to unfold an umbrella of control over the pastor who would venture into the role of a crusader for change.

This tension between local power groups and the pastor as change agent, however, is not a new one. When Francis

Asbury devised the circuit system (developed from John Wesley's model) in the early Methodist church, part of his concept was to move the pastor out of the local church or churches before his role of change agent could be compromised. Any preacher wishing to "locate" (stay in one church and not move every two years) was put under harsh discipline and often had to give up his ordination. The role of these early circuit riders was not to pastor as we know it; that role went to the class leader or local lay leader (patriarch/sponsor). The pastor's job was to "point out sin wherever it existed." He therefore had to be immune from local power which would naturally try to interfere with such an excoriation process, especially if church members were involved in the sinful practice being highlighted (a Methodist layperson owning slaves for example).

Modern pastors locate and are thus severely compromised in their role as intervenor as change agent. We must look then to a second traditional change agent in the American experience - the *revivalist* or *evangelist*. This most notable figure of Americana was the itinerant preacher who came each year to the local church. He or she came saying "all the things that needed saying", convicting the, "resident sinners," and generally throwing the fear of God into the locals. This was done in such a way that would have gotten the local pastor "run out of town on a rail" if he had made such pronouncements.

In the modern church we have become accustomed to making fun of the stereotypical traveling preacher. We envision the "shyster" behind the Bible as seen in an Elmer Gantry or Sister Amy. This image was reinforced by Jim Bakker and Jimmy Swaggart, or by the pathetic figure of the uneducated, shabbily dressed and ignorant pig farmer, "the Preacher" turned evangelist in the saga <u>The Grapes of Wrath</u> by John Steinbeck. The modern, middle class educated family would place little credibility in anything that even appeared to smack of such revivalism.

Unfortunately the abandonment of this office is akin to "throwing out the baby with the bath water." In looking to Paul, the author of the "how-to book" of the western church, he clearly delineates the offices of the church. He writes in his letter to the Ephesians:

> And he himself gave some to be apostles, some prophets, some evangelists and some pastors and teachers, for the equipping of the saints for the work of the ministry for the edifying of the body of Christ.[11]

Each of these offices, albeit their names changed, must be present in the church in order for the work of the ministry and the building or edifying of the body to take place. Each office, with the exception of that of the evangelist, is present and has

---

[11] Ephesians 4:11-12, NKJV.

continued active[12] in the mainline church.[13] Not only is this office vacant, but the task assigned to this office is not being accomplished.

Traditionally the evangelist was ascribed but one task, and that was to lead people to belief in Christ. Throughout the history of the church pastors were expected as part of their duties to be an evangelist to at least some degree.[14] In the modern era, while we may pay lip service to this task, most churches would be alarmed if they were to be assigned a pastor who was strong as an evangelist. Further, any lay person in the congregation who began going about trying to "lead people to Christ" would, at best, soon find himself or herself isolated from other church members and labeled a "religious fanatic."

Even the word "evangelism" conjures up reactions of extreme discomfort if it is voiced in gatherings, either clergy or lay. In 1991, the Evangelism Institute of the United Church of Christ came to Florida for its three year term. The Institute was touring nationwide to try to "rekindle the flame" in our spiritually dead and dying churches. I served as one of the

---

[12] The task of the Apostle is now carried out by missionaries.
[13] There is currently a fledgling attempt to organize, legitimize and promote this ministry in several denominations. Most notable are the National Assoc. of United Methodist Evangelists and The Assoc. of Southern Baptist Evangelists. Other attempts include the Francis Asbury Society. Participants are "on their own," usually taking up this work at great financial loss to their families, receiving little denominational support.
[14] 2 Timothy 4:5.

Renaissance or Ruin

directors of E.I. in Florida. In calling on our pastors and churches I was granted the warm greeting that I had come to expect from my fellow church members. However, after the initial salutations were exchanged and simultaneous with the introduction of the words "Evangelism Institute," a chord of suspicion and wariness sounded across the room. Participation in E.I. reflected this attitude in that less than one third of our Florida churches participated.

To demonstrate this sad state of affairs, this small attendance was taken as a good omen since participation was far less in other conferences. After the fact, the same reaction awaited the local church representatives attending E.I. when they returned to their churches of origin. The excitement of the event and the enthusiasm internalized by the attendees was soon squelched by peer pressure at the local level. This negative acceptance resulted in either a disintegration or a generous diluting of the intended work of the Institute.

If our churches are to be edified, growing spiritually in wisdom and in numbers, it is imperative that we reinvent the office of the evangelist. Most denominations have long abandoned the office and the acceptance of both evangelism and evangelist.

Leaders in any local church or denomination who expect their church to grow are going to have to "bite the bullet" on this one. Some person or group in each of our churches needs to take the responsibility to re-introduce evangelism, and create a willingness, even a desire, to add new people to the kingdom and to the rolls of the local church. Here again the pastor can't do it. He or she may be pressured by both the local power structure and status quo conscious denominational executives to remain neutral and non-threatening. Local lay leaders won't do it alone. There will be no end to the coercion applied to neutralize their effort.[15] The reintroduction of the evangelist, as ordained by God, for the building of the body, is the church's most efficient method and most immediate opportunity for effective intervention by an intentional outsider as change agent.

Note please that the people of the church are as in need of faith renewal as the people outside our doors. Evangelists are needed to *reevangelize* the body and to reacquaint once excited believers to the joy of reawakened faith. Liberation Theologian Ronaldo Munoz of South American fame put it this way:

> The object is a more lucid reevangelization of our faith in God, a reevangelization that, on our own collective historical journey, will make that faith at once more personal and more prophetic,

---

[15] Millions of dollars have been spent and elaborate programs of lay evangelism training have been devised over the past 15 years. Some, such as *Evangelism Explosion,* seem to work better than others. Most, however, have little effect in the local church. These efforts need to continue, but cannot supplant the need for professional evangelists whose task it is to light the fire of faith in the local congregants, clergy and lay alike.

thereby recapturing the best tradition of the people.[16]

Denominational bodies that have not promoted the revival of this professional office should consider doing so at once. Groups such as the United Methodists who have introduced a structure for the renewal of this ministry should pay more than lip service to men and women who wish to accept this call.

The office of the evangelist and the work he/she does is a major missing ingredient in the effort to bring the church back to life. Evangelists can convict, or if you prefer, convince us of our sinfulness (individual and systemic), and of our separation from God in a much more dynamic way because they are outsiders. The evangelist can introduce contemporary music and worship into the local church by bringing into that church the new methods and materials being accepted across the greater church. The evangelist can, as an outsider, introduce more spiritual vigor and change into a congregation in four days than can the local pastor in four years. Because of their "outsidedness" this can be done without instigating an extended inner church or church-pastor conflict. An immediate, effective, and scriptural way to introduce change into a local church is then to find, train, enlist, and support professional evangelists.

---

[16] Ronaldo Munoz, The God of the Christians, (NY, Orbis Books, 1990), 41.

The third interventionist tactic is to seek out the *parish consultant*. This person or firm is seen as an expert on churches and how they function. The PC (not to be confused with personal computer) usually has years of experience as a local church pastor, which, at the risk of seeming to equivocate, is often but not always helpful, depending on the personal outlook and motivation of the PC. He or she has been taught the art of asking questions of the church, questions such as, "Who's in charge here; let me hear your 'real' history, what kind of people are you, 'truly,' where do you 'honestly' want to go?"

PC's come in two basic varieties. One is the *para-church consultant* from an independent group or company. The considerations here are to determine which group most closely aligns to your type of church, and what exactly you need to accomplish. Some firms specialize in helping the local pastor redirect the efforts of the church. Others deal more with the lay people at the church level and clergy on the external level. Some specialize in fund raising only, while others have introduced a major renewal/evangelism component along with the group dynamics evaluation and redirection. Most firms charge substantial fees, however, others will work with the church for extremely small fees. Church leadership will need to be diligent in fact finding well in advance.

The second type of parish consultant is the *denominational consultant*. Here a much larger spread in methods and effectiveness can be found. The denominational PC may be an employee of the General Synod or Conference, employed by a regional authority or under a local conference or association. He or she may be a young career person trained in group dynamics, but completely lack experience in the church. Otherwise, and this is more often the case, the consultant will have been a long term pastor who has years of internalized experience to offer. The latter can render good and valid observations as to the real flow and direction of the church. The difficulty arises from the fact that this person may be almost completely unaware of the methods, instruments, and technologies available for the implementation of long term change.

A word of caution to the pastor, and the church, is in order here. Some PC's are little more than retirees or semi-retirees looking to make extra income. While they may honestly feel that their years of experience would be helpful, in reality they may have become so much a part of the status quo and have served so long as "prophets in the problem," they are not able to lend to the solution. Also, their effectiveness may be compromised in that they are under direction from the denomination or conference to accomplish an agenda far different from the needs of the church. Consequently, these folks are often extremely limited in what they can accomplish.

The effective parish consultant will need months of preparation, and data supplied by test instruments.[17] He or she will need expertise in developing an inter-relational history of the congregation. This person or firm will need skills in game playing and a plethora of audio visual actualizers focused on enlisting and inspiring people. The parish consultant, along with the evangelist (or these two offices combined in one person), can be the most effective method to rebuild a dying church, or move a languid church to richer possibilities in membership and ministry.

The ultimate results to be achieved by any intervenor in the end rests in the hands of the local church. There are two forces that will affect any recovery deleteriously. Unfortunately, both are present in the majority of churches.

>   1. A pastor is often opposed to change and resistant to new methods.
>
>   2. Core church members often would rather see the church cease to exist than to accept change.

These two power centers in the church must be open and above-board with any intervenor. In like manner the

---

[17] Interlink Consultants of Overland Park, Kansas specializes in tests for church leaders. University Associates San Diego, California has a panoply of human resource development instruments. Human Synergistics of Plymouth, Michigan offers trainers the best team building materials available. All must be used by trained personnel only.

intervenor is cautioned to pay particular attention to these persons during his or her process. If this negativity remains in the congregation, all effort for change may be for naught, regardless of the consultant's efforts.

This leads me to the final factor in re-directing the closed system church, and that is *the internal faction*. You'll remember Jethro came to the Hebrew camp as a change agent and delivered his message accordingly. That however, was but half the task. Moses and his select people still had to effect the necessary changes. Thus the internal leadership factor must be structured in such a way as to facilitate redirection and regeneration; otherwise, any effort (even by an accomplished intentional outsider) will be an exercise in futility.

The Internal Leadership Factor

All of the external pressure in the world cannot force change upon an organism that does not choose to accept it. In the case of a person addicted to drugs, all the counseling and group therapy available will not inspire a cure until the addicted person becomes convinced (bottoming out) that a change in lifestyle is necessary and decides to give up drugs.

Jesus said, "You shall know the truth and the truth shall make you free."[18] We can translate one meaning of that statement to form the basis of dynamic counseling. In discovering the truth by seeing events and conditions as they

---

[18] John 8:32.

actually are, a person, or in our case a church, is then "free" to make decisions to either attempt to revise the situation or acquiesce to it. When drug dependent persons see themselves and their lives in the light of reality, the pain of that existence often moves addicts to seek a cure. Likewise, the change agent's job is not to implement changes but rather to help the congregation see the truth, free from myth or fantasy. From that vantage point, the church will be free to either accept the status quo or take actions necessary to actuate change.

If the church does desire to facilitate change, a rough road lies before it. The church is little more than an extended family (the smaller the church the closer the family ties), therefore it is built on many close, complex, and strong interpersonal relationships. Edwin Friedman, in his now famous book Generation to Generation, deals extensively with this extended family relationship.[19] He reminds the reader that we can only change a relationship to which we belong. This, you will note, excludes intentional outsiders as the final element of change. Their role is simply to inaugurate the process, placing final implementation squarely in the hands of the constituency.

Unfortunately we are less likely to confront for change in a relationship to which we belong. This supports the outside but connectional position of the change agent. He/she must be

---

[19] Edwin H. Friedman, Generation to Generation, (New York, The Guilford Press, 1985), 27-63.

Renaissance or Ruin

an outsider in order to present the problem, diagnose the disorder and help formulate the solution. On the other hand, the change agent needs to possess some connection through ordination or other credentials.

Once the intervenor's task is completed, insiders, that is to say the church's leaders, must carry out the revisions and develop new standards. The difficulty arises from the fact that communities are based on balance and on a set of norms well known and trusted by all. It is rare that a group left to its own will unanimously agree and work for major change. If one or two leaders in the church adopt new postures, you can be sure that a type of symmetry will come into play. "All the emotional pushes and pulls" will attempt to locate at zero, therefore keeping the group in balance and maintaining "homeostasis."[20]

Often factors such as family secrets, unnamed agendas, neuroses, control, and manipulation also encourage the group to leave well enough alone. When altering any chronic situation, as the change is introduced, things will always get worse before they start to improve. Consequently, if the bellwether of the congregation should defy the norm and suggest a change in an important area, almost certainly severe tension will be the first result and the rest of the church will close the system rapidly in order to restore order.

It is for all of the above reasons and many more, I'm sure, that many experts warn that existing structures cannot be

[20] Balance.

asked to plan, on their own, a future that differs from the past. The leaders of the church are already well fitted into official slots. The only change in most churches is the occasional exchange of offices among the same group of people. One Southern Baptist pastor reported that he had served a church in his early days in the ministry where it had become "normal" to rotate its chair position on the Board of Deacons between three young men perceived by the church as the leaders. One was a banker, one a lawyer and one an engineer. After leaving the church, he used to enjoy wagering, in jest, with his wife as to who would be the chairman in the next year. After twenty-five years, each January when the church newsletter arrived he was reassured that homeostasis was being maintained because he had been able to predict the choice. These same three men, now elderly, continue to pass the Deacon chair position among themselves. Incidentally this once great Baptist Church has declined in membership during those same years from a 1965 high of 975 to a 1991 low of 115.

If all of these observations of the infra-structure are valid, how can church leaders effect change? The only effective answer is to form an ad hoc committee or "super task force" with new and different mandates based on a long term planning model. This *Strategic Planning Committee* should be a broadly based committee with representation from all areas of the church, reflecting all of the interest groups, age classifications, and longevity's in membership. This committee should work under nine expectations. They are to:

1. Openly challenge the status quo - question everything.

2. Recommend changes while realizing they will probably be disruptive.

3. Be made up of a substantial number of people that the congregation sees as inventive and creative, especially people who are dissatisfied with current affairs.

4. Plan in stages: immediate innovations (two to six years), and long term expectations (two or three decades).

5. offer one or two specific alternatives to every recommendation to change in the status quo.

6. Vary in opinion so widely that consensus is impossible and compromise is often the only alternative. Occasionally an open ended suggestion will come from the group.

7. Innovate and are not to be expected to mobilize resources; this is the function of the congregation as a whole.

8. Develop a goodly bank of knowledge in a particular area and attempt to retain it, they may lose touch with the church as a whole. The best antidote is to encourage gradual sharing of information with the church.

9. Present the alternatives and should not be expected to do anything. The church must mobilize behind their report. However, this group should deliver its final report in such a way as to insist action be taken on their work.[21]

Combining the initial work of the intentional outsider, usually necessary to begin the process of change, with the long term work of a Strategic Planning Committee, appears to be the most comprehensive method to examine the problems, renew the faith and interest, and create a working thrust in the local congregation.[22]

With the work of the change agent completed, the congregation introduced to God as God relates to the world in which the church now lives and the truth laid before all concerned, the congregation can either choose to stay a closed system and face certain demise, or they can move forward to rebirth. Remember that in the end, death or life for a local church remains each congregation's choice. No one enjoys the

---

[21] Lyle E. Schaller, Create Your Future, 26-29.
[22] For a complete treatment of this lay follow-up planning stage see chapter eleven dealing with Strategic Planning.

thought of standing on the sideline watching a church die, but suicide for a church determined to carry it out can no more be avoided than can the suicide of a resolved person. Every organism must choose to live.

Moses answered Jethro's call wisely, the Hebrew leadership did the same and the people of Israel re-opened the closed system. They began communicating with God and the world in which they found themselves. By using the structures herein suggested, the American church has its best opportunity to open its closed system. The problem of revitalization often seems overwhelming, but when tackled in faith, as Jethro so wisely stated, "God will be with you."

TRIGGER POINTS

1. How close do you feel God is to you in the living of your daily life?

2. Which of the following communities would you consider to be more "closed" to you if you were an outsider? A discount store; A labor union; An army battalion; An industrial corporation; A small church; A large church.

3. Of the five methods of introducing change to a closed system listed in this chapter, which would work best in your church? Why?

4. Would your church be willing to risk impaneling a long term planning team under the mandates suggested in this chapter?

CHAPTER VIII

STAND BEFORE GOD FOR THE PEOPLE

Hard Pan

Traveling through the region west and south of Jacksonville, Florida, in an area roughly bound by the St. John's River and the Okeefenokee Swamp on the east and north, and the Ocala State Forest and Interstate 75 on the south and west, one becomes immediately aware of the overwhelming scarcity of population. This land, divided into the political regions of Clay, Putnam, Alachua, Baker, and parts of Duval and Nassau counties of Florida is even now pristine, forest covered, and devoid of any real development.

For years I assumed this was due in part to the very hot, windless summers and the great number of gnats and sand fleas that inhabit the region. "Not so," say the natives. These people, who are the descendants of the rugged pioneers described in Marjorie Rawlings' Cross Creek, blame the low population on *hard-pan*. So also does the Florida Department of the Interior.

Settlers first made their way into this area in the 1880's and settled in an area stretching south of Jacksonville all the way down the St. Johns River to central Florida, to the region around Sanford (not far from Orlando). As the river lands became more densely populated, many hearty souls ventured to the outback and attempted settlement in the area mentioned above. When they began to drill their wells to get life-giving water, however, they ran into difficulty. Below the surface of this entire area there lies a hard, thick, almost impenetrable layer of clay. This harder-than-rock clay in most cases prohibited the drilling of deep wells by the early settlers. Without the benefit of modern diamond bits and high speed power drills, the homesteaders found it an impossible job to get to "good water" for their families. Fortunately for civilization, some hearty souls opted to exist on shallow wells of rancid sulfur water. Many thousands of others, however, found themselves unable to live with hard-pan and moved on to settle along the coast and lakes of south Florida.

As the hard-pan prohibits the drill from reaching the water below, it also does not allow the passage of waste seeping down from the septic systems (cesspools) to drift deep into the underwater purifying system. Therefore, the settlers soon found their own sewage contaminating their too-shallow wells, even if the two were separated by several hundred feet. This non-percolation of water up and sewage down, caused by the layer of clay, brought death and abandonment to settlement after settlement. Even now, this area remains sparsely populated due to governmental intervention and environmental impact restrictions due in part to the presence of the hard-pan.

No one knows for sure from whence came the hard-pan, but one theory goes roughly like this: Twenty million years ago the Gulf of Mexico was a great inland sea stretching from what is now the east coast of Florida (the famed coral ridge) westward to the Rocky Mountain range of the American West. It covered all of the central United States as far north as, and including, the Great Lakes. As the waters

Renaissance or Ruin

receded, a clock-wise current developed that swept north along the Rockies, east over the north central plains and south along the west side of the Appalachian Mountains. These formed the eastern beach of the sea. Thousands of types of sedimentary rocks were picked up by the moving current, each deposited along the route of the current which came to its lumbering end covering the area now known as north Florida. Because of the slow drift of the current here, the area became a swampy depository for much of this heavy residue. As the result of millions of years of receding waters and heavy environmental pressure, this residue slowly became compacted into a hard layer of clay with a density eight to ten times normal for its volume. Because of that density and compactness this subsurface layer became the hard-pan now lying beneath the surface of this otherwise beautiful and inviting land.[1]

I've chosen hard-pan as a most appropriate metaphor to describe the situation now facing the mainline church. The inflow of the numbers of new parishioners has decreased through the last forty years, much as did the water of the inland sea five million years ago. Those members who were left formed a core church. not unlike the settling of the particles carried by the dying inland sea. Pressure exerted by the receding numbers and shrinking resources compressed those members remaining into an extremely close body; this analogous to the environmental pressure on the minerals left by the recessing sea. Sociologically speaking, these left-behind members formed a "resolute residue." They gradually

---

[1] There are other factors, including the infusion of calcium sulfate, that causes the clay to become rock-hard within seconds of exposure to air. Miners in all areas of the south have actually abandoned shafts rather than attempt to cut through the clay layer. Geological Survey Florida Dept. of Interior, Tallahassee.

developing an "us and them" survivalistic attitude, and like hard-pan, these groups became impenetrable and unchanging. The church, like the Florida outback, may seem pristine and inviting, but the majority of our congregations are just as unproductive and unyielding as rural north Florida because of our hidden subsurface *hard-pan mentality*.

The question then becomes, *How does the work of the Gospel get down under such conditions?* The historical response, over the past forty years, has simply been to allow the young, the new, and the pioneers appearing among us to move on. Those entrusted to us by God have become the building blocks for both the Evangelical or Full Gospel movements. Our denominational and local leadership have opted to keep our existing communities intact and non-threatened by the influx of new people.

The results of this operating philosophy can be seen across the church. Since their peak in popularity in the 1950's, the Roman Catholic and mainline Protestant churches have lost members by the millions. The four major mainliners began only four percent of all new congregations founded in the decade from 1970 to 1980. By the 1970's, while mainline churches were beginning only fifty-five to eighty congregations a year, the gap in the need for new church starts, to accommodate the booming population, was being filled by the so called "new churches."[2] These non-mainline upstarts[3] received roughly half the newcomers into the church during the 1970's and 1980's. Independent churches received half of the rest, and groups like

---

[2] Lyle E. Schaller, <u>Different World</u>, 81-89.
[3] The Church of the Nazarene, Seventh Day Adventists, Assembly of God, Southern Baptists, Evangelical Lutheran Synod, Evangelical Free Church, Evangelical Covenant Church, Christian and Missionary Alliance, the Church of God (Cleveland, TN), and the Church of God in Christ.

Renaissance or Ruin

Jehovah's Witnesses and Latter Day Saints took most of the remainder.[4] It would appear from these statistics that the mainline churches are no longer in the business of encouraging, inviting, and welcoming new generations of Americans into their churches.

The second method of dealing with *hard-pan* (I've tried this one) is to drill through it. You'll remember that Moses was using this tactic when Jethro came to the camp. Moses was working twenty hours a day beating himself against the *hard-pan mentality* of the tribes, trying to get "these people" to do the "right thing." After observing this method of response, Jethro interjected

> You will surely wear yourself out.[5]

I have interviewed many discouraged pastors from mainline churches over the past seven years. If one psychological malady could be found common to all, "tired discouragement" would be that condition. One veteran Methodist pastor noted he was tired of the useless cycle. He said:

> I come to a church and see the possibilities in the community. I work diligently, pray faithfully, and things begin to happen. Sure enough, just like the scriptures promise, the congregation multiplies and grows in grace. Then as sure as clock work, three or four years go by, I begin to get a lot of hassle from both the church leaders and the conference, and the next thing you know I'm moved. The tragic

---
[4] The Latter Day Saints alone grew from approximately 4,800 churches in 1970 to over 8,000 churches in 1983.
[5] Exodus 18:18

thing is that immediately the congregation returns to its lower level of members, the conference seems pleased, and all is lost.

This now middle-aged pastor has since left the denominational church after twenty-two years of service, but I've heard his complaint from countless others who continue to suffer disillusionment.

These tired prophets are trying to drill through the *hard-pan*. They, as have I, have worked themselves to a frazzle because they tried to stand before God in place of the people. Jethro's instructions to any would-be Moses is to "stand before God for the people."[6]

This "standing before God for the people" is the third and final option for dealing with *hard-pan*. The object is to find a method of growing the Gospel where we are, while helping both the pastor and the congregation to stand fast. Also while attempting to grow the Gospel, we must find a way to end the senseless slaughter (metaphorically speaking) of thousands of devoted pastors. It's not productive to call pastoral candidates, encourage them, spend thousands training them and then destroy them after one or two pastorates, just to show the world we are trying to solve *our rigidity problem*. *Standing for the people* to dissolve *hard-pan*, can save ALL the people, ALL the churches, ALL the pastors; and at the same time glorify God. The question emerges of exactly how to accomplish such a task.

Leadership vs. Hard-pan

Although I expect to concentrate on the issue later, the one thing I must emphasize is that the church, or any other community for that matter, cannot be saved by one leader.

---

[6] Exodus 18:19

Moses couldn't do it with the tribes of Israel, Frank Shagroo couldn't do it at Eastern Airlines and one pastor or one devoted church member can't do it either. If the mainline church is to be saved, the *hard-pan* at all levels of the church must be dissolved by an entire generation of leaders. They should be willing to work together in all areas of the church, laboring in concert and confronting rigidity and closedness wherever it exists.

On the local level this means that lay leaders need pastoral leaders resolved to do the work of Christ and grow the church. Pastors - the days of one-person control is over. All leaders must work together as a ministry team. It also means that the pastor, as leader, needs to know with certainty, that if the proponents of the status quo rail against him or her, the conference and association leaders will stand with the pastor. The days of cowardice and opportunism, of caving into political pressure from local power groups, are gone.

Finally, national leaders need to be resolved to take the lead and support conference and local church people as they rise to the challenge. We need to move past responding to temper tantrums of some "important" local power figures. *Hard-pan* and the politics that is its bulwark is threaded deeply through all levels of the church. Those wanting to save the church should expect to find it everywhere. For this reason leaders wanting to dissolve it must also be found everywhere - Managing By Walking Around.

The first requisite for leaders, at all levels, this book cannot teach. When standing "before God for the people" Jesus said the leader must possess a deep and abiding love. Initially the candidate must love God. There is no hope for leaders in the church who will not:

- love the Lord your God with all your heart,
with all your soul,
and with all your mind.[7]

Do not take this requirement lightly; it is the source of a primary flaw in choosing Christian leadership. The church is plump with administrators, teachers, bishops, priests, pastors, conference ministers, deacons, local officers and members who exhibit little or no love for God. One elderly pastor openly confessed to me that he had lost his faith and love for God many years before but had continued to serve several congregations (not at all unusual). Many of us serve in churches with lay officials who do not regularly attend church, who give little or nothing to God's work. Often these people openly live lifestyles obviously devoid of love for God, God's work, or God's church.

I have in my library an old yearbook of a now closed Presbyterian Church. The book was commemorating the 100th Anniversary of the church with a special celebration held on June 2, 1893. Pictured in the book were the faces of the members of the session, the local leaders of that church. They were the richest and most successful men in Chester, Pennsylvania at that time and were doubtless chosen for that reason. There wasn't a non-prosperous non-influential man among them. From having an intimate knowledge of the city where the church was located, I have inherited the stories of the reputations of some of these persons. Some of them were slum landlords in the "red-light" district of the city, others were known for political or business chicanery. Scanning their collective backgrounds an assumption could be made that many of those in the leadership of this particular congregation had little love for God.

---

[7] Matthew 22:37, NKJV.

Renaissance or Ruin

With only a token number of members left in many of our churches, it usually seems impossible to fill the jobs. As a result our consideration of this most basic issue is quickly passed over -

- ✓ Is this candidate a believer in Jesus the Christ?
- ✓ Does he/she love God?
- ✓ Is the candidate seeking first the kingdom of God?

Too often the sole question asked by nominating committees is, "Will you show up and give a half-hearted effort to the job?" There is a saying in a church I recently served

If you can breathe - you can have the job!

In that same church a new nominee, who had never served in a church office before, came to her first board meeting, and was chosen, at this first meeting, to chair the board. In another church a lady who had been out of church for years joined the church in March, came to her first Women's Fellowship meeting in May, and was elected president of the group in June.

We are so desperate to "fill the slots" on our church boards and committees that no one dares to ask any qualifying questions. Obviously the very last question to be considered is relationship to God. One could not conceive of a corporate president being chosen to head General Motors or Dupont who had no love for, dedication to, belief or faith in the company or its product. Such a thing would be ruinous. Yet daily, in churches across the country, we often put whole leadership teams in place, ostensibly to serve Christ; yet many have little or no love for God, no dedication to the work of the Gospel, no knowledge of God's word or faith in God's message. Many of these teams have little or no idea what the overall mission of the church is to be.

In one church, three of the five main power figures in high office openly espoused having no faith in Jesus as the Christ. This won't work; it can't work. This neglect has been just as ruinous for the church as it would have been for the Dupont Co. The primary prerequisite, then, in considering leadership at all levels, is to qualify the person individually to establish, "Does this candidate love God, does this person believe in Jesus Christ?"

The second thing Jesus taught would-be leaders, is to

- love your neighbor as yourself.[8]

If a person is to stand before God as leader that person must not only love God but also stand before the people in love, with love.

In the book Quality In Action, Patrick Townsend and Joan Gebhardt give 93 lessons in leadership. Number nineteen is titled, "Love, Leadership at Its Best." This book has no connection to the Gospel and is not church related, yet take note as the authors offer this axiom:

> Love is what makes leadership work; it is what makes the difference between manipulating people and leading people. You cannot manipulate people into doing quality work.[9]

The authors continue to find many connections between leadership and love. Both have in common the act of caring about another's welfare. Also, both require a true interaction -

---

[8] Matthew 22:39, NKJV.
[9] Patrick L. Townsend and Joan E. Gebhardt, Quality in Action, (New York, John Wiley and Sons, Inc., 1992), 50.

listening and sharing - as well as a giving and a receiving. The leader and the lover both exemplify integrity, courage, and competence that are worth emulating by all parties involved. In both leadership and love, perception can be as important as reality. Both parties need to *feel* loved and cared for, as well as actively *being* loved and cared for.

Also, the reputation of the leader is important to the follower. Reputation strongly impacts the willingness to follow, even in long term relationships. The trait of *openness* in the leader is vital. Letting the follower know the leader's real self, the leader's real faith, real belief and real virtues are important to followers. The follower needs to know that the leader has his or her best interest in mind; in short, that the leader really loves the follower. Washington, Napoleon, and MacArthur are said by historians to have been military leaders who were believed by their followers to "love their men." To demonstrate how important perception is, even over reality, we remember that Napoleon did not pay his men, made them forage for food and abandoned them often. Unfortunately for Europe, the troops *believed* the charlatan loved them.

Lastly, forgiving and the willingness to forgive are also primary traits of a good leader and a good lover. God forgave us even though we were still sinners[10] in rebellion against God. In marriage it is sometimes impossible to get through the years without each partner doing substantial harm to the other. Likewise, other relationships in the home or the church are filled with daily sins and shortcomings in relationships. True love requires constant forgiveness of each other, and so does true leadership.

One common ingredient in *hard-pan* living is a lack of trust and the inability to forgive. If true love exists in

---

[10] Romans 5:8.

leadership, "Innovation and change (the true product of leadership) must be perceived as opportunities rather than threats."[11] If you love your child you encourage him or her to take the first step knowing there will be a fall, and yet you celebrate the fall. If you punish the fall the child may not try to walk again. The leader needs to encourage trust, and the only way that can be done is to share continuing forgiveness in love.

♦ *In the end it is Love that dissolves Hard-Pan.*

The Proactive Leader

The leader in standing before God and standing for his or her people, doing both with love for each, will by virtue of that love exhibit four proactive tendencies which can serve toward neutralizing the most stubborn *hard-pan* personalities.[12] An achieving leader possessing all the love in the world for his/her calling, however, would achieve little without a solid methodical praxis in leadership. This proactive leader will then need the following competencies, and be able to:

1. Direct attention

2. Search for meaning

3. Instill trust

4. Discipline the self.

Proactive leaders are willing not only to develop the vision for themselves, but they are also willing to risk communicating that vision. No group can climb to greater

---

[11] Kouzes and Posner, 77.
[12] Bennis, 19.

heights than its current existence, unless leaders are there to envision a world not-yet-in-existence. The *hard-pan* church, conversely, exhibits a-world-no-longer posture, and is impacted by that view of self. The corrective for this scenario are leaders who are willing to develop a vision where there is none and project or *direct attention* to that vision.

> Visions seen only by the leaders are insufficient to create organizational movement. They must get others to see the exciting future possibilities. Leaders breathe life into visions. They communicate their hopes and dreams so that others clearly understand and accept them as their own. They show others how their values and interest will be served by the long-term vision of the future. Leaders are expressive and they attract followers through warmth and friendship.[13]

In the church, the vision to be shared is God's vision of a world brought to God, made void of injustice and filled with love. Jesus reinforced the primary vision of a church of love. Any leader in that church is to exalt that vision. As Jesus left this world, bequeathing the church His power and His authority, He gave its congregation specific instructions:

> Go therefore and make disciples of all the nations, baptizing them in the name of the Father and of the Son, and of the Holy Spirit, teaching them to observe all things that I have commanded you;[14]

---

[13] Kouzes and Posner, 57.
[14] Matthew 28:19-20 (a), NKJV.

The common vision of the people of God should be a church filled with people seeking after God, learning to love themselves and all humankind, searching for righteousness and sharing justice with all creation. But to simply have and hold this vision isn't enough, we must share it and live it while coaching and exhorting others to do the same. Envisioning the future, projecting it openly, and enlisting others in creating it, are the hallmarks of a proactive leader.

Jimmy Carter, while serving as president, had one of the most dynamic visions for the future one could imagine. He articulated this vision well, but his failure came in not being able to enlist others to assist in carrying it out.[15] Conversely, John Kennedy also had a vision, he articulated it well, and for whatever reason, was able to enlist others to embrace it. If assassination had not brought that process to a standstill, Kennedy's dream of a great new society would probably have come near true. He was able to grab and direct the attention of followers; therefore, the vision was well on its way to becoming a reality. Interestingly, as past president, Jimmy Carter achieved one of the highest levels of leadership in the history of the nation. His work with the Carter Center, Emory University and Habitat for Humanity has earned him a huge following and worldwide praise. He has, during this latter era, begun to embody the vision of a world built on the godly principles.

The scriptures also give examples of this leader/follower visionary formula. On the day of Pentecost Peter was ready for proactive leadership. He believed, he

---

[15] Note should be taken here that when Warren Bennis briefly examines the Carter White House he is looking for leadership traits only. I and others in reviewing the data of the Carter years are studying leadership only. Many students, myself included, see Jimmy Carter as one of the most dedicated and brilliant men to ever have served this nation.

loved God and he had burgeoning faith. When he saw the vision, he shared it openly with all[16] and he enlisted others to accept that vision as their own.[17]

Today's proactive leader will also be in the vanguard in *the search for meaning*. The church needs a reason for being. To this end the proactive leader should first look at what the body is currently doing in each area in order to either validate or discard the practice. Habits often become an encumbrance to growth and a real energizer behind *hard-pan* living. Expending effort and resources just because "its always been done that way" is real fodder for pejorative power and guaranteed to accelerate group failure. The status quo, of which habit is a main building block, can only be challenged and dissolved if every program and practice the church offers is continually and critically reviewed. Searching for meaning in the present will often reveal that large portions of the life of the church are being eaten up by meaningless gestures.

In Philadelphia, where I grew up, one of the most annoying phrases used by my young peers was "just 'cause" ("just because" in the King's English). When asked, "Why are we going to a gang fight with ...," the answer was, "Just 'cause." In other words, there was no reason for the gang fight or stealing the car or vandalizing the subway, so teens were expected to follow along and do it - "just 'cause."

Christ-like living requires more than "just 'cause" actions. The mainline church has lost two entire generations of its children. Millions of these Twenty-first century people have grown so far from the faith that many basics of the faith are foreign and lost to them. The church persists in using language, liturgy, methods, and music with no regard to these

---

[16] Acts 2:14-21.
[17] Acts 2:41.

strangers in our midst. For example, the largest portion of churches in the United Church of Christ continue to use the Pilgrim Hymnal. This hymnal is leftover from a now dead denomination, the Congregational Christian Church, which joined to form the new denomination in 1957. Other UCC churches continue to use the hymnal left over from the denomination of their origin. Like these other song books, the Pilgrim Hymnal was compiled in the early 1930's, by people then in their fifties, who revered music presented to them in their formative years prior to the turn of the century.

If one inspects this hymnal, and most others currently used in the mainline churches, you will note the origin dates of the songs usually range from the early 1630's, and would be considered new offerings if they originated in the 1850's. Consequently, worship services in the Episcopal, UCC, Presbyterian and Lutheran churches are undergirded with music left over from the Anglo-European migration of the sixteenth, seventeenth and eighteenth centuries. These now outdated, minor keyed, and often morbid hymns are meaningless and repugnant to people reared in a modern American culture. Yet if a pastor or progressive layperson would suggest replacing the archaic hymnal with one of the new "upbeat" books available, the reaction from the pews would be akin to the threat of war.

Our congregations no longer sing music they like, but rather sing that which they are used to - "Just 'cause." A proactive leader in his/her church must be willing to openly challenge these outdated symbols and practices. These leaders will seek real meanings in order to recast the heart of the Gospel in language and symbols that can be understood by the world which we serve.

The search for meaning takes on a second face for proactive church leaders. They must not only be able to develop a vision, not only explain its true meaning, but also be able to create meaning in the life of followers. The church as a whole needs to do the same thing for the people of the entire world. It is not enough to explain that, "God so loved the world that He gave His only begotten son..."[18]. Leaders should realize that two generations of people, from both within and without the church, have grown up with no knowledge of the concepts of personal sin, repentance, and redemption to which this verse speaks. We should also be prepared to explain the meaning of the terms reconciliation, justification, forgiveness, saved, sinner, and regeneration. But even that isn't enough. The real goal is to help the people of the church and its world to internalize the love in the Gospel. This can only be accomplished if the church and its members can relate, themselves, to the story of salvation. The people of church must answer the question "What is the meaning of the message for me?"

The invitation to search for real meaning and the offer of innovation to help open the Kingdom will be meaningless to the *hard-pan* personality. For people accustomed to living paranoid, counter-productive, reclusive lives, the call to courage, abundance, and openness is frightening. The proactive leader then must help these followers find the meaning of the love of God as it can be shed "abroad in their hearts."[19] Warren Bennis, from whose book Why Leaders Can't Lead much of this material is taken, quotes Alexander Haig's coinage of the term "tangibilitated" to describe the leader's function as searcher for meaning. Bennis is suggesting

---

[18] John 3:16
[19] Revelations 5:5.

that the proactive leader must bring the myth and the dream to reality for the follower in order to turn the abstract into the tangible.

The third task of the proactive church leader is to *instill trust*. As previously mentioned, this may be the hardest task of all. Reflecting on the unloving personality and the high level of insecurity exhibited by large numbers of the core membership of our churches, one can appreciate the enormity of the task of introducing trust to a non-trusting community.

The world in which we live has seen every institution, every bastion of what was previously viewed as sacrosanct, ripped apart by scandalous revelations. In our society, the very words "trust me" are seen as the indication of an impending "rip-off." In spite of this suspicion and lack of trust in institutions and authority, people are hungry to find leaders they can trust.

In a landmark survey, Ron Crossland and Boyd Clark of AT&T's Cincinnati based Sales and Marketing Education Center administered a test asking 2,615 middle managers what traits they consider when evaluating the "followability" of a leader. Traits such as independence, loyalty, determination, and ambition - those traits that lead toward productive success - were well down on the list, placing 20, 19, 17, and 16 respectively. Traits that led were in order of their importance:

1. Honest   83 percent

2. Competent   67 percent

3. Forward-looking 62 percent

4. Inspiring   58 percent

You'll note that the first trait, seen as most important in a leader, was *honesty*. In other words, these followers were saying, "We want a boss we can trust."

Millions of people gave money to PTL, only to find that beneath all that seemed "holy" was much that was unholy. People have repeatedly voted and worked for political leaders, only to find that there was never any intent to fulfill the promises their candidates had made. Even the systems we trust have let us down.

Thousands of known violent criminals are freed from prison each day having served only a fraction of their sentences, only to commit greater and more serious crimes, often within hours of release. During the period beginning in 1986 and going through the recession of 1992, hundreds of firms, many large "blue chippers" went belly-up, taking with them the pension money viewed as a sacred trust by thousands of retirees. It seems we are surrounded with anything but trustworthy people and institutions. No group or community, however, can long survive without trust.

When Jesus came amongst us He said, "You believe (trust) in God, believe (trust) also in me."[20] In order to prove His trustworthiness He gave up His life. When Paul carried the Gospel to Europe he said in essence, "Here is God's message - trust me." He gave up his life to serve the kingdom as a prisoner, proving for all time that not only he, but the Gospel of God could be depended upon. The would-be leaders of the church today may not be asked to face the cross or a prison cell, but they are being asked by their people to be constant and true to the message - to be people worthy of trust.

In order to be vested with this trust the proactive leader must be willing to live as a Christian twenty-four hours a day,

---

[20] John 14:1.

allowing his or her life to be an open book. Evangelist Jimmy Swaggart blasted sexual promiscuity, but behind closed doors he acted out in darkness the very immorality he condemned publicly. I know of pastors who preach against consuming alcohol and serve churches which strictly forbid its consumption; yet many of these same pastors and their parishioners drink alcoholic beverages at private and public affairs.

The important thing here is not the alcohol. Jesus drank wine, I drink wine, many churches ask only responsible moderation of their members. If a leader in one of these churches drinks alcohol moderately, that's his or her business. But trust is violated when an institution says one thing, i.e. "Alcohol is evil," its public image matches this, yet secretly, on the sly, the leader and members practice something else. An older pastor said it this way, "Say what you believe - believe what you say - do what you believe and say."[21] The proactive leader can only elicit trust from followers who have become *hard-pan* through a lack of trust, if that leader is honest about who he/she really is.

The final trait of a proactive leader in the turn of the century church will be *discipline of self*. Coming out of the age of "the great impersonal systems," this self-discipline, self-actualization, self-criticizing seems foreign. During the 1940's and 50's our society tried to develop business and governing systems that were free from human influence and individual personalities. This was the great age of the systems

---

[21] The choosing of alcohol as an example would relate more to the conservative church. In the mainline church a more appropriate example would be to cite the Gospel's call for righteousness in its members, and then to examine the business lives and dealings of the church's leaders. Often one set of ethics is assented to in church, but, when profit is involved, Christians adopt a separate ethical standard.

manager trained to assume command and maintain a system of mechanized intellect.

This condition came about due to the lack of trust our species placed in itself, probably due to failures in our humanness. These failures resulted in system breakdown (WWI / WWII). We, however, have discovered that we cannot invent a system that works without people input. One of the problems that face our people in their search for human credibility is that we were instructed as children to go to the man in the uniform and badge when we're lost. Unfortunately we've found out that anyone can don a uniform or buy a badge. In other words, we've been taught to trust the people brandishing the symbols of the system - to stand for us against that very system - only to find that each of these people are not worthy of our trust. The result is a general lack of trust in anything bigger than ourselves, including the church, the pastor, and the lay leader.

Many years ago I operated a security guard agency. One of the greatest difficulties we had was to teach our officers not to put faith in someone simply because the person was wearing a particular uniform or driving a certain type car. Undercover supervisors would routinely be allowed to pass by security posts by being dressed in pin striped suits and driving up to the gate in a BMW. The guards were quick to stop and question others not brandishing these superficial symbols of success. White, clean shaven, well dressed executive types passed without a challenge.

Those ascending to leadership have become so accustomed to fitting into a pre-made slot, putting on a title or a badge, expecting certain things to happen automatically, that we place others into leadership situations expecting positive results. We assume that whoever accepts the title of lay leader or pastor will instinctively offer valid leadership and that the followers will cooperate without a second thought. We've come to know differently, but nevertheless we expect it to be otherwise.

When Oral Roberts retires, most expect Richard Roberts to take his place, and supporters actually are expecting him to get the same results as did his father because he holds the title of "son." The same is true with Billy Graham; many assume his son will fit into the slot of one of the great evangelists of the ages, just because he's a Graham. Churches likewise expect an untrained, uncalled, often uninvolved and inexperienced person to be a leader just by assuming the office of moderator or trustee, or just because the person is a member of the church's extended family. Not only do we fail to ask ourselves, "Are these intended leaders godly people," but we fail to look at their lifestyle, their discipline of self.

The leaders of this age will need to be far less "systems people" and more personally accomplished as individuals. They will be more willing to critique themselves and seek training constantly than were their predecessors. Today's leaders must be willing to know themselves. The leaders of the 1990's will need to evaluate their strengths and nurture them. They will need to openly admit their weak points and be prepared to overcome them. The people of our society are acutely wary of a person who is blind to self, and who is therefore seeking things only for self.

Kouzes and Posner, in their book The Leadership Challenge, refer to this overall theme as competence;[22] as a matter of fact, they increase it's importance by entitling it "value-added competence." While admitting that technical

---

[22] Kouzes and Posner, 19-20.

Renaissance or Ruin

competence is important, they say that this does not create a leader and this is not the competence of which they speak.

A good machinist may be just that - a good machinist. A competent leader of a machine company would be well served by becoming a proficient machinist; but additionally, this leader needs to bring something else to the position. That something else is value-added competence that which we have called *discipline of self*. It involves the pushing of one's self beyond just machinery, moving to a level competence which is as spiritual as physical. It moves beyond superficial symbols and meaningless titles to a "deep flow" living experience.

John Wesley was a good preacher, a devoted Christian, and almost punitive in his quest to reach Christian perfection. During his lifetime from 1702-1796 there were hundreds of great theologians, great preachers, devoted Christians, and those seeking holiness before God, but only Wesley set England afire. There are many reasons for his success, but self-discipline or value-added competence is the closest thing to a name that embraces all of them.

- ✓ He was credible in the eyes of the people.

- ✓ He directed their attention toward God and self.

- ✓ He joined their search for the meaning of life.

- ✓ He earned their trust by self sacrifice.

- ✓ He struggled to be honest about himself.

The theory goes that if one can't be honest with one's own self, one can't be honest with others. Discipline of self is then imperative in the development of value-added competency and the final intersection on the road to proactive leadership.

As Leadership Develops

I am going to claim success in our quest for leadership by not saying, "If" leadership develops, but rather, "As" leadership develops. I will assume that the faithful of the church will not ignore the warnings presaged in the first half of this work. I shall further assume that intelligent, learned, concerned men and women at all levels of the church will rise to the challenges facing the mainline church and move forward in proactive leadership. I shall take it for granted that bishops, conference executives and staffers will be willing to forsake the current illusion of job security. I shall be presumptuous and believe that many pastors will take a deep breath and chance being dumped on the sidewalk in order to do the right thing.

Finally, I have faith that lay men and women will risk estrangement from fearful mates, loss of friendship from immature church friends, and "lonely nights on the farm" (strained family relationships) in order to save the church.

As these sacrifices are made, "What immediate results can the church expect?"

Warren Bennis has evaluated organizations that have leadership openly operating at all levels and has found four distinct phenomenon present therein. Essentially Bennis says that solid leadership initially produces the following results:

> 1. People feel significant.
> Everyone feels that he or she makes a difference to the success of the organization. Where they are empowered, people feel that what they do has meaning and significance.

2. Learning and competence matter.
Leaders value learning and mastery, and so do people who work for leaders. Leaders make it clear that there is no failure in valid attempts, only mistakes that give us feedback and tell us what to do next.

3. People are part of a community.
Where there is leadership, there is a team, a family, a unity. Even people who do not especially like each other feel a sense of community.

4. Work or ministry is exciting.
Where there are leaders, work is stimulating, challenging, fascinating, and fun. An essential ingredient in organizational leadership is pulling together rather than pushing people toward a goal...Leaders articulate and embody the ideals toward which the organization strives.[23]

It is of significance to recall that Bennis is writing of leadership in the business world and to a secular audience, yet almost every goal of community in the church setting is set forth in this secular document.

Leadership principals similar to the ones we've been examining were introduced into a declining company named Teleflex. The new CEO, Bill Black, introduced a strong people philosophy and the company's productivity soared. The program allowed people to be people - not personnel. It was discovered that people like to work as long as they are guided to a mutual understanding of the objective, and that people

---
[23] Bennis, 23.

have egos and development needs. If these needs are satisfied, great commitment results. Further, Teleflex's people developed a working climate that was challenging, invigorating, and fun. Finally, at Teleflex people are invited to work in an atmosphere of trust. In a trusting relationship people will take risks, thus growth occurs. Growth is rewarded, which results in increased self confidence and renewed leadership.[24]

Leaders in the church, both lay and clergy, are seen by author Leighton Ford as shepherd-makers. He notes that "shepherd is a key biblical term for the leader who empowers others."[25] He postulates that Jesus laid the model others throughout church history have followed. That model is one of empowering people to reach their full potential both in and out of church life. Quoting Klaus Bockmuehl, Ford restates that, "Shepherding people means to help them grow; it demands thoughtfulness about how to make the other one great and it implies nothing less than the act of true friendship for others."[26]

Leadership in the church apparently involves more than meeting goals and getting the job done. It means more than carrying out the work of the Gospel. If we follow the model of Jesus' ministry we first help people grow for their own sake; the result is that the job WILL be done, the kingdom WILL grow and the world WILL be changed.

You'll remember that Moses was working as hard as he could and doing it all by himself. Jethro saw the horrible waste of this tactic. He told Moses to get the people involved. He acknowledged that Moses was doing two things right. He was

---

[24] Peters and Austin, 206.
[25] Ford, 163.
[26] Klaus Bockmuehl, Living by the Gospel, Colorado Springs, Helmers and Howard, 1986. As quoted in Leighton Ford, Transforming Leadership (Downers Grove, Ill., Intervarsity Press, 1991), 163

standing before God and he was doing it for the people. But to this Jethro now added, "With the people."

The dissolving of *hard-pan* in our local churches and national bodies will lead to the renaissance of the church of the Gospel. However, it will take much more than the traditional methods of setting goals, involving people, providing material and training. It will require God-centered, people-focused, proactive leadership. Further, it will require a great deal of love and sacrifice to permanently dissolve the *hard-pan* attitude held by the *resolute residue* in our congregations. Leadership that makes people feel significant, teaches the truth of the Gospel in the context of our contemporary world, presents discipleship as an exciting way of life, and creates loving community, will be more than a match for the evils of the past. Our closed systems will become open as our leaders

♦ *stand openly before God for their people.*

TRIGGER POINTS

1. Can you cite cases where families or firms have developed a *Hard-pan*, unchanging attitude? What was the end result?

2. Are you familiar with any of the "new" church groups growing across the country? What are some of their characteristics?

3. Can you name common chords and themes between leadership and love?

4. Are most people you know proactive or reactive? Which are you?

5. What are the dangers in being reactive?

6. What are the dangers in becoming proactive?

CHAPTER IX

BRING THE DIFFICULTIES TO GOD

Upon Jethro's arrival at the Israeli camp, he immediately noticed that Moses was caught in an age old trap. The people were bringing their difficulties to him and he responded by handling each problem, soon many problems, finally mega-problems. Before long, he was wearing himself out and no problems were being solved.

Any person in a position of authority can relate to the subtle danger of discovering oneself in leadership, finding that not only "the buck stops here," but so also do the pennies, quarters, national debt, and responsibility for the third world. Unfortunately society is replete with people who delight in orchestrating situations, attempting to "triangle"[1] others into a "take responsibility for me" relationship. In this way they can shift the blame to another when things fall apart. The same paradigm exists within organizations.

In one of my first pastorates I was assigned a typical small charge of under eighty people, an older church with no vision and little hope for the future. I, in true crusader fashion, waded in, attacked the situation, and, as Moses did, took on all

---

[1] Edwin H. Friedman, <u>Generation to Generation: Family Process in Church and Synagogue</u>, (New York, The Guilford Press, 1985), 35-39.

the difficulties "single-handedly." I theorized that once the people saw what could be done, they would rise spontaneously and take over the leadership themselves. Moses probably presumed the same thing 3700 years ago. It did not work for Moses, it didn't work for me, and it won't work for you either.

The first thing that the pastor or a critically positioned lay leader of the congregation must realize is that the buck does NOT stop here. From "here" it goes two ways. First it travels out horizontally, and then moves in all directions; that is to say, to all the people of the congregation. The people of each local church are solely responsible for the failure or success of their particular church.

When I was a junior in high school, a boy named Rick transferred to our school. Chester High School was a tough, port city school that bathed in the "excitement" of gangs, fights, and street crime. Rick was a real milquetoast from the suburbs and spent his days at Chester High in fear of physical confrontation. In order to avoid a possible fight himself, he would play people off against each other. He would approach one boy and tell him that another kid was saying bad things about him. Of course, the hearer would become angry and say threatening things about the third party who had, to this point, said nothing. Rick then ran to the third party and related all the second boy had said. After several hours of this Rick would arrange a time and place where the unsuspecting "toughs" would meet. There you would find Rick yelling, "Fight, fight!" while running away for safety. Rick, like many others, was always willing to sit safely on the sidelines, taking no responsibility, all the while manipulating others into negative relationships.

The local church is little more than one big extended family relationship. All of its members, its leaders, and its pastors are "triangled" in several ways. Everyone finds themselves tied together in deep and multi-level relationships, three dimensional and triangular in shape. In such a situation problem solving becomes almost impossible. There are always two or three people involved in what appears on the surface to be an otherwise simple scheme. To compound the situation, these people may be triangled with others, thus creating many layers of relationship. The modern local church leader, not unlike Moses in the Exodus story, often finds entangled dramas strongly resembling a knot on a small child's shoe, seemingly comprehensible but filled with unseen complexities.

Rabbi Edwin Friedman relates the following story illustrating this situation in his book Generation to Generation:

> In one particular parable called "The Bridge," a man suddenly realizes what he wants out of life, but is told he must set out immediately or his opportunity will be lost forever. Hurrying on his way, he meets another while crossing a bridge. The other asks him if he will hold on to the end of a rope. The protagonist says, "Yes, but only for a moment," because he is on a very important journey. This man hands him one end of the rope, but the other is tied around his own waist. And as soon as the protagonist takes hold of one end, the other man throws himself off the bridge. There then ensues a dialogue between the two in which the man holding the rope says he has to go, and the other just keeps answering passively, "I am your responsibility."[2]

---

[2] Friedman, 266.

The "Bridge" exemplifies the relational pattern of the local church. You could multiply these two men by the number of people in your congregation, pass out as many ropes, and you would soon have a situation where each person is connected by rope to every other person. These dual relationships subsequently become three-sided or "triangled" because there is always another point of fact, or a third party in any relationship between two people. It could be man (A) to man (B) with point (C) being an unspoken profit motive. Another example would be woman (A) and man (B) serving as chair and member of the trustees, respectively. A triangled relationship might occur by the manipulation of his father (C), the church's big giver. Often leaders, particularly pastors who are generally perennial optimists, recognize the depth of a church's problems at about the same time everyone in the choir starts yelling, "It's your responsibility!" Simultaneously, these onlookers "dive off" the metaphorical bridge above (cease interacting or withdraw support), rendering the "fixing" of the situation impossible.

The only hope for the creation of proactive, goal-achieving leadership in the closed system of the relationally triangled church is to share the "difficulties" over a greater plane. We can only do this by expanding the base of involved persons, *before the people*, and involving God more dramatically, by openly *bringing the difficulties to God*. This literally involves the power center surrendering some of their turf and inviting many more people into leadership.

The first step is to ask *what is going on here?* This book is written in an attempt to help our congregations see their local church, to whatever degree is applicable, as a dysfunctional organism, whose infrastructure is locked inertially into *pejorative power relationships*. This untenable scenario in turn intensifies the personal dysfunction of its members, as well as the community as a whole. Put simply, the invitation is here extended for each congregation, through self-critique, to recognize the places where they regularly make decisions and carry out programs that are harmful to the overall success of the church and its people.

The second step is to *recast these problems into achievable objectives*, thus harnessing the kinetic energy of the church, now working unproductively, into a forward moving, task accomplishing power dynamic. To the degree that leaders (clergy or lay) are unaware of the global feelings, ties and power motivators at work in the congregation, they will try to bring the difficulties onto themselves. They assume that they possess the skills necessary to bring the congregation happiness. Most pastors are particularly vulnerable to this trap because of the rescue complex that fires the pastoral psyche. They are often intimidated and made to feel inadequate if they cannot solve the problems of their congregations. At this point pastors become easily threatened. It needs to be continually recognized that the problems in our congregations are far bigger than any pastor or local leader. They transcend the local church, the community, and are endemic upon an entire generation. Therefore, we cannot hope to solve the problems of xenophobia, exclusionism, social paranoia, and *hard pan* syndrome by attacking them solitarily.

We began this section cautioning the leader to pass the problems and difficulties out from self and on to the largest portion of the congregation possible. By focusing on problems as being outside of any individual, the people can approach difficulties in safety. This frees those in close relationships to redefine particular difficulties, rather than attempt to challenge interpersonal relationships. In working out the day-to-day problems facing the church in a methodical, team oriented, goal-achieving way, strength and confidence begins to develop. As the result of their work begins to take on "tangibility," pride and self-confidence is built. In other words, working with specific problems as a community can become the key to solving a much deeper social and community crisis.

The Dysfunctional Church

We've spent much time developing the underlying causes of the severe problems facing our churches as we enter the Twenty-first century. Many of these areas have never been opened to public scrutiny. Dysfunctions in our infrastructure, power politics, hard pan syndrome, and triangling to avoid taking responsibility are the major culprits. In one sense, we have thrown the "skeletons," hidden in the closet of the church universal, out of the laboratory of the anthropologist and the sociologist, into full view of the world. These psychopathologies need to be examined in far greater depth than can be done in this one volume.

Even though many of these problems are really of a societal nature and reflect major civic dysfunctions, they have produced particular symptoms impacting the church which are definable and dissectable. By using process planning, strategic planning, and adaptable leadership methods, as reviewed in this book, these socio-pathologies are workable in the congregation. We cannot, in our local church setting, tackle the underlying causation of human dysfunctions that have taken centuries to develop, but we can turn the problems we face in our church from the subjective into the objective and bring them one at a time "to God before the people."

It should be anticipated as leadership develops that new goals and programs will surface. Subsequently, new direction and new leaders will emerge; thereby replacing social paranoia with community-wide ministry and efficacy . Let us take some time to analyze symptoms of social dysfunction peculiar to the church. These symptoms have been named "church blight." They were first exposed in Lyle Schaller's somewhat older work Parish Planning. In the commentary below I shall add some observations of my own, but overall his theory that "church blight" can be diagnosed by observing certain patterns in a local church remains intact. These symptoms as elucidated by Schaller and amplified with my comments are as follows:

1. *Emphasis on institution, not God.*
   A) Security becomes the reason we attend. We feel safe and we keep the institution alive to have the church as our umbrella. The serving of God, preaching and teaching the Gospel, and ministering to the people of the community, are paid lip service only. In a recent poll,[3] a list of 10 cohesive forces that hold a typical mainline church together did not include a religious component at all.

   B) Church survival is the underlying reason for all of our actions. When we seek members we're not looking to lead people to God or to enter into community with new friends; instead we are recruiting needed members to meet the budget.

---

[3]   Lyle E. Schaller, Strategies for Change, (Nashville, Abingdon Press, 1993), 19.

2. *Ignoring future consequences of current actions.*
Decisions are made in this type of church with no thought to future growth. The next generation doesn't matter when making decisions. The only factors considered are money and maintenance of the status quo.

3. *Sunday School convenience scheduling.*
The church school failure phenomenon of the 1950's, that of scheduling Sunday School at the church hour, has proved universally disastrous. Christian Education in this environment is seen as a child's activity and not entered into by any significant number of adults. Sunday School here would be viewed as an activity separate and not vital to the church as a whole. Entire families and persons of all ages are denied the opportunity to mature beyond the teen years. Here, youth view Sunday School as childish because adults do not attend; therefore, they also drop out as soon as possible. The entire church enters into a belief compact that implies teaching the Gospel and learning one's faith is anything but a life-long experience.

4. *Planning for yesterday.*
Everything from parking lots to budgets are based on what was previously achieved with no thought to move beyond it. "We've always done it this way" or "we've done that before,

and it didn't work so we're never going to try again" are symptomatic remarks from officers of a church stuck here. Hymn books are twenty years old, no new methods are tried, and the church is generally trying to recapture a world which is no longer.

5. *Decisions made for leaders, not for congregations and communities.*
When this symptom is present, the cadre of the church makes decisions seemly oblivious to the congregation as a whole. The language used in official meetings says "we and they." Officers and core members see themselves as "we," the providers and controllers, while they look at the general membership as "they," the obligees and outsiders. "What do they want from us?" "We do our best for them and they don't appreciate us." Here, the core church members see themselves as a berated handful "doing all the work around here." There is almost never churchwide active community ministry in this situation.

6. *Means become an end in itself.*
A church began a yard sale eight years ago because the church had slipped so far financially that sheer existence had become the battle cry. For the first several years it worked, bringing in as much as $2,000.00. As the years progressed, however, the receipts grew smaller and smaller

until in 1994 it took in less than $800.00 Income from donations also rose dramatically during that period, due in part to the teaching of tithing and a 30 percent increase in attendance. The yard sales cluttered the buildings for three months each year; and at one time, decisions on building usage were determined solely by yard sale storage, even to the point of canceling Sunday School for lack of space. The yard sale had become firmly ensconced into the life of the church even though it had an overall deleterious effect. The yard sale itself had taken on its own "divinity." Events can easily become icons in the church. This becomes dangerous when the doing of the events supersedes the real purpose of the church or impedes the progress of the congregation. One can test how firmly entrenched such an event has become by proposing a study to find out if that event currently holds any valid purpose in church life. If an uproar occurs, you may have an icon on your hands.

7. *Numbers replace participation as the only goal.* Smaller is not better, and increasing numbers should be one of the major objectives in church planning. To those who object it should be emphasized that we're looking to bring in numbers of PEOPLE. However, many churches try only to bring new people "in." They boast to be ever growing, but never plan for the assimilation of the new people.

Whenever the pastor is out in the community making people contact, while the existing congregation is unsympathetic and remains uninvolved in the prospecting, you will find this symptom of blight. The real long term success of a church depends on growing numbers of involved, participating, ministering people. There are certain questions that can serve as barometers that we might consider asking. As your church grows, are the small groups growing in attendance and in involvement? Are the fellowships growing in attendance and frequency? Are more folks involved in outreach ministry? Are the new people accepted onto the church's committees and boards? A "No" to any of these signals a problem.

8. *Meetings - reports - goals take place of results.* In bodies where this condition exists, meetings are held, data is collated, decisions are made, goals are set, and that's the end of that. The purpose of meeting in this context is to provide a social gathering only, therefore once the meeting is held, the purpose is accomplished. These churches "meet to meet." Many church boards believe that once the action or project is OK'd, their job is done and the congregation is responsible for carrying it out. True leadership sees problems and situations as opportunities, not as crises. They:

✓ research the topic

✓ make a decision

✓ get as many involved as possible

✓ get the job done. Getting the job done is the key expression.

To Schaller's list I will add one more.

9. *The church supports itself on other than the donations of its congregation.*
Many older churches exist on rents received, donations from businesses or government for performing specific services or, more usually, on the proceeds of an endowment. If there was ever a curse in disguise, endowments are that curse. Churches must support themselves from donations received from across the entire living congregation in order to stay vibrant. Even churches which exist off the huge offering of one big giver find themselves dying a slow death and not able to determine why. If the people of the church allow any source other than their own bank accounts to carry their ministry, the congregation's sense of ownership will disappear, blight will set in, and the death watch can begin.

There, of course, may be modification in the symptoms of blight and particulars may vary slightly from church to church; however, these basic nine symptoms are fairly universal, easily identifiable conditions that many churches experience.

An invitation is therefore extended to each reader to use this list as a guide in the examination of the reader's home church. A constructive exercise would be to allow each congregation to critique itself to see if it has become a victim of church blight.

Process Planning

It is one thing for an intentional outsider such as Jethro to suggest taking the difficulties to God before the people; it is an entirely different prospect to determine just how the local leader serving a church suffering from blight can do that on a regular basis.

The late Arthur Adams, a pioneer of church leadership, developed a model to be used in the local church in the decision making process for just such a purpose. He called this method of leader interaction "focused brainstorming."[4] To date his suggested planning process is the best method I have seen for beginning to tackle, on a daily basis, the acute problem of churches stuck in chronic failure through lack of solid leadership practices. Unlike strategic planning, which is designed to redirect the congregations efforts on a long range basis, focused brainstorming is a way to alter the course of the church's future as it is directed in the regular meetings of the church's boards and committees. Adams' model can be drawn as an oval or circle with six specific points of entry.

- Problems

- Possibilities

- Projects

- Patterns

---

[4] Arthur M. Adams, Effective Leadership for Today's Church, (Philadelphia, Westminster Press, 1978), 50-57.

- Purposes
- Prospects

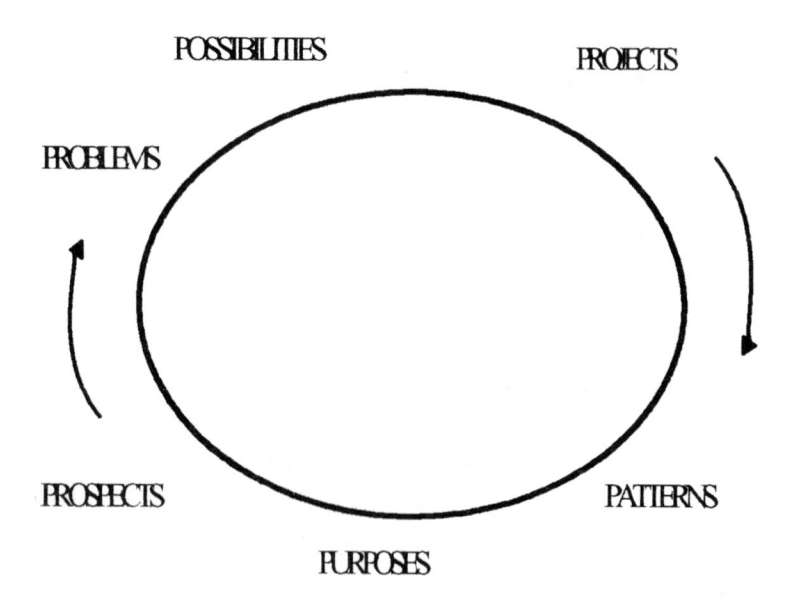

```
         POSSIBILITIES          PROJECTS

PROBLEMS


PROSPECTS                              PATTERNS
              PURPOSES
```

Church leaders often assume that the solution to an ongoing problem must come from their personal knowledge and experience base. This often leads to frustration and combat as each committee member takes the responsibility for securing an answer to a given problem, all the while seeing themselves as inadequate Each participant is therefore threatened by other points of view. The local church leaders, like Moses before them, are trapped in an endless cycle of problem solving and infighting rather than accomplishing ministry.

Renaissance or Ruin

In taking Jethro's suggestion to "bring the difficulties to God," the leader in any group can lift the burden away from his or her self, and pass it on to "God before the people." This maneuver can be executed by using Adams' method, based on a team's response to a problem, to reach consensus. Employing focused brainstorming allows solutions and ideas to generate from the entire group, avoiding the limited response that can come from a solo player.

Let's look at a case where a crisis faced a church and the governing body *did not* use focused brainstorming. A committee at St. Mary's Church was faced with another in a series of seemingly endless problems. The city had determined that they needed a larger parking lot to avoid traffic problems and complaints from the neighbors. The church had owned the land for years, but it was undeveloped. Like many churches founded in the 1940's and 1950's, St. Mary's had planned one day to expand on the land. Growth had stopped a generation ago and church decay and "blight" had since set in. The land lay fallow.

The current problem in parking had been ironically fostered by a rather sudden two year pattern of growth brought about by a new pastor, and some favorable demographic changes in the neighborhood. As in all churches in failure, however, money had taken the place of vision as their *raison d'être,* and no one on the committee could appreciate the reality of the opportunity facing the church.

As the committee came together to face this life and death issue involving $2,000 and twenty new parking spaces, they had no problem solving model to follow. Leadership didn't have a chance, so the result was crisis management. Crisis management handles problems by attacking the symptoms of a problem, seeking to make it go away by any means; usually neutralizing the symptom while ignoring the real problem. This "quick fix" method is taken in an attempt to restore order and happiness (homeostasis). The committee at St. Mary's dealt solely with the situation by attempting to neutralize it. They chose to petition the city to reverse its order, basing their request on interference of church by state. The city caved in, St. Mary's didn't have to build a bigger parking lot, and the status quo was maintained.

Take a moment to relive that fateful trustees meeting, this time using Adams' method. First, the moderator of the meeting might write on a drawing board the six steps in Process Planning. It should be done in such a way that observers could see that the only way of carrying out the meeting process was to go from step to step until all six categories were covered. An oval or circular design works best for me, with each of the "P" words posted around the perimeter.

The moderator begins with the category *Problem* and asks the group to develop a mutually agreed upon definition of the problem to be discussed. In this case the group could have chosen - "The city is trying to make us spend $2,000.00 to build a parking lot we don't want." At St. Mary's this is exactly how the problem was stated. As you can see from the defining stage, the trustees at St. Mary's automatically attempted to invoke "crisis management" instead of leadership in the very tone of the definition. This is a normal human defensive reaction.

In crisis management there are only two stages, "Problems" and "Solutions." Under this scenario, committees move directly to "solution." Having achieved neutralization of the defining statement (problem all gone), they would feel satisfied that their job was done. In St. Mary's case, getting

Renaissance or Ruin

"the city off our backs" would qualify as a solution. In reality there is one last hidden step in crisis management, which could be labeled "Ramifications." This would help those using that system to see what they've actually accomplished, which is usually nothing.

Following Adams' plan, however, the next area of discussion would come under the heading *Possibilities*. Here several options could be developed and listed for all to see: "Build the lot - fight city hall - cancel all the new programs to reduce traffic - close the church."

Once there is a good sense that all the options are listed, the next category, *Projects,* is tackled. Here the group would discuss other projects going on in the church to see if there is anything currently in motion that would impact this decision. At St. Mary's some of these factors would have been:

1. A church growth committee that had become active,

2. New services had begun,

3. Over twenty new members had joined,

4. The church school was beginning a long term series of popular lesson,

5. Two new rental tenants beginning to use the buildings.

Once the interaction begins to abate and all influencing factors are listed, the moderator would focus on the next in the series of touchstones.

Patterns investigation helps to determine what is happening around the church as a result of ongoing projects and other activities. During this discussion it would quickly become apparent that the church was experiencing rejuvenation in property use. The head usher would perhaps chime in, "Our attendance is up to over a hundred on Sunday morning." The property chair person could add "the people complain that the Bible lectures are held the same night that the new tenants AA and Alanon are meeting, causing a terrible parking and rest room problem." The worship chairperson could add that the same thing is true on Sunday, "We've got plenty of chairs, but our parking lot is over-full."

This is an excellent time to slide into the next category, *Purpose*. The meeting leader now could interject "What are we here for, why do we exist, I mean, what is our purpose as a church?" The answer will come in a myriad of guises, but when all the answers are written on the board under the Purpose step they should all quintessentially say - *We are in the business of reaching people*.

Natural evolution should lead on to the last step, *Prospects*. Again, using our hypothetical example of St. Mary's, the flow in the meeting dialogue will congeal around the prospect that "The more people, the more cars, the greater our success." The Prospect in this case should lead to the consensus that the lot is needed if the lectures are to be attended, the tenants are to remain, income is to increase, and if the church is to continue to grow. Without the lot, the Prospects are that all this will end. If done in this manner the decision will have been reached, not by a powerful official, not

Renaissance or Ruin

by political trade-offs, but by being objective and following a process of productive consensus. Quite literally, this committee would have stood *before the people bringing the difficulty* (problem) *to God.*

Note that the end result is diametrically opposite the traditional Problem - Solution - Ramification model.

At first, following a disciplined plan such as Adams' Focused Brainstorming method of Process Planning seems cumbersome compared to the usually spontaneous informality of the church meeting. Observations of these "free - unstructured" meetings, however, indicate that one or two persons usually dominate the discussion and the outcome of the meeting. We have come to realize in the past few years that every meeting needs an agenda; we now need to realize that seeing problem solving as an end in itself is self defeating.

Problems are challenges, problems often indicate a surge in the growth of the organism, a tangling of an ever unreeling line leading to the future. Problems are a sign that maturation and development are taking place, and not an indication of failure, or disaster to be dealt with in a defensive - crisis mentality. Focused Brainstorming is by far the best method I've worked through for introducing leadership into a local church meeting curriculum. It can be used by the trained professional and by the untrained lay person alike. It can be used in large meetings and small. It can be done as an effort to eliminate attacks on particular people, or the dreams and goals of groups in the church that find themselves juxtaposed to one another.

A cautionary note is worthwhile at this point. A person holding power pejoratively will naturally scoff at the prospects of introducing discipline, order, and process into a meeting. This type of power holder operates best in spontaneity. The controlling personality detests working in a planned, orderly fashion because planning, order, and discipline become the control factor rather than his or her threats and intimidation. Several people present at initial meetings where process planning is to be introduced should be prepared to move into focused brainstorming even over opposition. In other words, be prepared for a temper tantrum or two.

The Healthy Church

We have spent a large portion of our effort to date looking at the symptoms and situations that reign, to one degree or another, in many of our failing churches. Let me now juxtapose these symptoms in a blighted church against a few signs and symptoms of healthy churches. These healthy church characteristics can replace those of blight by the introduction of well defined leadership and by leaders willing to bring the difficulties to God for the people:

1. *Theology* - The church-alive is first of all a theological institution. The Christian church that has the mandate for success is <u>God centered</u>. The talk, the songs and the minds of its people are ever God-seeking and Christ-focused. The <u>name of Jesus</u> is on everyone's tongue, and more than any other activity, the worship and teaching of His love and Lordship pervades every area of the life of the church. People are not only open about Jesus at the center of their lives, they are verbal about their faith. These folks usually don't invite you to their church to see the beautiful organ or the great swimming pool. You are

invited to "hear our preacher talk about *Jesus.*" This is a church of personal and living faith.

2. *Philosophy* - means "a system of principles for guidance in practical affairs." For Christians involved in healthy churches, Jesus is their guide; their philosophy is doing, giving, and sharing. They teach the giving away of the Gospel and the sharing of the gifts of God. Here is where the liberal so called "social gospel" church got into trouble. The living church will not talk about social action, but they will do it. The blighted liberal social gospel church will talk a lot, but do nothing. The secret to success is in the doing.

One healthy store front church in Miami, Florida has given away over 20,000,000 pounds of food to the poor in the past six years. Another independent Gospel Church in Jacksonville has sent and is continuously sponsoring fifteen missionaries, workers, and medical people in Haiti. A maverick denominational church (United Methodist) in New Jersey sponsors as many as five missionaries all over the world, separate from its United Methodist apportionments. This same congregation also gives full support to one of its native sons who is a missionary for Wycliff Bible Translators. Independent Baptists are operating homes for children, alcohol rehabilitation centers, and unplanned pregnancy centers. Other independent or casually affiliated denominational churches run food kitchens, clothing centers, and drug clinics. All this from churches that are growing by leaps and bounds. The living, breathing church gives and grows. The old "dreadnought" down the block waits to grow, then maybe they'll give. The philosophy of the vital church is love - people - caring centered. not self - money - fellowship centered.

3. *Economy* - The living, growing church ALWAYS exists on its own offerings received fairly equally from throughout the church. Tithing is not a bad word, it's expected.

While there are no statistics, of which I'm aware, that cover all denominations and churches, I was privy to an informal poll taken several years ago from a fairly representative cross section of churches. Of ten churches polled, all were more or less equal in economic resources per family when viewing the entire congregation. In other words, each church had about the same percentage of persons falling into each of the four income categories (low-income, middle low, middle high, and high income). Six of the churches were relatively lifeless and were seen by their pastors as being in trouble. Four were rising stars, growing and vibrant.

One common trait shared by the six failing

churches was that less than five percent of the people were tithers (incidentally, most of these pastors did not tithe either). In the four growing, alive bodies the tithing families ran from 27 percent to 50 percent of the congregation (ironically, all the pastors also tithed their income). The operating income of a successful church must come almost exclusively from the pockets of its members; not ever from yard sales, bingo, endowments, rents collected or annual bazaars.[5]

4. *Ethos* - The reigning underlying and fundamental concept of the living church is that it exists as a tool - a utility - an implement to be used and even used up in the work of the Kingdom. The living church doesn't hold its building in reserve or consider itself as a sacrosanct or Holy place. The more blighted a church, the further along in failure, the more deteriorated, the more protective of its property it becomes and the more exclusive it feels about itself.

A good example of this is a Baptist church in one of the neighborhoods of Philadelphia. It was populated by a remnant congregation of

---

[5] Fund raisers are not harmful to the church's economy if the proceeds are given away in ministry and do not accrue to the benefit of the congregation. A Catholic church in Hollywood, Florida raises over $150,000 per annum by holding a 3-day carnival. All this income is used to help poor people get back on their feet. St. Maurice is an exceptionally successful church in all areas of its ministry.

less than twenty people, almost all elderly women. The neighborhood had changed ethnically and now the church stood almost deserted. Its roof leaking prodigiously, its carpets were in ruin. The church was generally in a condition of abject physical failure, nigh unto death. The mission council of the denomination decided to reach some of the "locals" for Christ by stocking the wretched basement of the building with pinball machines to attract the neighborhood youth. Unfortunately, to access the cellar the kids would need to transgress the "holy" space of the closed, decaying sanctuary, an act unthinkable to the congregation. A solution was sought and found; the kids could use the basement, but they would need to enter the play area by sliding down the abandoned coal chute from the back alley.

In this case, the reigning ethic of the congregation was to hoard - not share; be exclusive - not inclusive; be separate and alone - not together and with the local people. Needless to say, ten years has passed, the playroom is gone, the congregation is gone, and no one was saved for Christ, in this life or the next.

The healthier congregation doesn't become upset ("have a cow" in the vernacular) if little fingerprints appear on the wall of the fellowship hall. An alive, growing church is going to have ice cream on the floor, pop cans in the men's room and noise in the sanctuary. The sanctuary is a work area, not a holy place of forbidding taboos. The pastor will be "Dick" or "Rev. Bill, the preacher" or "the prof," not to be confused with the Reverend Doctor Artimous L. Finnley III who pastors Tombstone Tabernacle. In the church-alive there is nothing holy, as in haughty, about the church place; it is a work place where people come to be transformed into saints of God.

5. *Leadership* - The church-alive is administrated by God-centered <u>leaders</u>. This is diametrically opposite to the failing unit's propensity to choose "keep(ing) the status quo <u>managers.</u>" Jesus said that all of us (churches not excepted), need to choose either mammon or God, that no one can have two masters.[6] He could have been challenging our church officers of today to choose either being a leader or accepting management.

Leadership in the growing, alive church consists of old people and young, long-time members and brand new converts. They all share one common denominator: they are leading the congregation toward God, not toward some sort of business centered goal. The entire infrastructure of this living leadership dynamic

---

[6] Matthew 6:24

is based on moving human beings, all human beings - from a self-centeredness to a God-centeredness. Therefore, all of their leadership decisions should reflect that goal. Requirements for office reflect little thought given to the "most right" person for the job and have more to do with a person whose "heart is right" for the job. These churches realize that an unconverted CPA will make a far worse church treasurer than a Jesus-loving, godly person with only a high school diploma.[7]

6. *Moral Codes* - There are exceptions to the following statement that: All growing, living churches teach and exhibit a well defined moral structure. There are exceptions, I'm sure, but I have never come across one. The old line liberal idea that anything goes, and every and any belief is alright is no longer palatable to the American family in the turn of the century church.[8]

I heard a story recently of a lady who called her pastor on Monday morning. She asked if she

---

[7] The first treasurer in the Christian church was eminently qualified to manage money, his name was Judas Iscariot.

[8] Like most pastors in main line denominations, I think of myself as a social liberal. I have come to realize, however, that the" anything goes" concepts of the 1970's and 80's are bringing our people to ruination. We as a species need limits on our behavior, and the church is the place we must come to learn those limits. If liberalism is not to be lost forever, our churches must come to grips with this need, and begin to address responsibility as well as rights.

could have a list of what her church believed. The pastor was astounded, saying "Mary, you've been a member here all your life, you should know our beliefs." She related that she had gone to a family reunion the day before. One of her sister-in-laws had become a charismatic Christian and was so excited, espousing to all what marvels she had been hearing at church. Another chimed in and told of the Evangelical church that she and her husband were attending in the town to which she had moved. She, too, was excited and related some of the doctrines that she had found to be comforting.

When asked by her friends what her church taught, however, Mary could only say, "I'm a Protestant and believe what they believe." On further questioning she found herself frustrated that her church did not guide her in what is right and wrong. She had been forced throughout the years to develop her own code of morality. This had been done by trial and error, working through one affair, two divorces, bad credit from overextension, and a now controlled drinking problem. She was embarrassed when she realized that her church did not help her define her absolutes (right and wrong).

The tragedy is that many mainline pastors would be as hard pressed to develop a code of morality as would most denominations. Our prevailing doctrine has come to be, "to each his/her own," and "consenting adults should be able to find their own way." The truth of the matter is that we cannot. Our families and our single adults, having been reared in this sea of moral mush, are stumbling and hungry to hear some basic moral imperatives that can be traced to God's word.

I do not advocate a return to "Victorianism," and I am far from a Christian rightist, but we must be prepared to meet people and their needs where they are. The hunger of our people is so great to hear basic right from wrong that we need not be surprised when they seek the answers in other faith families.

In actuality, many denominational statements do exist that are well able to serve as a basis for moral-ethical formulation. These, combined with their biblical base, could satisfy the needs of our people to have an authoritative basis on which to build their lives. Our problem is our reluctance to examine these base beliefs for fear of offending someone. The church alive delivers God's word to God's people. Their need is for direction, not ambiguity. If they do not receive a stronger source of moral/ethical teachings than that which is available from their own psyches, the people of this generation will continue to live and die in terror. Our people know what they need - the church that survives will be the one who "delivers the goods."

7. *Citizenship* - in the living church is primarily and fundamentally in the kingdom of God. The members consider themselves not members of an institution, but really see themselves as disciples and followers. They are not spectators, but rather they themselves are priests. Their leaders feel ultimately responsible for the souls of those around them.[9]

The members of dying churches consider themselves many things. Perhaps when asked, " what are you," they would respond, "Oh, Methodist of course." Perhaps when asked some would say, "Well, we're United Church of Christ." Still others would think of themselves primarily as belong to the First Baptist Church. The members of the thriving, vibrant church will have none of it. When asked where their allegiance lies, their answer would always be, "To God, of course." No reticence here.

In a class of United Methodist ministers in the New Jersey conference, the leader of the class was lamenting the great numbers of closing churches in that conference. After a while one of the pastors stood and indignantly asked if, "Are you trying to say that WE are responsible for this turn of events?" The class leader

---

[9] Hebrews 13:15-17.

retorted by asking, "Who do you think should be held responsible?" The pastor answered that "it is no one's fault, it just happened." In the community where that man served, two United Methodist churches had closed in the prior six years, and the remaining one was almost void of communicants. Ironically, during the same period one Assembly of God in that same community tripled in size from 120 members to over 400, and a Liberty Baptist Mission had opened and achieved phenomenal success, hosting close to 200 each Sunday. All this in a town with a static population. Who was responsible? The problem isn't the blame, it's the unwillingness of leaders to accept responsibility.

It is obvious from this review that the two growing churches had leaders who were convinced that their citizenship was firmly established in the Kingdom of God. They would believe that being a member, deacon, or pastor was of little consequence outside the call to be responsible for the souls of others. Like being a citizen of any other domain, these leaders feel that they must shoulder the burden that God has given the church of Jesus Christ.

In most of our mainline traditional churches we feel no such responsibility. We exhibit irresponsible apathy. There is no urgency because we teach there is no hell. There is no excitement because with us there is no heaven. There is no reason, because there isn't a God who walks personally with us. Thanks to wholesale belief in the "Big Bang" theory, many of our preachers and laity have become deists. With no citizenship in God 's kingdom, there is no duty to serve that kingdom

The important points for the leader, hoping to create a living church family, are to

- help the people bring their difficulties out into the open,

- give them to God in sight of the people,

- focus the energy of the people and the power of God on the possibilities, not the problems.

Church leaders can no longer ignore the blighted church and conclude that time will take care of the problem. Likewise, crisis management in use to solve the immediate problems by the quick fix method will only serve to prolong the dying process.

The publishing of the above lists, comparing the blighted church to the healthy church, will help leaders in failing mainliners begin to see the gap between their church and successful ones. It should be hoped that in viewing the comparison, the pain of failure will create a call for change. Process Planning for week-in and week-out goal management and Strategic Planning for the long range must be used to carry the new vision to a new reality. This *proactive leadership* is the only method of bringing the church to a new level of hope. Let the church see the prospects for their own future, both bad and good, and encourage them to share it amongst all the people.

TRIGGER POINTS

1. Study the nine symptoms of a blighted dysfunctional church. How many of these symptoms are present in your church?

2. Study the list to the characteristics of the church-alive. How many of these characteristics prevail in your church?

3. Can you think of concrete proposals that would cancel out church blight and/or introduce rejuvenating characteristics to your church?

4. Using a problem currently facing your church, "run" it through the six steps of Process Planning, beginning with the Problem point. Keep pressing forward until all steps are covered. How does the picture look after the completion of the exercise?

CHAPTER X

TEACH THEM THE STATUTES SHOW THEM HOW TO WALK

Mary's committee was practically non-functioning. Everyone in the church was angry. She had been elected chairperson of the committee on Christian Education at St. Jude Church and the results of their work was close to a disgrace.

She was fortunate in that there were several public school teachers on her committee who also taught Sunday School, the pastor taught adult classes and her budget was ample. Despite all of these factors, however, attendance was very low, Sunday School brought few results, and the entire area of Christian education was in general disarray.

As could be imagined, the parents of the Sunday School children were upset, so much so that several families had left the church. The church council and church officers were outraged about the situation, but felt powerless to intervene. The pastor was beside himself because Mary would rarely speak to him. The students of all ages were disgusted, and the Board of Christian Education itself was even more angry (a reaction to shame). No one really knew with whom to be angry, yet everyone was almost sick with frustration.

Mary was particularly angry with the pastor, "It's all his fault," she would say in meetings in an attempt to triangle him into responsibility. The board was angry with Mary but could not voice their feelings because she was a life-long friend to some and to others she was an important member of a small but powerful coalition in the church. The children blamed the teachers and the rest of the church didn't know who to blame. When Paul wrote to the church at Ephesus telling them that their spiritual gifts were to be used for the "building" of the body, and every part thereof,[1] it is doubtful that he envisioned such a state of affairs.

St. Jude's Christian Education committee, and the church as a whole, is but one of the thousands of churches whose greatest single corporate emotion is fear. In St. Jude's case this fear of failure and of innovation was exhibiting itself as anger. *It's worth noting that the emotion of anger is virtually always the product of fear.* The first question then, is to ask "what in St. Jude's case was producing such fear that resulted in that anger?"

In Mary's case it was fear of failure. She was so afraid of failing at her task that she could not bring herself to tackle it. This was compounded by the political reality that if she did succeed, her friends in the power coalition would ostracize her. This group was extremely loyal to the former pastor and at the same time suspicious of the new one. They had decided to play a waiting game of non-cooperation in order to encourage the new pastor to leave, thereby demonstrating their power. Christian Ed's continued failure was an important part of their scheme. Mary was caught in the middle.

When the pastor tried to prompt her to take the leadership and bear the responsibility necessary to complete the

---

[1] Ephesians 4: 11 - 12

task, she reviled him, seeing him as a threat forcing her to face her fear of failure. The committee too, was gripped by fear. All the members were afraid to challenge the deadlock for fear of being rebuked by Mary or one of the board members who opposed the pastor. The parents and the other church members were afraid to confront Mary and the other board members for fear of rejection, or of being exposed as ignorant of the workings of Christian Education. Therefore the fear of failure, or rejection by the inner ring, actually caused failure, which begot system-wide failure, which naturally resulted in universal anger. The anger here was because everyone, including Mary, wanted the Sunday School to blossom but *their own fears kept it from happening.*

When Moses found himself in a similar paralyzing cycle of failure, Jethro came with his series of antidotes. He interjected knowledge and confidence, forces mutually exclusive of ignorance and fear. Fear of failure bred from a base of ignorance as to how to be a leader, how to get people to complete the task, and what is expected of a leader, is a basic cause for failure in our church and other social systems. Jethro said,

> You shall teach them the statutes and the laws, and show them the way in which they must walk and the work they must do.[2]

Many people who accept jobs in churches, civic organizations and industry feel the bottom line is to "get the task completed." They forget or do not realize the second part of the equation of leadership, that of *employing the talent of the people under your care or command.*

---

[2] Exodus 18:20.

Mary was an excellent "doer." She had run her own small business for years, but she was accustomed to using her talent as an experienced and dependable worker to get the task completed. Even in a small church, however, the task is too broad for one person to attempt to accomplish by himself/herself. Also, since one of the major tasks of the church is to help its people grow spiritually (edify the body), leaders must not deny any worker under them the opportunity to complete their own task of ministry. Thus when solid leadership is practiced two goals are realized simultaneously,

- Completion of the task

- Empowering of the worker who completed the task.

In this manner the immediate need is satisfied, however the long range goal of growing a stronger inter-generational ministering community is met as well.

We can adapt Jethro's wisdom and apply it to the two things that need be accomplished among all church leadership. **First**, *Teach them the statutes*, and **second**, *Show them the way they must walk*. This should go a long way to correct the capricious and ineffective management of ministry now almost universally practiced. In examining these two imperatives we shall find the key to methodical leadership development within the church.

Teach Them The Statutes - Developing Leadership

Statutes are rules, often so basic to the working of the whole society that they are formed into laws. According to the dictionary definition, statutes can be either governmental ordinances for all to obey (laws) or they can be internal rules for an organization to order its affairs. In the case of Moses, Jethro's advice was aimed at helping the community become one of order and law because, as Jethro so aptly observed, chaos and anarchy were reigning in their absence.

Every organization requires an infrastructure comprised of a group of people who work in a setting based on order. Leadership, the entity designed to build and grow an organization, must, of necessity, also advocate and follow certain patterns, rules, or statues for the creation and maintenance of the infrastructure. What Jethro was suggesting was for Moses to stop trying to carry out the statutes by himself and to select others to be leaders beside him. First, however, Moses had to disseminate the statutes or rules under which this new creation, leadership, was to operate. Once this knowledge was imparted, the participants (fellow leaders) all could operate under a single banner; thus growth and order could follow.

No one social organism can be expected to define the ordering of leadership for all other type organizations. White collar enterprises would require different statutes than would a retail enterprise. The military is different from the civilian sector. The church is different from the secular world. However, upon examining various sources and writings from different disciplines and work areas, it is amazing to find how many characteristics and principles on the establishment of leadership are similar and interchangeable. The church has at its disposal the oldest written record of a code of leadership standards known to humankind. This is found in the Holy Scriptures. However, these standards are often difficult to extract and formulate into one easily quotable, learnable code. In an effort to make these biblical principles more recognizable, let us look at some of these precepts as they are found in other area of society.

The United States Marine Corps prescribes eleven such principles of leadership which have been translated from the Guidebook for Marines. These exhibit a more demanding style than most church volunteers would accept. Nevertheless, let's look at these eleven principles:

1. *Take responsibility* - A leader must be willing to assume responsibility for both self and the actions of fellow subordinate workers.

2. *Know yourself* - Constantly seek self improvement through self evaluation.

3. *Set example for others to follow* - This applies to self conduct in both private and business life.

4. *Develop your subordinates* - Allow your subordinates to handle the details of their assignment while encouraging them to complete their task.

5. *Be available* - Answer requests for advice, stay aware of the progress of all activities, however, do not crush the self initiative of followers.

6. *Look after the welfare of your subordinates* - Know and be interested in the welfare of your team mates, make sure they receive all personal help.

7. *Keep everyone well informed* - Make sure your followers have complete, truthful, and ever progressive reports of the state of the task force.

8. *Set goals that are achievable* - Intangible and global goals sound great, but are immeasurable and unimaginable. Be reasonable in setting objectives.

9. *Make sound and timely decisions* - Base decisions on factual information. If a decision is wrong have the courage to admit it and change it.

10. *Know your job* - No one is an expert in the area of each job needed to be carried out. However, be open to learn, go to seminars, read books, and be ever learning your field of endeavor.

11. *Build teamwork* - Assign projects to entire team. Set individual objectives all of which come together to create a whole. The creating of a team is as important as completing the job.[3]

As a former business executive I can attest that anyone following these principles, all things being equal, could not help but to succeed in the secular world. These rules, however valid and effective they may be, could not be expected to be followed by the volunteer executive in the church, even if that

---

[3] Townsend and Gebhardt 1992, 29.

person ascribed to them in his/her daily business life. They would be just too demanding.

Also, for the upper level business executive or for the church leader there are some missing pieces. Things such as innovation and vision and experimentation are not mentioned in the Marine Corps statutes mainly because these qualities are not expected or even encouraged in a military setting.

This having been said, it has been theorized that one of the reasons for the current problems facing American business can be traced to the fact that some of these military rules, devoid of innovation and experimentation, have bled across into business management principles. This is due to our great military successes and the resulting large numbers of former military officers who have migrated into the board rooms of major US firms. For these ex-military leaders, systematized standardization becomes more important than vision and innovation.

One glaring flaw I found in my journey as a candidate for the United Methodist ministry was the importance conveyed to a new seminary graduate, when accepting his/her first charge, to consider, first of all, your predecessor and your successor. The instructions given encouraged you not to achieve so much so as to put your forerunner in a bad light. Also, great performance would make it too hard to find a successor to fill your shoes.

Consequently, the United Methodist Church appears to place great value in a standardized mediocrity, and rewards that above vision or accomplishment. The Methodists aren't the only ones who obey that unwritten law, it's just more easily enforced here due to the strong connectional system.

Ten Commandments of Leadership

Apparently, if we are to introduce regenerative leadership into the church we shall have to go beyond the admirable traits expected of the military executive. James Kouzes and Barry Posner come remarkably close to giving a set of statutes on leadership perfect for the church. While originally designed for the business setting, if followed by our church leaders these "Ten Commandments of Leadership" will go a long way toward developing the basis for a successful cadre of church leaders.

The authors postulate that leadership can be learned through imitation and emulation using these statutes:

1. *Search for opportunities*

2. *Experiment and take risks*

3. *Envision the future*

4. *Enlist others*

5. *Foster collaboration*

6. *Strengthen others*

7. *Set the example*

8. *Plan small wins*

9. *Recognize individual contributions*

10. *Celebrate accomplishments*[4]

---

[4] Kouzes and Posner 1988, 14.

Britt Minshall

At a glance, one can see many similarities between this list and the Marine Corps list. Number four, "Enlist others" equates to "Build teamwork" in the first list. "Set the example" in the "Ten Commandments of Leadership" is identical to the Marine Corps idea of "Setting the example for others to follow." In one way or another, two-thirds of both lists can be closely matched. There are, however, several differences which in our case could spell the difference between success and failure in a church.

For example, the commandment in the second list to *Search for opportunities.* Remember that the definition of leadership given earlier in this book calls for the leader to "move on before," thereby creating forward movement for the community and systematic change. We also need to realize that the chance to do this will not usually be dropped in one's lap. Our churches exist inertially. That is to say they just keep going in the same direction, relishing the lack of change. If a leader wishes to move the congregation on to greater things, that leader will have to dig, push, and hunt for an opportunity to challenge the process. This is precisely why I touted the benefit of Adams' "focused brainstorming" earlier in this work. It forces the church administrators on an on-going basis to dig, push, and search for opportunities arising from encounters with everyday challenges. Leaders are supposed to be pioneers, they are about innovation and change.[5] James McGregor Burns writes:

> Attention may continue to center in the predictable, visible matters of technique and process and personality rather than in the prospects and nature of fundamental, substantive alteration in people's lives and welfare and opportunities of "real

[5] Kouzes and Posner 1988, 30-33.

change." Political leadership, however, can be defined only in terms of, and to the extent of the realization of, purposeful, substantive change in the condition of people's lives. The ultimate test of practical leadership is the realization of intended, real change that meets people's enduring needs.[6]

Here one can see that change is not for change's sake, but change in this sense is the opportunity to improve the condition of the species, in our case through moving the church closer to its call from God.

Several years ago I became involved in a chess game with an opponent that was "tit for tat" my exact match. We became so entangled in each other's moves and so defensive in our play that we could have continued forever in a dead heat with no winner or loser. After nearly an hour it was obvious that something had to give. A change in the status quo had to take place. Any change, good or bad, would have been preferable to a slow death by moving of knights and bishops back and forth. At that point, I deliberately moved my queen's bishop into the path of his king's knight, my bishop having no cover or back-up. Rollicking laughter emanated from my opponent who exclaimed, "I knew it, what a foolish move, you're going to lose that bishop." He was right, but it was worth the risk, even to take a loss to create forward movement and finish the game. Eventually my opponent lost the game, which brings us to Kouzes' and Posner's second radical commandment to challenge the process, *Experiment and take risks*.

---

[6] Burns 1978, 461.

For obvious reasons this instruction is not in the military list. Often lower grade officers who experiment and take risks go to one of three places: Arlington National Cemetery, the disciplinary barracks, or to Ft. Leavenworth Federal Prison. The military reserves this commandment for its highest level officers. In the stagnated business or church situation, however, no such prohibition exists, nor should it. Members can become so defensive (fearful of losing relationships for example), that unless the leader is willing to take risks and push for trying something really new, the stalemated game of slow decay could go on for years.

Patricia Carrigan's story of tremendous success as the first female assembly plant manager in America is told in her article Up From the Ashes. After becoming the executive and operational head of a failing General Motors plant, she realized great change had to take place or total failure and eventual shutdown was assured. The union and the management had become involved in a stalemated struggle that was going nowhere. She began several programs at the plant, but her eventual success was due to her dedication to four principles on which she based her management philosophy. Principal number one was, "To change, take risks, accept responsibility, and become accountable for our actions."[7]

Taking risks, however, is something most of us have difficulty with, especially in the church. The most adventurous entrepreneur becomes submissive to the whole body at a church board meeting. The risk of loss of extended family and security in relationships is often overpowering.

Researchers in group dynamics have found that in small groups which have been together more or less intact for

---

[7] P. M. Carrigan, "Up From the Ashes," *Organizational Dynamics Practioner*, (1986, 18) 2.

periods of five years or longer, the performance levels are extremely low. The best performing groups are those who have been together for three years or less.[8] There are several reasons, but the bottom line seems to be that as time goes on groups become more and more a closed system, cutting themselves off from the rest of the society, the church, or the company; they - the group - become their own world. In this setting close relationships supplant accomplishments as the number one priority.

Also unsaid is the underlying threat that if one begins to introduce new ideas, take risks, or experiments with new things, the homeostasis or balance of the group will be threatened. Business has now learned that the makeup of groups need to be "shaken up" or changed periodically just to keep the unit pliable in its thinking, open to new challenges, and effective in the market place.

In most churches, however, the cadre or core group of the church tends to remain intact for decades. Jobs may be changed from one person to another, but the sponsors (the patriarchs and matriarchs and their satellites) always remain the same. In this static setting there is little room for risk-taking.

There are two possible antidotes for this fear of risk-taking.

> 1. The church could adopt a policy that each committee is to report at least one new experiment it has tried each quarter or twice per year. This must be accompanied by,

> 2. A fun time to celebrate "bloopers."

---

[8] Kouzes and Posner 1988, 58

Non-successes will happen if risks are taken, but if no risk is taken, failure through stalemate is certain. The problem is that when a church leader, clergy or lay, takes a risk, the specter of failure ever clouds the horizon. Failure is anticipated and often engineered by the rest of the group.[9] Once the failure is realized, the other sponsors in the group chastise the experimenter, under the guise of comforting, for the risk taking. The church record is amended for all time to reflect the risk, the mistake, and the official repentance of the one who strayed. The object of all this retribution is to kill the desire to challenge the process by experimenting with new programs and ideas.

The greatest risk a leader in most of our churches will need to be willing to take is the risk of the temporary loss of friendships. If, however, the leader perseveres through one or two non-successes with deliberation and confidence, others will often follow. R. H. Macy failed in retailing seven times before his store in New York became a success."[10] Likewise, in the middle of great success J. C. Penney went bankrupt, but picked himself up and started over again going on to even greater heights.

Technically speaking, Paul failed over and over. Either he was being run out of town by the very people he came to help or the opposition was having him tossed into jail. He lost battle after battle and yet by persevering and continuing to risk all, he won the war. *Absolute failure comes not from non-success but rather from not trying.*

The third significant difference between the military list and Kouzes and Posner's leadership list is that *Envisioning the*

---

[9] Note what happens in the average family of smokers when one tries to quit. The others will blow smoke on the repentant one's face, offer free cigarettes and try to temp them back into the fold.

[10] Kouzes and Posner 1988, 63.

Renaissance or Ruin

Future does not appear at all in the military model. The next commandment in this area, *Enlisting Others* is very relevant to the Marines, therefore it does appear as item number four on that list. If any organization should own both of these two themes as a part of its very essence, the Christian church should be able to claim that designation. By the same token, if any organization ever operated without these two leadership commands, the mainline church of the 1980's and 1990's can claim that distinction as well.

The very first sermon preached in the Christian church on the day of Pentecost in ancient Jerusalem spoke of an envisioned future. As Peter stood, filled with the Holy Spirit, he delivered God's first instruction to the infant body using the Hebrew scriptures. From the prophet Joel Peter read:

> And it shall come to pass in the last days, says God, That I will pour out My Spirit on all flesh; Your sons and your daughters shall prophesy, Your young men shall see visions, Your old men shall dream dreams. And on My menservants and My maidservants I will pour out My Spirit in those days; And they shall prophesy.....[11]

These menservants and maidservants of whom Joel prophesied and about whom Peter spoke, sit in the pews of our churches today. What is missing is the seeing of visions and the implementation of them.

If my proposal that the antidote for the status quo is proactive leadership is to be taken as true, then the first task of a leader is to create, form, and share a new vision for a new future. Literally to *see visions and dream dreams*. The person who holds a vision for the future but fails to articulate that

---

[11] Acts 2:17-18, NKJV.

vision to the community may be classified as a dreamer, but never as a leader.

The church leader's task is to *envision the future* in a way different from the past and then be willing *to enlist others* in the community in the conversion of that vision into reality. It then becomes the responsibility of the community to either accept or reject that vision.

A note here is important. While the second task of the leader in this area is to enlist the community in making the vision a reality, the leader cannot be responsible once he or she has, with perseverance and belief, shared the vision of the future, if the group rejects that vision.

Jesus came and shared his vision of the Kingdom of God and was soundly rejected by the ecclesiastical infrastructure (the leaders of the Jewish religious community). His instruction from God was to stay and to suffer the ultimate rejection - death. Few of us are called to that degree of loyalty to vision or community. Conversely, all visions for the future are not compatible with every community that is privy to them. For this reason I suggest that if visionary leaders so strongly believe that their dreams should become reality, and if, subsequently, their community of origin continually rejects implementation, it is incumbent on that leader to seek another community power base which will accept and sponsor that dream. The important emphasis here must be on humankind's receiving of the leader's gift and not the survival of one particular faith community.

When Jesus began preaching, He first spoke in His local synagogue at Nazareth. The result is well known. The people rejected Him out of hand, sparking the comment from Him that, "No prophet is accepted in his own country."[12] As a

---

[12] Luke 4:24.

result of this rejection Jesus moved to Capernaum and began to deliver his message there.

A more contemporary example occurred in 1960. The man who developed cable television came to the seashore town of Wildwood, New Jersey. He was a poorly dressed inventor with little money in his pocket. He told the community business leaders that he could make it possible for the television stations from Philadelphia (one hundred miles away) to be seen in the homes and motels of this remote seaside village. He demonstrated his equipment and shared his vision with business and government leaders and asked their help in financing the operation. He also proposed that if they would allow him to run his cable, and if they would buy the equipment, these people and their community would share in the anticipated revenues from other proposed systems nationwide. After much arguing the leaders rejected the offer. The CATV visionary moved on, finally finding a community in California who accepted his vision. As a result, Wildwood did not receive cable television for twenty years and never shared in the profits. Those who accepted and developed the vision began to see the benefits immediately and better yet, realized millions of dollars from their modest investment in CATV.

The leader's only imperative is to share the vision with belief, thus allowing others to enlist with the leader behind the vision. I do not think I exaggerate when I say that the thousands upon thousands of failing churches in America have no vision at all. I say further with confidence that the rejection of futuristic planning by these same churches, introduced by new pastors and/or concerned lay people, is now a matter of habit.

Visions are more than programs thrown haphazardly out of denomination headquarters in big white and blue envelops the pastor receives semi-monthly. The hope from "congregation central" is that by spending millions of dollars for pretty bulletin inserts and millions more on shining multicolored posters, that somehow, someone will rise to the occasion and lead the church to a response. While this happens occasionally (pastors here or there have a special interest) most of the posters languish in a back room closet or perhaps special collections are taken realizing microscopic revenues. In all of this however, little world changing is accomplished. The dangerous side effect of these half-hearted campaigns is that local congregations are often lulled into the false belief that something truly global and dynamic is taking place.

Likewise, ideas brought forth in board meetings are not necessarily visions. Most ideas, good as they may be, are voiced, bounced around, and voted upon. It is irrelevant as to which way the vote goes however, because even if the idea is adopted it never gets implemented. If by some stroke of luck some ideas are set in motion, most are done poorly and abandoned quickly.

An idea in itself is never a vision. A *vision must be seen*. The very word means that some person can actually picture what this program or thing will look like. A vision is, in that respect, real. It has color, emotion, names, smells, and form. A vision must be perceptible by the visionary as a picture of what the future should look like and also promoted by that person to bring about that future.

A vision is also *future oriented*. It requires a stretch from the present and is well out in the future. Ideas and existing programs attempt to fit themselves into the existing milieu; therefore, they are often regressive rather than progressive.

Renaissance or Ruin

A perfect example of this occurred at St. Mark's Church. The Sunday School had always been very small and taught by two or three people. Someone had a *Vision* - "By moving the Sunday School hour to other than the worship hour, and developing new curriculum we can double our Sunday School numbers." It worked! Sunday School became an exciting, growing entity. However, this growth presented problems. For one thing new teachers were needed. Naturally conflicts erupted between the new teachers and the old (forward movement always creates conflict). Soon someone had an *Idea* - "Let's put the Sunday School back to the original hour and get rid of the problem." The difference is easily discernible:

- the *Vision* portrayed a dynamic, effective, successful future

- the *Idea* solved a problem by returning to past behaviors which restored a failure

Thirdly, a *vision sets forth a more perfect existence*, a shining example, an ideal of something that is not yet, but could be. Visionaries are said to be idealists. Supporters perceive their visionary leader as moving toward a newer, better world. Critics see the same visionary leader as a "troublemaker" and speak of "the idealist" with disdain. The truth is that without visionaries there can be no future. One hundred years ago the telephone, the motion picture, radio, airplanes, and most other material things we now take for granted were visions in someone's mind. Edison, De Vries, Einstein, and others were seen as dreamers. Without them, however, life as we know it would not exist.

Here as elsewhere the relational nature of the structure of the church presents the greatest challenge to its future and its leaders. The smaller the church, the greater the problem. People in these small units can, on occasion, support a person who brings forth a new and better ideal. For the most part, however, small groups are not able to internalize any radical departure from the norm. This is especially true if the new ideal impacts the size or balance of the group.

This leads to the fourth basic characteristic of a vision, and that is *its uniqueness*. It is different, it's new, and therefore often threatening. Think carefully about the vision Jesus presented to the leaders of the religious establishment. He taught salvation through direct loving relationship with God rather than with works or paying tithes to the temple. Jesus' entire concept of having a love relationship with God, and being open and loving to all people, was unique indeed. Paul extrapolated this somewhat vague idea into a new command - salvation comes through faith and faith alone, and this salvation was offered to gentiles as well as Jews. This concept was so revolutionary that most people still have difficulty accepting it.

Visions, in order to be unique, are not necessarily earth-shaking, but they need to be unique to that body.

Clarence Jordan, a Southern Baptist minister, had a vision that was unique to the 1940's and 1950's. The vision was that black and white people could live together in the same community even in the racist environment of Mississippi. This idea would not have been unique in France. It would be more unique in Chicago or New York, but in Mississippi it was so revolutionary that it was viewed as dangerously radical. Consequently, it took years of struggle for the Koinea Community to come to fruition and its existence was threatened for years. Clarence Jordan was a visionary; he saw

Renaissance or Ruin

a picture of something from the future that he felt could be, he carried the vision openly and repeatedly to others, he was repudiated and censored, but in the end his vision became reality.

To these four qualities of a vision featured in <u>The Leadership Challenge</u>, I will add, for the church community that a vision must also be *unselfish*, and *godly*. When we sit in our meetings, tossing about ideas on ways to make more money; not to give over to missions, but rather to meet our every day obligations by having yard sales or rummage sales, visions are not being shared. These kinds of ideas do not meet the test of unselfishness and are therefore regressive if anything. Ideas of ways to make our church better "for us" do not meet the criteria of an unselfish vision.

- ✓ A plan to open a needed care center for Alzheimer's patients - *that is a vision*!

- ✓ A plan to hold a cross denominational crusade for Christ - *that's a vision*!

- ✓ A plan to double the size and effectiveness of the Sunday School - *that's a vision*!

- ✓ A suggestion to send ten percent of each week's collection to the starving in Somalia, Haiti, or Rwanda - *truly this is a vision*!

The final test I'm adding to identify a vision is *godliness*. In the body of Christ a vision need not be only seen as futuristic, idealistic, unique, and unselfish, it must also meet with God's standard of kingdom living. A few years ago at the height of the "sexual revolution" a large denominational church in Tennessee entered into a "ministry." The members decided to produce video films of their married couples having sex. The notion was to show Christians viewing the films that they could experiment with different sexual positions and not be in defiance of God's will. Basically, they were correct, God is not Victorian and I believe dictates not what married, consenting adults do in their marital relationship (within reason). However, the vision of publicly screening sexually explicit films of Christian people having sex is anything but godly. Therefore this was not a vision from God for the church, but rather an idea straight from Satan and for propagation of hell.

There is a place for visions to be openly introduced in even the most routine of business meetings. Thinking back to Adams' "Focused Brainstorming" planning process you'll remember that one of the entry points to the process is *Possibilities*. Here, often coming on the heels of the prior step labeled *Problems*, is the perfect place to introduce a vision that could change the entire method of church operations. Using a "continuous improvement" method such as "I Power" is particularly applicable here.[13]

In Washington D.C., St. Peter's Baptist Church was laboring with serious long term problems. The church was in a racially changed neighborhood. The parishioners, all white, had moved out to Chevy Chase and other suburbs many years ago. St. Peter's facilities were built during the 1950's and

---

[13] "I power" was developed by Martin Edelston and Marion Buhazian, both of Boardroom Publishers in New York. Its principal is to tap into the inherent intelligence and superior knowledge of the people of a particular company, department or church encouraging employees or members in a perpetual and systematic way to be continually improving the community's performance and workability. For a complete treatment of this particular method of continual improvement strategies, see Martin Edelston and Marion Buhagian, "I" Power The Secrets of Great Business in Bad Times, (Ft Lee, NJ, Barricade Books), 1992.

Renaissance or Ruin

featured the best of everything, including a large recreation center (basketball, game rooms, etc.). The problem first manifested itself in the "trashing" of the property by vandals each night. A serious problem? Yes. A leader with a vision, however, was ready to move the situation from *Problems* to *Possibilities*. The visionary, Jim H., stood and courageously suggested:

> Let's open the gymnasium at 7 p.m. Friday, and keep it open until 6 a.m. Sunday morning. We can contact the Police Athletic League and other groups to staff it, and we'll pay for the maintenance costs.

His proposal met all the tests of a vision.

- Jim was *able to see* and *project the picture* of the gym filled with street youth.

- There was nothing like this program now available - it was *future oriented*.

- It promised a win-win for both youth and church, literally *a more perfect existence*.

- The idea was new and innovative; it was *unique*.

- The church would be giving itself away in service to others *unselfishly*, and

- the plan was ministry in the truest sense of the word - it was *godly*.

Surely here was a Kingdom inspired vision being presented to the Board of St. Peter's church. What a vision!

The response from the board was predictable -

> Too expensive, ridiculous, the building is ours, not theirs.

As could be expected the backlash came. But the visionary leader kept on creating the word picture. He gave financial statistics and kept pressing his point.

Finally, after eight months, opposition caved in. A serious long lived *Problem* had turned into a *Possibility* (vision) which soon became a *Project* with the facility open all weekend long. Three hundred neighborhood kids, who formerly roamed the streets in darkness because their parents worked throughout the night hours, now came to enjoy the facility. The interesting side effects for the church were two fold.

1. The cost of maintaining the gym was actually less than the cost of vandalism, which incidentally ceased, and

2. many people from not only the neighborhood, but from all over Washington and the suburbs, upon hearing the story, took an active interest in the church. These people either offered financial support or, even more astonishingly, came to join St. Peter's as part of the congregation.

In the midst of the deepest darkness the brightest of visions often occurs. Leaders who become familiar with these statutes begin to "take responsibility, know one's self, search for opportunities, take risks,' and 'envision the future."[14] These are the people who will save the church.

However, the other end of the equation is that these leaders must find ways to activate the other half of the list of "commandments for leaders" given above. These commandments move leaders out of self and instruct them to interact with others in order to complete the church, literally to make it perfect. They include, "enlisting others, fostering collaboration, recognizing individual contributions,' and 'celebrating accomplishments."[15]

If we use the Marine Corps list, these commands would translate to "developing their subordinates (fellow workers), set achievable goals,' and 'build teamwork."[16] At this point they should be willing and able to involve the strengths and capabilities of others.

Jethro had taken time to instruct Moses, who in turn was willing to take stock of himself. He then implemented Jethro's programs involving the entirety of the people. This last step, however, that of working with others, was then and is today the most difficult. One of the parishioners at a seminar I taught summed it up in a question she asked, "What do you do if your committee doesn't want to move forward - how do you activate them?" In answer to that question Jethro and I use two different languages but say the same thing.

Show Them How To Walk

Up to this point in Jethro's dialogue with Moses, his main concern has been the leader, Moses. We have focused on the inner psyche and mind set of the leaders in general. This process involved background history, a study of the dynamics

---

[14] First five of the Ten Commandments of Leadership.
[15] Kouzes and Posner 1988, 14.
[16] Townsend and Gebhardt 1992, 28-29.

of groups and a thumbnail sketch of what God expects of a leader. The reader's reactions to the text may have vacillated from absolute agreement to argument, on to anger and back again. Until now however, I'm sure we will all agree the focus has been with the leader and the performing of the acts of leadership.

A leader without followers, however, cannot exercise leadership. Leadership can only be practiced in community, and, while you as leader may now be aware of the principles needed to reverse the blight upon your church, the question will arise - "How do I do it?" It is helpful to know that the leadership statutes say to "enlist others and strengthen others" or to "build teamwork and foster collaboration," but the question remains - *how can that be accomplished in a volunteer organization?*

In this setting the leader can't threaten loss because there is no salary. Unlike the Marine Corps the church leader has no brig or punishing demotion to hold over the head of a fellow worker. How does the church leader work with others? Keeping the principles we have discussed in mind, I should like to share one technique of transforming principles into praxis, literally *to show you as leader - how to lead.*

The easy part of our job is to inform leaders that they should enlist others, build teamwork, foster collaboration, and generally build leadership skills. It is quite another to find a method that will tell you how to accomplish that task. There are among us a small percentage of people who have, from birth or shortly after, been endowed with the blessings of natural leadership. Unfortunately, if the church has to wait for a squadron of these gifted ones to breeze through its doors, it will be gone from the picture.

Renaissance or Ruin

The church as well as the business world needs a panoply of leaders now and in every generation, and at all levels. Historically, the church found its leaders among the members of each generation who had been blessed by a profound encounter with God. As a result of this experience they desired to serve God in more pragmatic ways. The circumstances of life in that bygone era lent itself to this leader recruiting method. Agrarian or small town life offered few distractions or other challenges to potential leaders. Talented young people who were not destined to receive a large legacy did not have a multitude of industrial, banking, or commercial pursuits to choose as alternatives. Therefore, some of the most intelligent and gifted leaders of each generation made the church either their life's work or a serious avocation.

On the lay level a pronounced sense of paternalism often served to recruit local people with talent into lay leadership positions. In this way those with power gained outside the church could focus their benevolence toward lay leadership roles in the church and exercise their natural leadership talents there. Today's circumstances are different. The most talented local professionals in contemporary society can exercise their altruistic tendencies, receiving greater notoriety and seemingly better results, by serving in charitable organizations.

From the clerical standpoint, careers in the church are seen as the least likely choice for bright young men and women. Persons with leadership talents can find many places in the business and government sector to exercise these talents. They can fulfill their spiritual needs (if that's even a concern) as a spectator to the 700 Club, and serve God in civic clubs such as the Kiwanis or Rotary.

In days past as many as 80% or 90% of the young people of the community were reared in the church, thus becoming familiar with vocation as an option. Now well under 30% of society's children are ever exposed to the church and most of them only superficially. Therefore, vocation is never considered an option. While we seem to be coming to the end of this so called secularized image of religion or "religion of the modern era," it will be decades, if ever, before the church is again seen as a vital place where someone can invest their leadership talents and expect any type of return.[17]

In the light of all this, we can assure ourselves that Buster Crabbe[18] will not come, leading the Foreign Legion, and that thousands of naturally talented, born-again, spirit-filled leaders, on fire for God, are not poised at the side door of old First Church waiting to save the "old girl" in her final hours. If this salvation is to be accomplished it will have to be carried out by the people best equipped to do the job - the faithful of the church.

An additional enigma facing our people is a deleterious anti-leadership attitude and suspicion of authority that has become endemic among the American people in the wake of the Vietnam War. Even our natural born leaders are in retreat, not to mention those who are moldable into leadership roles. Bureaucrats and non-innovative managers are in the forefront of society. Warren Bennis writes:

> Two hundred years ago, when the nation's founders gathered in Philadelphia to write the Constitution,

---

[17] This refers more to receiving satisfaction, since the church is not normally viewed as a place to secure a financial return.

[18] For the sake of our younger readers, Buster Crabbe was a well known movie star of the 1940 through 1960 era. One of his most famous roles was as a commander in the French Foreign Legion. He became a prototype of the rescuer of people in distress.

the United States had a population of only three million people, yet six world-class leaders contributed to the making of that extraordinary document. Today, there are more than 240 million of us, and we have Ollie North, the thinking man's Rambo. What happened?

As eighteenth-century America was notable for its geniuses, nineteenth-century America for its freewheeling adventurers and entrepreneurs, and early twentieth-century America for its scientists and inventors, late twentieth-century America has been notable for its bureaucrats and managers.[19]

Let us work under the assumption that each reader is either a natural born leader or, better yet, a would-be but as yet unrecognized leader in God's kingdom. The primary factors necessary to actuating leadership have been covered in the preceding chapters. These are a knowledge of the problem and the corrective actions needed to be taken. Next we reviewed the rules by which a leader must play. Now we shall explore the key to effective leadership - *how to lead others*.

Adaptable Leadership Theory

This is where the *Adaptable Leadership Theory* can, for the average person, became the tool for the creation of leadership in our churches at all levels. The basic concept that fires the furnaces of Adaptable Leadership is:

> To achieve as many goals of the group and actuate as many dreams of individuals in that group as possible, employing the efforts and ideas of as many

---

[19] Bennis 1989, 33.

people as can be involved.[20]

The onus to date has been on the leader's ability to lead. Here we shifts to the follower's propensity to execute the tasks common to the completion of the assignment.

Adaptable Leadership first became the focus of attention at Ohio State University over two decades ago and was later brought to light in the work of David Sawyer, Ph.D.[21] This Adaptable Leadership Theory and its well known offspring Situational Leadership Resources was developed by Paul Hershey and Kenneth H. Blanchard of Leadership Studies, Inc.[22]

The first component of the theory (now a discipline in practice) focuses on the follower in a given situation. The follower here becomes a "significant other" and a part of the equation that will determine the final outcome in any exercise. It is theorized that each person or group of people possesses a measurable *Task Maturity* (TM), e.g. the person or group's degree of ability to accept an assigned task, be responsible to undertake it and bring it to a successful conclusion. This process also take place under a measurable *degree of supervision*.

For example, Bill is a trustee at First Church of Philadelphia. He is by trade a blue collar worker at Lyons Shipbuilding Company accustomed to carrying out small tasks assigned him under his foreman's supervision. At the church, the Board of Trustees assigned him the task of being in charge of the auditorium seating set-up for an upcoming conference. He was told at the trustees meeting that the conference was

---

[20] Minshall 1992, 36.
[21] Sawyer, 1986.
[22] *Situational Leadership* is a registered trademark of Leadership Studies, Inc. of San Diego, CA.

Renaissance or Ruin

scheduled for Saturday morning at 10 a.m., how many seats to be placed, and the required seating arrangements.

This meeting of trustees was held ten days prior to the conference. Tom, the chairman of the Trustees heard nothing from Bill and assumed the job would be completed. Naturally, he was aghast when he arrived the morning of the conference an hour before the doors opened to find no chairs in place. Bill arrived shortly after, sporting a big smile and offering remarks such as, "Well, I didn't know when you wanted it done' or 'if I should get help." "I didn't have a key to the building, you know..." Needless to say Tom, Bill, the custodian, and the first twenty conference attendees spent the next hour frantically setting up the chairs. The conference began a half hour late and everyone was generally unhappy. This type of scene is repeated over and over in the church, causing visitors to wonder if church folks are just bumbling half-wits, or at best these observers give a condescending nod followed by the remark - "Well what do you expect, it's only a church".

This story exemplifies a typical case of a follower with a *low task maturity level* (1 or 2 on a scale of 4). Bill is not accustomed to completing tasks on his own and must not be expected to do so. The usual pattern of response to this situation is that Tom in the future will never again ask Bill to complete a task and will poke fun at Bill behind his back. Bill's self image, perhaps already low, will drop slowly and soon Bill will drift away from the church. Tom will internalize that age old adage "I'd rather just do things myself, you can't depend on others." At this point he will no longer be a leader, but rather a good worker doing all the work of the Trustees himself. Consequently the leadership base of the church is reduced by two and the core leadership of the church is lowered by one, further sealing off the cadre from the rest of the congregation.

An illustration of a person with a *high task maturity* (3 or 4) is found in Helen, who was elected as a member of the Altar Committee two years ago at Trinity Church. Helen is a head dispatcher for the Metro transit system responsible for continually evaluating traffic patterns in the city and dispatching additional buses and trains to necessary locations. Accustomed to operating without supervision and on a busy schedule, she was reluctant to accept the job of taking care of the altar, but wanted to serve the church, so she accepted the position.

She promptly contacted the church office and secured a list of every service scheduled for the next year. She scanned a book to learn what colors represent which season for the paraments. She contacted the florist and arranged for flower delivery at certain places at certain times. Finally, she phoned the pastor, Worship chairperson, organist, and custodian, exchanged phone numbers with them and arranged for a continual communication pattern.

Needless to say, the Worship chairperson and the rest of the sanctuary staff never had to worry when Helen was in charge. Once she was notified of an event they could be sure when they arrived that the job would be done. This is a perfect example of high task maturity

The first response of the reader is to say, "I'll recruit all Helens for my board and my job will be easy." May I suggest you not waste your time; that would be an impossible task. Task Maturity, perhaps better labeled "Follower Readiness"[23] varies in all persons according to circumstances.

In the two cases above, Helen (TM4) is able, willing and confident. If she had been unwilling or insecure, her ability would not change, but her TM level would drop at least a point

---

[23] Leadership Studies, Inc.

(TM3). One can see that not just ability, which is not so pliable, but also attitude which is easily varied, impacts the follower's readiness (TM level). Even Jesus picked twelve board members with varying task maturities. Some, like Peter, dropped the ball every time he got the chance (TM 1 or 2), while others like James and John were operating on level 4 all the time. Others apparently disappeared at Pentecost, leaving their TM levels as unknown and, of course, one turned out to be a traitor and thief. Therefore, attempting to enlist only the "very best people" is probably a waste of time, you'll do better to work with those you have.

The completion of the task then must rest with some force outside the follower. That force is *the adaptability of the leader*.

This introduces the second component of the *Adaptable Leadership Theory*, the *leader behavior style*. Hersey and Blanchard postulate that each person not only has a normal task maturity level, but also each leader possesses a primary style of leadership which is normal to his or her personality. This primary style can be categorized into one of the four classifications used in their instruments developed to support their Situational Leadership program.[24] The four are:

1. *Telling*

2. *Selling*

3. *Participating*

4. *Delegating*

Basically, the *Telling* leader, *Leadership Level One* (LL1) can be likened unto a Marine Drill Instructor or a crew boss on a work gang. He or she simply tells the follower(s)

---

[24] Leadership Studies Inc.

what to do and supervises the work closely. The follower is not expected to think on his or her own and is discouraged from creative thinking or planning. Persons with low level *task maturity* (TM1) respond well to this type of leadership and under its imposition can accomplish many tasks. Conversely, persons with level 4 task maturity (TM4), such as Helen, do not function well under such close supervision. Therefore if a telling style leader (LL1) does not adjust his/her leadership style they will excel when leading the(TM1) types but "run off" the level 4 follower(s).

The next lead style level (LL2) on the leader style box is labeled by Hershey and Blanchard as *Selling*. This has nothing to do with the act of selling such as of cars or furniture, but rather indicates a prodding style. This type of leader keeps close contact with his/her followers, checking their progress repeatedly and pushing or encouraging each follower on to the goal. Tom needed to be this type of leader with Bill in order to get the job done. Unfortunately Tom did not realize he had to adapt his lead style to the individual with whom he was currently working. Tom, a business executive, continued to use his accustomed "Delegating Style" (LL4) to which poor Bill, a (TM2), could not relate. Bill needed the close interaction found in the selling (LL2) mode. I personally would label this level of leadership (LL2) as "Coaching" rather than selling. Incidentally, Helen a (TM4) would find it annoying and somewhat distracting to work under this type of supervision; Bill, on the other hand, finds it absolutely necessary.

Next on the leadership style sequence is *Participating* (LL3). At this level the leader sees his/her role as a stand-by person, to participate in the accomplishing of the task only when necessary. This lower level of supervision would be

Renaissance or Ruin

welcomed by Helen, but Bill may have some difficulty with it. The "Participating" leader often waits for a call for help or indication of assistance needed from the follower(s). Thus this style of leadership only works with a follower whose task maturity level is high enough to allow him or her to ask for assistance (TM3 or 4). Bill probably did not meet that requirement, therefore a *participating* leader would have difficulty bringing him to completion of the task.

Finally, Tom's style *Delegating* (LL4), is generally used at the highest levels of supervision. CEO's, for example, would be dealing with people with high task maturity levels (TM4). At this advanced level, once a corporate decision is made the leader needs only assign or delegate to each executive under him/her the general goal to be achieved. Persons with high task maturity (TM4) such as upper level executives will draw their own game plan, pick their workers, set the objective, and bring the plan to completion. This *Delegating* style leader often becomes frustrated when dealing with the average worker (TM1 or 2). He/she is so accustomed to dialoguing and working with well placed high achievers, that in the church setting this (LL4) leader will assume that "people are so lazy" or "these people can't do anything." On the other hand, if an (LL4) leader lucks out and inherits a couple of (TM4) board members, this threesome can leave the rest of the church behind by envisioning, developing, and executing extraordinary projects in unheard of time. They may actually be so efficacious that the congregation will become disheartened.

It may seem that we have reached a stalemate. Are we to test the entire congregation and assign only (TM4) high achievers to (LL4) high level leaders and let the rest of the church do lawn work and take out the trash? Not on your life!

I suggest rather that we envision the church as the supreme learning place, the place to go on to perfection, to enhance our skills, as well as our quintessential selves. Thus we come to the *adaptable* part of A.L.T. *It's this adaptability that enables the successful leader to lead.*

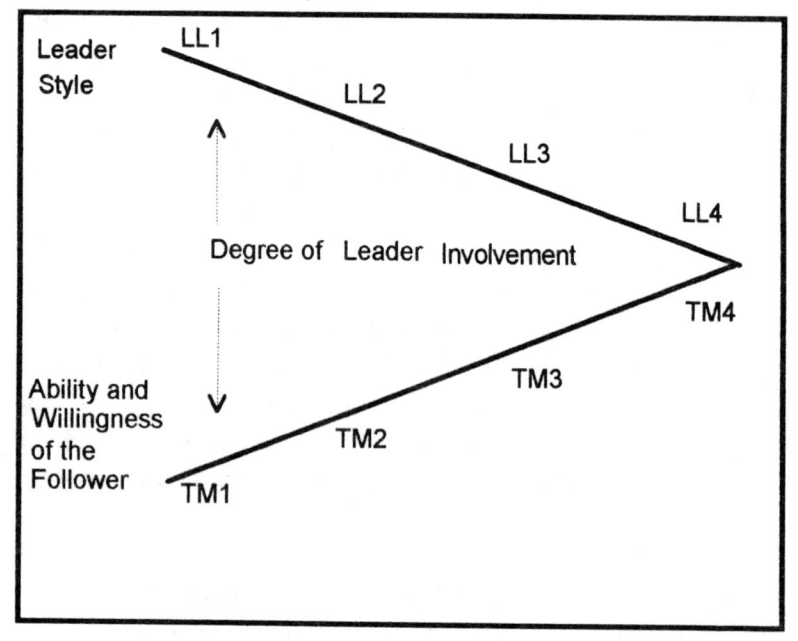

```
Leader      LL1
Style
                LL2
         ^
                      LL3
         |
                              LL4
         |  Degree of Leader Involvement
         |                           TM4
Ability and              TM3
Willingness  v
of the           TM2
Follower   TM1
```

Style of Leader Involvement Appropriate for Each Task Maturity Level

The customary resolution to the problem of the mismatch of leaders to followers is to expect the followers to do a better job and to increase their TM levels on their own. When this does not take place, most churches follow a predictable pattern. The cadre of leaders pick and choose again and again a small group of people in the church with whom they can work and gradually the church becomes divided into two groups.

The first is the involved leaders and accountable workers, "the cadre" or in the vernacular - *the clique*. The second is *the people of the pew*. Their only function is to attend church and give money. It is seen as far too much effort to reach out beyond the inner circle of the clique of "old chums" to involve more of "them" (pew people) who have such a difficult time in working with "us."

This widely accepted solution is one of the major defects in the inner personal relations within the church. This solitary flaw goes a long way to bring about the "closed system" that is killing our churches. The right and productive resolution to the dilemma is found in doing precisely what we don't wish to do; that is,

♦ reach out to *THEM*

♦ to join *US* until

♦ *WE* are all responsible for the church's future.

Since it is too much to ask all followers to change, *Adaptable Leadership* presents the notion that the leader needs to become adaptable to the followers' differing needs for leadership. Let's look at an example.

Tom runs his own small business. As we know, he is the head trustee at First Church, Philadelphia. In his business pursuits he has five long-term employees who know well their fields of endeavor. Throughout the years, following a pattern of normal attrition, Tom's small firm has settled down to work well with Tom. He is a Delegating Style leader (LL4), quite unaccustomed to having to prod anyone to complete a task. On the Board of Trustees at church Tom has five members. Bill, the newest member, only became a church member four months ago. He's still afraid of his surroundings and shy by nature at all times. His normal work setting requires little personal initiative and that becomes apparent when assigned a task at the church.

Mary and Joe are also trustees, but they've been at the church for several years and are not intimidated by the setting. Their personalities and secular work settings are different from Bill's, requiring performance of more self-actuated tasks and far less supervision than Bill. They both have TM levels of 2 or 3. As chairperson, Tom is more comfortable with them. Unlike Bill, they will receive an occasional chore to do; nothing important, mind you, but a small job here and there. While Tom will never give Bill a job again, because he "refuses to baby-sit a grown man," he likewise will not engage Mary or Joe very often because he "doesn't have time to push or prod or check back too often."

Finally there is Larry. His TM level peaks at 4. Tom knows all he has to do is mention a needed chore to Larry and it is as good as done. Of course, Tom chooses Larry for every important task and many lesser ones. Tom is more accustomed to this level of follower since his employees are all (TM 3) and (TM 4). The rest of the board sits idly by while the "Bobsey Twins," as Tom and Larry are known by the congregation, run the church.

The jobs get done, yes, but the rules of leadership are broken at every stage. No one in the group is serving God as he or she volunteered to do. Bill, Mary, and Joe are outcasts and at each meeting their TM levels drop lower and lower reinforcing any negative self-image they may already have. Tom and Larry are getting their strokes from each other and the congregation who sees them as both heroes and martyrs. The resulting "prideful control" experienced by the pair is strangely reminiscent of the Pharisees of Jesus' day who did their works because they loved to receive the accolades of the people.[25]

Gradually Bill will drift away from the church, secretly vowing never to darken the doors of the church again. Mary and Joe will slowly retire to the pew to be "Sunday only people" at first, but later they, too, will disappear. Tom and Larry, the "dynamic duo," will settle into a pattern of languid maintenance management eventually trying to exclude any change, excitement, or challenge from "their" church.

Leadership in this scenario is drastically reduced, participation by the congregation decreases sharply and eventually membership dwindles. Only Larry and Tom are constants eventually in control of the show. This doesn't fly well juxtaposed with the primary imperative of leadership in the church, that of:

> Serving God by achieving as many goals of the group and actuating as many dreams of individuals in the group as possible, employing the efforts and ideas of as many people as possible.[26]

The mandate of the church is not only to get the job done, but to also involve as many members as possible. The task is not only to get the assigned job done, but also to create more disciples and for each of these to grow in spirituality and ministry. Each task and work of the church is a source of exponential growth, not only for the Kingdom, but also for the congregation as a whole.

If Tom and Larry alone deliver food to the geriatric center, then Tom and Larry alone minister to the residents. If

---

[25] Luke 11:37-44.
[26] Minshall 1992, 36.

all the trustees deliver the food (admittedly requiring more effort on Tom's part), five people meet the residents, witness the love of Christ, grow in grace, minister in God's shadow and increase in task maturity. Each time Bill, Mary, and Joe do accomplish a task, their sense of self and ability to complete a function increases. Eventually even Bill will be able to accept the job of setting up the chairs for a conference and get it done with increasingly less supervision.

The focus here is on the follower; however, the responsibility is that of the leader. That responsibility is not to get the job done at all costs, but rather to be willing to adapt his or her leadership style (LL1 - LL4), to the task maturity level of each individual follower (TM1 - TM4), thus allowing that follower to complete the task to the best of his or her ability. A word of encouragement is needed here. Adaptable Leadership doesn't anticipate that a leader needs to adjust to all persons in the body - "be all things to all people" so to speak, but rather it addresses each leader with respect to the people in his or her immediate charge. In Tom's case it would refer to his willingness to adjust his leader's response and degree of contact to each one of his board members - Bill, Mary, Joe, and Larry - to help each of them perform their tasks well.

For Bill (TM1), Tom will need to work as a coach (selling) or even a Drill Instructor (telling); LL2 and LL1 respectively. Tom's remark was correct; he does need to be a baby sitter with Bill. Bill's task maturity in the church setting is indeed child-like. This is where Christian love in leadership comes in, remembering the axiom previously stated, "Love is what makes leadership work."[27] If Tom enters into dialogue with Bill exhibiting or feeling resentment, then that interaction becomes manipulation and it will have no positive effect.

---

[27] Townsend and Gebhardt, 1992, 50.

Renaissance or Ruin

Tom's leadership behavior needs to be further adaptable. Mary and Joe need to grow in task maturity and be included in the work of the ministry. Tom, therefore, needs to adjust again, adapting to meet their respective follower readiness. Since their TM levels are 2 and 3 respectively, Tom needs to be a coach (LL2) and a participator (LL3), thus be open and available, and not consider that an invasion of privacy.

With Larry, Tom will need no adjustment; they go together like "birds of a feather." Tom will need to be acutely aware that this could spell failure in his leadership style. He will need to deliberately push away from the natural tendency to give Larry the important jobs because it is the easy way out.

In his relationship with Larry, Tom may need to be honest and open in apprising him of the need to share the work with a greater number of board members and help Larry through that period of adjustment. Even here the task of the leader is not easy. One of the leadership commandments previously noted, "Keeping everyone well informed," comes into play at this point. If he doesn't do this the Board of Trustees may gain Mary, Joe, and Bill, losing Larry in the process.

Great leaders are not those boasting delegating (LL4) scores, although in the management structure of big corporations these people usually sit in the highest chairs. Truly great leaders are those who love the body, are excited about the task, and develop their followers to deliver their greatest potential.

Many leaders are mono-styled leaders and therefore can function in only one mode and in one arena. A good example can be found in the wartime Master Sergeant. He may be decorated as an outstanding leader of troops in battle, but when peace comes and the discharge is granted he fails as an executive in a manufacturing company. The situation has changed, but the sergeant hasn't. On the battlefield he was a teller (LL1) and the troops were trained to respond to that kind of military discipline. Death or prison was the price of disobedience.

A great leader is one who is adaptable to the circumstances and people with whom he or she works, and the church needs great leaders. For the person truly interested in achieving a high level of effectiveness in ministry and leadership, instruments are available to determine one's primary style of leadership and to gauge one's adaptability or rigidity level.[28]

It would appear that accepting a ministry in God's church will require more work in the future than in the past. Perhaps God is asking believers to invest as much in Kingdom building as we do in personal enrichment. It seems likely that churches that survive the upcoming "Fin de' siecle" (turn of the century) will not be churches whose congregations view them as the community hangout, a place to bury the bodies of their dead, the place to dump old furniture or the place to drop old clothing for the rummage sale. Likewise, congregations who view God's service as a second class endeavor, employing their leftover non-vital efforts and abilities, will not survive the millennium. The church of Jesus Christ is not the place to dump ourselves when we wish to hide from the world in which we live.

---

[28] Pfeiffer and Company International Publishers, 8517 Production Avenue, San Diego CA, serve as the distributors of Situational Leadership materials cited herein. Other lead style inventories are also available from them and other venders. The American Society of Training and Development, Alexandria VA, will have a complete list of approved organizations offering this material.

Renaissance or Ruin

Those hoping to enter into the Twenty-first century as ministers of Jesus Christ (lay and clergy) will need to take risks, investing time and self in that leadership effort. Just any-old-thing will no longer suffice.

Jethro told Moses, "In order to survive you must teach your people the statutes and show them the way they must walk." The Adaptable Leadership method and the commandments for developing leadership echo Jethro's instructions.

When speaking of one of America's greatest leaders, James MacGregor Burns writes:

> Woodrow Wilson called for leaders who, by boldly interpreting the nation's conscience, could lift a people out of their everyday selves. That people can be lifted into their better selves is the secret of transforming leadership...[29]

Through Adaptable and Dedicated Leadership development the people of God can come to have "life and have it more abundantly,"[30] transforming not only the church, but also the hurting world in which we live.

---

[29] Burns 1978, 462
[30] John 10:10, NKJV

Britt Minshall

TRIGGER POINTS

1. Compare the *Eleven Principles of Leadership* (USMC) with the *Ten Commandments of Leadership*. Develop a consolidated list for your church.

2. Which principles do you recognize as being in continuous use in your work place?

3. Which are regularly practiced in your church?

4. Can you recognize your Task Maturity and your Follower Readiness level at your secular job? In your church assignment?

5. What do you think your primary lead style is: teller, seller, participator, delegater?

6. Poll you team members. What do they see as your primary lead style?

7. Is there a discrepancy?

CHAPTER XI

THE WORK THEY MUST DO

Reverend Jones had pastored at Pilgrim Church for thirteen years and six months when, in January of 1988, he announced to the council that he would be leaving after the Easter service. He had reached that magic point in the pastorate, somewhere between twelve and fourteen years, beyond which it is usually taboo to hang around. He realized that the future was fraught with danger and he was one of the very few long term pastors who was willing to take the plunge and leave while he was still considered a saint.

At the same time Jones was approaching another ominous plateau, that of fifty-five years of age. He realized it was going to be exceedingly difficult to secure a pastoral appointment beyond that age. A third driving personal force had also come into the picture, he had by chance found an empty pulpit near the home of his children who lived almost a thousand miles away. "Now," thought he and his wife Laura, "We can be close to the kids."

Jones' pastorate had been very successful. The first three years had been rocky, but once the opposition settled down or left, the congregation had begun many programs, built a fellowship hall, sponsored a new church start, and achieved statewide notoriety as a vibrant, giving, ministering church. Now, as the council listened to Jones' resignation speech, the members sat motionless, an effete collection of stunned church leaders. What were they to do now, and how were they to do it?

Typical of many pastorates, as the years had progressed people sympathetic to his style of planning and operating had come into power and the administration of the church began to take place more by acquiescence than by struggle, pull, or tension. Most pastorates start as did Jones', but truly successful "long term" pastorates (those lasting between 7 and 10 years) almost always settle into a pattern of allowing the pastor to "make the balls" that the congregation is to roll. Jones and his bunch were no exception.

The church had implemented his ideas, but they had been, after all, his ideas. The church supported the long range plans, but those plans originated in Jones' mind. While the church was congregational and had to voice approval, that was all they had done. The congregation had simply "approved" his dreams, goals, and objectives. They carried them out with efficiency and vigor, but they had never "owned" them.

Interestingly, in most cases, the picture we've painted is a prototype of a very successful church. Any unit with a strong, universally revered leader can do wonders and achieve success beyond its size. There are, however, three inherent dangers in this model:

>1. This entrepreneurial model often stays small, usually a one-celled unit.[1] One strong

---

[1] Many writers point to the new hugely successful mega-churches such as World Harvest of Ohio, Crystal Cathedral of California, and Coral Ridge Presbyterian in Ft. Lauderdale, Florida to support this model as the best one for growth. The strong long-term pastor units, however should be looked at as aberrations. They are in reality mini-denominations and cannot be cited in this study.

Renaissance or Ruin

solo leader can only carry from one hundred to about two hundred people.

2. This type of congregation becomes so identified with one pastor, it becomes "Rev. Jones' church." The community rarely sees the ministry of the people. The people of the church never accept a new pastor easily. Jones may be succeeded by two or three "short-termers" whose lives will be made miserable at Pilgrim Church.

3. The people of the church develop an impotency in envisioning, dreaming, planning, and executing their own dreams. They become workers for another's dreams. As good as these programs may be, they are still someone else's dreams, thus the congregation's creativity is rarely challenged.

It is this last point, that of developing a congregation's visions and converting a community's dreams into ministering realities, that we plan to address in this segment.

When Jethro came to Moses' camp, (note I said "Moses' camp," not the Israelis' camp) he found a hopeless situation. Not unlike Jones, he found his son-in-law attempting to "be all and end all." Moses was the father, the leader, the planner, the visionary, the judge, and the manager. The result was a systemic travesty. No one can be "all of the above" and serve as a leader. Bedlam and "grid-lock" were the outcome. Jethro found a system in failure.

To this point in our journey we have examined four of the leadership instructions Jethro gave to Moses. He said:

>   1. Be Godly.

>   2. Communicate with God.

>   3. Teach the people the laws of God and the rules for living.

>   4. Show them how they must work with each other.

And now we shall look at another:

>   5. ***Show them the work the leader must do.***

What we plan to look at is the method under which we organize our churches. Should we continue to follow the accepted method of hiring strong pastors who can survive the three year onslaught of opposition, eventually becoming vested with the directing and planning of movement of the church?

When Pastor Jones left Pilgrim Church the congregation followed the pattern of most churches losing a long term "successful" pastor. For two years the people fell into depression. Programs came to a standstill, attendance dropped (in the end to 30% of its former high), and the officers fought among themselves for control. As pastoral candidates were interviewed none could measure up to the set standard. When, after sixty interviews, a candidate was chosen to come and meet the people, an opposing group formed with the vow to "Get rid of him" sight unseen. Fighting and bickering followed. The church hired and fired two more pastors in the next five years. Never again would the church blossom into even a shadow of its former self. *Why?* Because it was never its "former self" - *it had been Jones' self.* The church had never become a dreaming, planning, and executing organism in charge of its own destiny. Rather it had gathered to support someone else's dream.[2]

There is an alternative method of directing the future of the church. This method combines the high degree of efficacy associated with the strong pastor-leader model above, joined with experiences designed to develop a strong self motivated congregation. It requires determination to set into place and a courageous pastor and resolute people. It demands much more effort initially than simply letting Rev. Jones, or a lay patriarch/matriarch run the show.

Another prerequisite is "guts." In the traditional all too comfortable pastor/ruler model, the pastor becomes responsible for failure if a plan goes sour. The pastor becomes "triangled" so to speak, with the entire church assuming the responsibility for the failure of the congregation. In this case the faint-hearted parishioner can pass the buck - "God will punish the pastor, we can point to the pastor, we can fire the pastor' or 'the world will ridicule the pastor." If an attempt is made to deviate from this model, the congregation and its leaders will need to venture forth with both effort and courage. At the same time, the pastor will need to recognize that vigorous lay leadership is a source of threat to the "pastor self" and be willing to proceed in spite of it.

---

[2] In every case the Pastor is not the usurper of the dreams of the church. In a greater number of situations a strong patriarch/matriarch is in complete control of the church's destiny. In either case the outcome is the same, a congregation with little ownership, scant enthusiasm and no leadership development.

This new method replaces a person or a position with a specialized team. This plan features a uniform structure upon which all major activities of the church will hang in the future. It becomes a systematized method of developing ministry that uses all proactive leadership skills and interposes them with the fervent call of the Holy Spirit to go out into the world and share the Gospel. This future oriented model is a radical departure from ancient tribal management techniques involving a strong leader (chief) and submissive followers. It follows Jethro's imperatives to Moses, and through my research in organizational dynamics, I find it to be an absolutely necessary innovation for incorporation into American church life. This future inventing mechanism is called *Strategic Planning*.

The Basis of Strategic Planning

The idea of broadly based future planning in an enterprise is not new. It, however, is very different from the way communities run in the natural order of things. Likewise, while *Strategic Planning* as an identifiable packaged product is a very new concept, the components of the process have been used as alternatives to both anarchy and despotism since the dawn of time.

Any study of history will reveal *anarchists* forming one parameter of organizational management, while *despots* have been ever present on the opposite shore. Both sides continually pull society in their respective directions. Despotism thrives on the very foundation of natural law, with its foundation of rule by the strong and obedience of the weak. Jones' church, Moses and his people, and most small businesses operate under this premise.

Renaissance or Ruin

While despotism is seen in derogatory terms today, it was probably the first method of administrating a group. The most powerful hunter or warrior of the prehistoric pampas was ceded the right to rule over the affairs of the tribe. Challenges would be offered to that ruler periodically by another would-be ruler who would either be met and overcome, the challenger being banned or killed; or the challenger would win, and the former ruler banished or killed.

Abraham ruled his tribe under this structure as can be seen when Lot offered a challenge to his authority. The only answer was for one or the other to leave or be vanquished. Lot left to avoid a problem.[3] After the split Abraham was free to exercise autocratic rule again. As we read this chapter in Hebrew history, we do so with cultural bias and find it hard to accept Abraham as a despot or as an autocrat, but we must understand that these terms have pejorated with the advent of modern democracy. The reformation period, coupled with the period of scientific enlightenment, saw, for the first time, the notion being raised that perhaps rule and future direction could be shared by all.

Many denominational models work precisely this way today. A church having had a strong entrenched lay leader with a history of absolute control, can expect the judicatory to send or assign several pastors, each of whom will stay but a year or two in an attempt to broaden the leadership base.[4] The victims in this scheme of "Religious Roulette" are the pastor's families

---

[3] Genesis 13:8-13.
[4] In recent years this situation has taken an ironic and tragic twist. Pastors who have served churches for many years are retiring and taking up residency in the very churches they pastored. More than just a violation of ministerial ethics it creates an impossible crisis for the church as the former pastor remains as the chief administrator and now additionally becomes the all powerful lay ruler.

that come close to being destroyed as these pastors are thrown like lambs to slaughter until one's prowess wins out. One Church of God (Cleveland TN) has sent nine pastors in ten years, each one being torn to shreds as the denomination attempts to find one who can "dethrone" a strong patriarch who has practically destroyed the church.

Returning to the ancient Sinai, Jethro was most precocious in trying to encourage Moses to share responsibility 2,000 years before the modern era, making Jethro the inventor of a shared planning dynamic. During his conversation with Moses, Jethro instructed Moses to select, from the people, men of good character, godly men, and place them in charge of smaller groups of people, letting them have the authority to judge (rule and manage) the people. This would obviously include some long range planning as well as execution of those plans.

Later Jesus would discourage despotism when He tackled the reigning ethic of group management during His lifetime. He sought to revolutionize status quo management techniques before they became a part of the church which was to be born of His followers. He taught:

> ...You know that those who are considered rulers over the Gentiles lord it over them, and their great ones exercise authority over them.
>
> Yet it shall not be so among you; but whoever desires to become great among you shall be your servant.
>
> And whoever of you desires to be first shall be slave of all.

For even the Son of Man did not come to be served, but to serve, and to give His life a ransom for many.[5]

This statement came on the heels of a confrontation with James, John, and their mother, all of whom were laboring under the accepted premise that leadership constituted rule by the strong over the weak as was widely accepted in first Christian century. In Matthew's account the three came to Jesus with their ambitions in hand. They attempted to grab the positions of authority in the "new" kingdom by flaunting their strengths and bragging of their ability to rule over others. Jesus, however, rebuked that system for believers, and for Kingdom living, by saying - "So it shall not be among you."

The first church sought to establish His words into reality as they came together to form their management, planning, and operating systems. The first meeting of the church was filled with prayer and a seeking of one accord. The business was conducted among a group of equals, looking to the future, and seeking consensus as they picked a replacement "director" for the vacancy left by Judas. One person or faction did not appoint a replacement as would be the case in an autocratic system, but rather nominations were accepted, debate ensued, and a decision was reached by the entire group. Matthias was chosen and was appointed to the ministry of apostleship.[6]

As time progressed, disputes among the members of the community forced an analysis by these leaders to determine what was wrong in the working program. It was decided to do some reformation and the group again planned together. It is noteworthy that the leaders did not respond to the crisis by

---

[5] Mark 10:42-45
[6] Acts 1:20-26.

down-sizing leadership, but increased the leadership power base, this time from twelve to nineteen as seven others were brought into authority and ministry with the election of the first deacons.[7] Indeed this early church, while replete with disagreement, was "of one heart and of one soul."[8]

It becomes obvious, however, that the church was still existing in a world of a different tradition of authority. Within 150 years, Victor the First was appointed the thirteenth Pope, and he aspired to consolidate rule in his person only; thus the long process of authority concentration began.

Perhaps the fall of Western Roman civil authority or the fear generated by the accompanying invading northern European tribes gave impetus to authoritarians. Perhaps Jesus' concepts were just too radical. Whatever the reason, autocratic rule soon became as accepted in the church as it had been in the world. This universal acceptance of strong central authority vested in one person is exemplified in the title given the greatest emperor on earth at the end of the first Christian millennium. The Byzantine emperor was officially titled "Ruler of all The Empire and "Despot of the World."

As the Renaissance, the Enlightenment, and later the Reformation took place, however, this type of rule came into disfavor. Gradually over this past five to seven hundred years, battle lines have been defined and drawn down the middle of the field of debate as to how things should be run and who has the responsibility to plan the future destiny of the people.

On one hand, the Aristocracy clings tenaciously to the premise that rule should be left in the hands of the fittest few. The aristocracy in America is not titled "nobility," nevertheless

---

[7] Acts 6:1-6.
[8] Acts 4:32.

they are present. These perennially successful ones often subscribe to an oligarchical governing structure.

This system is especially apparent in the church. It embodies the concept of power and rule closely held by a small number of "sponsors"; usually led by one or two power holders who feel, or at least suspect, that their positions in the church are divinely inspired, many times based on their advanced status in society. They postulate that those who have the power to rule (the source of their power is irrelevant) can rule the best because they have the power and ability to see further, know more, and posses the ability to "get things done."[9] These movers and shakers would say they receive their power, perhaps from God, or simply because they obviously deserve it, having fought the challenge of life and having victored. They theorize that rule, planning, and authority come from the top - execution and obedience originates from the bottom. Aristocracism is simply despotism in the hands of a ruling class of "Social Darwinists," rather than a sole ruling person.

On the other side of the debate one views pure democratic "Plebeianism," rule of all the people, by all the people. The American Constitution, as amended, ekes of it and yet the authors of that document were "aristocracins" and probably never envisioned a government by "all the people," but only the blessed few. It should be noted that this author is not so naive or idealistic to believe that our society is truly government by plebiscite. It is rather a system of republicanism impacted by vast and competing power complexes at work.

In theory and in constitution, however, most American churches, especially churches embracing congregational polity, are constituted as a union in equality of all the members. In

---

[9] See Plato's The Republic. Here the Guardians served this purpose, selected, however by birth rather than by achievement.

actuality none operate under total democratic principles, because, say critics, it has been found that it does not work as well as delegating authority to a group of lesser numbers.[10]

As despotism and aristocracism have their down sides, so does this glorious ideal of perfect democracy. Despotism's downfall is its tendency to lead to tyranny by the ruler and indolence for the people. Representative democracy, on the other hand, leads to exclusivity for the chosen representatives and political maneuvering, squabbling, and isolation for the mass of the people.

While Plebeianism has ever increased to the betterment of society, it seems to have hit a temporary snag in its development. Perhaps the human "arche-psyche" has not matured enough to accept the responsibility of a continual forward movement. Presages illuminating a future of daily voting by phone or computer on all the issues before the nation on a given day will probably never evolve. Corporations in which the employees are the sole owners and operators have been tried on a limited basis but for the greater part will probably remain more a theory than a practice.

Ideally it sounds great to think of a church in which all members are equally gifted, equally know and love God, and wish to surrender in loving relationship to the whole body to the same degree. In this setting long range plans could be

---

[10] Within the local church, Southern Baptist and United Churches of Christ are probably the most autonomous and congregational in polity. Compared to other churches in other parts of the world, however, all American churches are extremely democratic. At the national level things often change. The UCC and the United Methodist, for example, loss all specter of representation of their local churches and pastors. Their "representative democratic" systems have created a power elite that completely controls these denominations. The result is that the rank and file have abandoned the hierarchy and are completely non-supportive and isolated from these once mighty systems.

made in short order because all would be "in one accord." Implementation would be an easy task, all members would give what was necessary and do all that was required to complete the task in an unselfish, humble way. The Kingdom of God would most surely have arrived.

However, to the date of this writing it has not yet come to pass. Therefore in devising any scheme for long term congregational mission, an eclectic and broad based support and involvement system must be included. *Strategic Planning* and the subsequent execution of the plan of ministry offers a combining of the forces and the people of the church (Aristocracins, democrats, idealists, and realists) into a viable planning and ministry team. As in the business community this method offers the best hope to create a future dynamic able to do the work of the Gospel.

The Process of Strategic Planning

The idea of strategic planning as a process able to be modeled and followed is relatively new. As human evolution moved beyond the general/troops, owner/employees level of small operating units during the period from 1880-1920, two things became apparent:

    1. Larger organizations cannot "bumble" along without a plan of operation and development, and

    2. As business and the world became more complex, input from more than one person, be he/she all powerful and intellect or not, was no longer able to "cut the mustard" in a competitive world.

Armies that learned this lesson, involving experts from many fields including business, military, and intellectuals - won their wars. Single officer-led military groups became bandits and lost wars. Enterprises that began to collect data from their consumers and the market, involving employees, managers, and customers in a long range examination of what should and should not be done - grew and prospered. Operators of organizations who wanted to maintain control, doing things like they had always been done, soon stagnated into oblivion.

In the History of Strategic Planning section of J. William Pfeiffer's book <u>Strategic Planning, Selected Readings</u>, he divides its evolution into five major stages of development. Taken from Hax and Majlif's 1984 classic book, these are:

1. Budget and financial control

2. Long range planning

3. Business strategic planning

4. Corporate strategic planning

5. Strategic management

The authors began their chronicle in the period of the 1890's and carried their developmental process through the 1980's.[11]

I offer this to exhibit the sophisticated development of this entire process. There are other ways to historically divide strategic planning developed by persons in many diverse business, governmental, and military ventures.

---

[11] A. C. Hax and N. S. Majlif. <u>Strategic Management: An Integrative Perspective</u>, Englewood Cliffs, N.J., Prentice Hall, 1984.

In the business climate of the current period strategists agree that we have moved into yet another stage in the development of strategic planning. This stage, which I shall call *strategic leadership*, involves a greater innovative component then ever before. In the declining situation in which the church finds itself, this strategic leadership is not only advisable, but necessary for our survival.[12]

The model of strategic planning that I have chosen to share with the church is a modified version of that developed by Pfeiffer and Company in 1985, labeled *Applied Strategic Planning* (ASP).[13] I've chosen ASP as my base departure point for two reasons. First, J. William Pfeiffer designed it to be equally applicable to both business and the non-profit sector. Second, this plan, unlike others, is easily adaptable to a church setting and it incorporates implementation factors that ensure a tangible result at the end of the process. Conversely, many plans heretofore available to the church were long on theory, required reading mountains of material, and had little to offer in the end.

---

[12] The reader will hear talk in the market place that the age of Strategic Planning is at an end. It is being touted that we are now entering the era of Strategic Action. For the American corporate community this is true. Our great corporations became heavily involved in Strategic Planning in the early 1980's at the low point in American productivity. The recent rebound in the viability of AT&T, Ford, GE, WMX and a myriad of other firms is the direct result of intensive Strategic Planning. It is time for these companies to move ahead into action. The church, however, has been isolated from this process, therefore we are only at the beginning of our time of crisis. For us the era of serious Strategic Planning is yet to begin.
[13] J. William Pfeiffer, Strategic Planning, Selected Readings, (Pfeiffer and Company, 1991), San Diego VII-XXXIX.

Britt Minshall

Getting Started - The Job of the Church Council

Step One

Planning the Process

The first step is often given little or no thought because it seems so elemental. To politicians and power brokers this step is seen as the most important of the eight steps. Manipulating-controlling personalities know the value of "working the back room" at this stage. This term was used for years in New York and northern New Jersey machine politics. Before legislation could get to the floor of the legislature, the outcome had already been decided behind the scenes in back rooms by "Bosses" influencing who would be on committees or in charge of setting agendas. The local church, state conferences, and national denominations are no stranger to this chicanery. The entire complexion of the Southern Baptist Convention has been altered during the past ten years because of the exerted efforts of the fundamentalist faction using this methodology.

Realizing the inevitability of this process of preparatory negotiating within the American paradigm, the strategic planning theorist put aside idealistic rhetoric and legitimized this step in the process in order to render it an honest part of the process.

There are, in most settings, five issues that must be resolved before real planning can begin. Make no mistake, their resolution is imperative for the continuation of the process. How they are resolved may well determine the success or failure of the venture, because they deal with the very philosophy of the life of the church. These five preliminary issues are:

1. How much commitment is there to the planning process?

2. Who should be involved?

3. How long will the process take?

4. Where will the meetings be held?

5. What is the Planning Team expected to accomplish?

How much commitment is there to the planning process? If the congregation is all for it, but the pastor is threatened, there is little hope. By the same token, if the pastor is all for it but a number of prominent leaders aren't supportive, there is even less hope. The key people in the process including the pastor, the most powerful players in the church and all of the chief stakeholders must initially be involved and committed.

It is important to air and handle objections at this point. Two objections will often be heard. The first will come from the fundamental faction, very spiritual folks, who will say, "The Holy Spirit is in charge; He can't be muzzled or anticipated." These folks may quote Jesus saying,

> Do not worry about your life...which of you by worrying can add one cubit to his stature...therefore do not worry saying, What shall we drink or what shall we wear?[14]

---

[14] Matthew 6:25-31, NKJV.

This group will be far less prevalent in the mainline church than in the more conservative congregation. Other than allowing opportunity to study this objection in the light of an examination of the text, there is little one can do to belay this feeling. Jesus never cautioned against planning. It becomes rather obvious, when looking at His yearly itinerary, that His annual road to Jerusalem was well laid out and apparently well planned, even to advance knowledge of his Bethany lodging at the home of Martha and Mary.

One might interject that planning is not worrying or being "anxious" as is a popular rendering of the text. "Worry about," as Jesus used the term, meant to dwell on it, turning it over and over again, even to being paralyzed from acting by the debilitating process of continual anxiety. One of the beautiful by-products of planning is to be free from acting out of worry, which is after all, crisis management. By conjecture and statements in the Gospel, we are assured that Jesus had well thought out and planned His final trip to Jerusalem, otherwise the events in the garden at the time of His arrest would have invoked crisis management and panic. It is far easier to make a productive, righteous, just, and godly decision concerning one's future in a setting of meditation and planning than at a time of trauma.

The second objection will come from those threatened by any change. Inherent in the very term Strategic Planning is that the goal is to move the church from one place to another. The status quo maintainer will therefore be the big critic in most church settings. A concerted effort should be made to offer peace and assurance to these individuals that their particular roles in the church are celebrated and that they are needed in the new scheme of things. Folks with advanced paranoia will, however, not be assuaged under any circumstances.

Part of the validity testing for the church at this juncture will be seeing if there is enough concern for the future of the church to continue to press forward even over the threats of these most adamant persons. Commitment to this process means more than just lip service, it will require commitment that may elicit sacrifice.

The next question to be answered during this first stage is *Who should be involved?* The question one hears most frequently is, "We have boards and committees in our church, why not just use them?" Many are concerned that only a few people in the church are in possession of sufficient information to handle such a task, and that leaders should work through the system.

Ever since World War II, organizational dynamics practitioners have realized that an existing team, vested with the normal executive functions of an organization, are unable to deliver when it comes to re-definition of an organization's goals. Whatever the normal function of an executive team, that function it can carry out, but planning for the future is not part of that function.[15] In other words, just as trustees have a definite function - say property management - so also do planners - and that is planning. Therefore an entirely new committee must be formed.

The make-up of this new group is vital. J. William Pfeiffer, looking at the business scene, sees a group of seven to

---

[15] This concern is also discussed in Lyle E. Schaller's book, Create Your Own Future, as cited elsewhere in this work. However, serious attention needs to be paid to the writing of Robert A. Walker, The Planning Function in Urban Government, (Chicago, University of Chicago Press, 1950) which provided much of the information behind these concepts.

twelve participants which should include the CEO, at least at the outset. Likewise, in the church the pastor should be involved as a full and equal member, but not as the moderator. Beyond this, business experts caution that the make-up take into consideration four factors, which are:

- The size of the organization

- The structure

- The various stakeholders

- The organization's history

This would be no less applicable to the church intending to enter the process.

Size does not impact the make-up of the group as much as the other factors. Ten to twelve members should probably be the number for any planning group whether it be a 150 member church or a 150,000 employee corporation. In the large corporation there would be several planning committees involved, dividing and sub-dividing the task by department or function. Structure, therefore, is more important for business than for a church, but nonetheless must be considered.

Chrysler Motors would make sure that manufacturing, personnel, marketing, and administration would be involved in the process. In like manner it is important to represent the major boards of the church on this committee: trustees, worship, education, and outreach (others if applicable) should also appear on this committee. In this way data becomes available from these ministry areas, and once decisions are made a way of implementation at the board level is in place.

The assurance of stakeholder involvement becomes a cloudy area to define. A planning committee was formed at St. Jude's Church after a particularly innovative pastor left. The people placed on the committee, for the greater part, were stakeholders; long term-members who wanted to undo the innovations begun during the prior five years.

Perhaps the way to proceed should be to eliminate those *who should not be involved*, working on the assumption that "stakeholder" is too broad a category.[16] First, the *status quo seekers* should not be on the committee. They are recognizable from your daily encounters with them. Clues to their identity might be found in such remarks as, "Our parking lot is ample, if you can't get a place, park on the street,' or 'The Sunday School has always met at church hour, leave it alone." Here one can hear an inability to see beyond the present and an absolute acceptance of it.

The second type to be avoided is the *sour on the future* person. They say things like "When my kids grew up in church in the 1960's we didn't have fancy Sunday School material, these kids today get too much." One such person recently suggested that the education committee of his church should search though the church basement and drag out the old Sunday School materials from the 1970's. He remarked "that stuff was good enough for my kids, it ought to be good enough for yours." This "sour on the future" person is highly dangerous to a church's future. It is wise to remember that yesterday has no future, only a past.

The third type of person to exclude from the planning team is *the malcontent* or "old obstinate." "Our church is too large...too liberal...has too many new faces...spends too much money," and on and on. You may know them, you may be

---

[16] Lyle E. Schaller, Create Your Own Future, 39-40.

married to one of them, but for God's sake leave them out of the process or it is doomed.

Number four on the list is the pastor's *number one opponent.* Many times this person will feel that, "All will be rosy if only this pastor will leave." Actually the planning process is designed around the laity's desires for the next generation. The period covered should project far beyond the tenure of the current pastor. Unfortunately for the church, this type of dysfunctional person is so "hells bent" (good word) on firing the pastor that he or she would gladly scuttle the future of the congregation to achieve that goal.

Finally, avoid the *nostalgia nuts* who want the chance to prove to the world that the church can once again serve "only this neighborhood," as it did when, "every member walked to church on Sunday." This person dreams of going back to pre-World War II ethics and modes of living - "Let's do it like we did when P. J. Grimly was our pastor back in ought six." Nostalgia nuts are fun to converse with, but their desire to live in the past and protest against the world today, renders them unsuitable for the work of this committee.

In order to counter accusations that I am blaspheming the past, I need to offer an adjuration concerning historicity. The history of the mainline church is laudable; one of the primary reasons it must be saved and regenerated. However, the richer the history, the more it desires to live on and smother the future. It would be unrealistic to suggest that a church could expect to "cut off" its past and take a completely different direction, and in most cases that would be equally counter-productive.

The older the church, the harder the task becomes of envisioning the future. What I suggested is to remember that the past is terribly addictive, and every opportunity to create an

Renaissance or Ruin

original future will need to be exercised, or the past will automatically resurface and try to live again.

In trying to create the future, the factors that impacted the past remain ever present. The physical setting of the church may not have changed. The environment surrounding the church may be very close to the way it was in 1955, or 1855, or in some cases 1755. A graveyard or a 200 year old building may dominate the landscape.

Younger people and newer members will be more attuned to the current physical setting and the current environment than older members will be. The past is bound to effect strategic planning.

- If tomorrow is to receive equal billing with yesterday - it will require a lot of deliberate hard work.

The third issue to resolve is *how long will the process take to complete?* Here a sharp difference appears between the church and the secular scene. According Pfeiffer's Applied Strategic Planning scheme, a period of ten to fifteen, six-hour days are set aside for the initial phase of the process. After this start-up period he sees a period of nine to twelve months overall, involving two or three days every six weeks. According to my calculations this means that ASP calls for a total of approximately 35 to 45 day-long meetings. There is a drastic difference in both time and commitment that can be required of a church member as opposed to a business executive. Also the planning process in the church, while often tedious, is less complex than that of a multinational corporation.

I suggest about twelve meetings be planned initially to cover the process beyond this first organizational stage, which takes place in council rather than in the planning teams realm. After this preparatory work the Planning Committee can be impaneled and they can move rapidly to begin their work as a closed committee at stage two. The initial schedule of meetings for the Planning Committee may be as follows:

- Meeting One - 3 hours - *Plan Process* Review - Begin Scanning Values

- Meeting Two - 3 hours - *Scanning Values*

- Meeting Three - 3 hours - End Scanning Values - Begin Mission Statement

- *Church-wide meeting* - 4 hours - Collect data for Operating and Mission Statements

- Meeting Four - 3 hours - *Formulate Mission Statement*

- Meeting Five - 3 hours - Review Dreams and Ideas of Individual Church Members

- Meeting Six - 3 hours - *Develop Dreams* and *Design Prototype Programs*

- Meeting Seven - 3 hours - *Performance Audit and Gap Analysis*

- Meeting Eight - 3 hours - Gap Closure and redesign of program models.

- Meeting Nine - 3 hours - Integrate Organization Plan - Contingency Planning.

- Meeting Ten - 3 hours - Meet With Boards to Set Goals for *Implementation*

- Meeting Eleven - 3 hours - Plan Implementation and *Kick-off*

- Meeting Twelve - 3 hours - Review progress

Additional follow-up meetings should be held for one or two months with boards and committees to evaluate performance, define the "gaps" between the plan and the actual implementation, and devise new gap "closing" techniques.[17] When the programs are running well, this planning group must be permanently disbanded to avoid the formation of yet another super board that will soon lose its effectiveness.

The schedule of twelve meetings to cover the eight stages of Strategic Planning is only a "dream document." An extremely healthy church, with a congregation of well differentiated leaders, could conceivably go through the process in twelve meetings. Some churches in the opposite camp could meet for twelve months and still be concentrating on the mission statement. I read recently of a church that had planned twenty meetings, but as of the fifteenth meeting the process had become bogged down.[18] At this point outside guidance should be sought. Usually if this type of protracted snag develops, a power struggle has supplanted the planning process as the goal.

The important thing to remember when looking at a time frame is not to allow more than fifteen days to lapse between meetings.

---

[17] A complete treatment of these terms and a formal explanation of each step will follow as this chapter proceeds.

[18] Lyle E. Schaller. Create Your Own Future, 35.

- The planning process for churches is best carried out in fairly frequent meetings in a concentrated five to seven month period.

If much longer is taken and the congregation gets bored, the thirst for future planning gets lost in the mire of everyday existence.

The fourth issue to be covered in the initial planning process is *where will the meeting be held?* In the business setting and often in the church setting, retreats are chosen to facilitate these events. Unlike businesses, the church cannot usually sustain the retreat setting long enough to make it effective.

During the past few years planning retreats have become popular for churches. All leaders (not a planning committee) go away for a weekend to the mountains or the seashore to "hash out" the future. Almost universally these planning retreats become mini-vacations, but do little for the local church. Church-wide or leadership-wide planning retreats may serve to improve one's tennis game, but they do almost nothing to impact the future of the church.

Cottage meetings (meetings held in different member's homes) were initially thought to be successful for planning; after all, they do well for prayer and Bible study, why not for planning? Soon the problem becomes a struggle between hosts to see who can outdo the other in the elegance of the hors d'oeuvres. This, coupled with the inevitable distraction of "drop-in friends" and child "tuck-ins," soon lead to a series of failures.

I suggest that each planning committee meeting be held in a different part of the church, attended only by the team members, but that the church provide a meeting ready setup. Serve coffee, crackers, soda, turn on the air conditioning or heat, but turn off the phone. By having the meeting first in the sanctuary, next in the high school education room, next in the nursery, and so on, the committee can get a sense of the fullness of church life. One older planning team member sat in a child's chair one night at a meeting I chaired, and laughed saying that he hadn't been in this elementary school room in twenty years, not since his children were this age. He couldn't believe the deteriorated condition of the facility. Out of that realization he went into the actual program planning with a new appreciation for the needs of the younger children.

The fifth and final question to be addressed is the issue of *What is the planning committee expected to accomplish?*" The church or the council needs to be both encouraging and explicit in the formulation of this commission to the team. They should be reviewed at the initial meeting of the strategic planning committee and then they should be kept before them for their duration.

Groups involved in strategic planning seem to eventually arrive at one of two destinations polemic to each other. If the instructions to the planning team are laced with cautionarys, its make-up too conservative, and they are continually viewed with suspicions that their final report may be too radical, then the final outcome will surely be a suggestion to continue business as usual. Rarely will new directions "well up" and grow exponentially from a group that sees itself being told not to innovate.

Conversely, a planning committee that receives encouragement to blaze new trails, and feels the support of the church to accomplish something new and different, will often return with an astonishing selection of "trail-blazing" programs.

Gary Hamel and C. K. Prahalad in an article found in the Harvard Business Review called this inaugural trust -

strategic intent.[19] This is more than just ambitious dreams. It is a delivery to the planning committee by the congregation, a commission to capture the essence of what it would take for the church to once again succeed in 1) *glorifying God*, and 2) *bring a sense of accomplishment to its members.* This strategic intent instructs the planning committee that they are vital in the process of encapsulating the future into workable, definable, and definite programs. The commission should also ask the planning team to include achievable targets through which the congregation can once again work toward life changing ministry.

Finally the church will need to realize and impart to the committee that their work is expected to involve a *sizable stretch* for the congregation. They need to understand that current capabilities and resources will not suffice. The congregation will have to become innovative and inventive. Old resources will have to be used in new ways, and new resources will have to be developed. In other words,

> the pastor, the governing organizations, and the congregation need to assure the strategic planning committee that *they are anticipating, and excitedly expecting, to have to reinvent the church* in order to set in motion the planning committee's recommendations.

This frees the strategic planning committee to explore hitherto unachieved heights for the church.

If these five issues of planning the process are done properly, the next seven steps that lead to implementation have an excellent chance of coming to a healthy and dynamic

---

[19] Gary Hamel and C. K. Prahalad, "Strategic Intent," <u>Harvard Business Review</u>, May/June 1989.

conclusion. As the committee settles in to do its work, the eyes of the entire church should be upon them. The prayers of the church should be surrounding them each time they meet. From the beginning the team should invite as much input as possible from all sources. At the same time they should share with the church monthly the ideas so far developed and be keen to receive reactions to the work as it progresses.

One last note on the stage one planning process. "It is the rare and exceptional organization that can manage the planning process effectively without consultation help."[20] There are several sources available to help a church go through the process including para-church agencies, denominational experts, and conference executives; even business consultants could be considered. There is one drawback here: often the church will "perform" for the visiting dignitary and then disregard all of his/her suggestions in the absence of such an outside agent. Here as elsewhere the most valuable work the planning team and the congregation can do is work openly and honestly.

---

[20] J. William Pfeiffer, Strategic Planning, Selected Readings, XV.

TRIGGER POINTS

1. Would there be strong objections in your church to a long-term planning effort?

2. Circle 12 of the following categories that you feel should be on your planning team:

Pastor	Trustee	Bd. Chr. Ed.
Spirit. Life	Missions	Outreach
Worship	Board (other)	Moderator
Youth	Staff Mem.	New Member
Member	Leader	Other____

3. Write a Great Commission for your planning team. In it:

☐ Acknowledge where the church has been.

☐ Proclaim your present state - good and bad.

☐ Instruct them to describe where you can and must go.

☐ Tell them to search out and define the environment in which the church now lives.

☐ Ask them to invent new programs and recommend any other actions that must be done to reinvent and redirect the church for viable ministry in the community.

4. Begin intensive and regular prayer groups to focus on the future of your church as a ministering center of the Gospel of God.

CHAPTER XII

GROWING INTO GLORY

The Planning Team's Agenda

Step Two

Scanning Values

First Church of Melbourne found itself in the grips of a moral dilemma which divided the church not just down factional lines, but divided families and generations as well. The church had been given securities in a company whose main business was the production of alcoholic beverages. This type of gift and the resulting furor is common to the church. Many times securities are received from companies with other controversial ties such as doing business in South Africa during the apartheid era or treating migrant workers unfairly.

A congregational meeting was called to settle the issue as to whether to sell the "liquor" stock or retain it in the church's portfolio. This meeting was an astonishing exercise to all parties. On one hand, there were those interested in keeping the stock. They said to sell the stock would be hypocritical since most people in the church consumed liquor. These folks saw the stock as a clear cut issue of finances. The stock gave a return of $22.00 per quarter and held a value of

$920.00. That, said the "Keep" group, made it a good solid investment. The church needed the money; thus, it was a dollars and cents issue to this group, or so they said.

Others in the church had a severe problem retaining the stock, believing that a church had no place owning this type of investment. They viewed the church as a model for society. It is the job of the church, said the "Sell" group to voice, in its worship, educational process, and corporate social life, a moral statement and set a standard of values for community.

This example typifies a bottom-line issue that must be settled in every group before it can fully function. For the church at Melbourne, indeed any church, and even for the private sector, money is not and should never be thought of as the primary issue. In the above case the $22.00 per quarter meant nothing; the church's budget, though strained, was over $100.000 per annum. The real issue between the two factions in this case was control.

In an in-depth survey forming part of the basic material for Tom Peters' book, In Search of Excellence, circa 1980, it was found that a company's success was directly tied to product value and quality, *not price*. This was validated later in a study completed in 1983 by McKinsey and Company for the American Business Conference. In 43 out of 45 cases, the winning companies victored by delivery of a product, "that supplies superior value to customers, rather than one that costs less."[1] I postulate that *money, or the lack of it, is not the real problem in virtually any church failure.*

All this is said in opposition to Carl Dudley's observations, one that most pastors agree with, that money is the major issue among small congregations.[2] I hypothesize that

---

[1] Tom Peters and Nancy Austin, Passion for Excellence, 53.
[2] Carl Dudley, Making Small Churches, 62-65.

Renaissance or Ruin

the lack of funds is used as the reason to meet and work out one financial emergency after another. Also, it can be the primary excuse cited for not being able to compete for new members with the "rich church over on Main Street that has all those fancy programs." Money, or the lack of it, is a tool to keep the pastor under control. The insufficiency of cash (not its abundance) is the primary source of power among most of our cadre and the principal excuse used by congregations not to exert themselves in ministry. In other words,

- *the scarcity of cash has replaced value in the product we are offering.*

Ironically, it is not a case of money being "the commodity" offered that becomes the focus of the value standard of the church; it is the absence of "it" that becomes the focus of values, goals, programs, and all future discourse.

- *Money or the absence of it can NEVER be the basis of ANY "value system."*

The question to answer then is, "How does this strategic planning committee, vested with the responsibility of creating a new entity, deal with the values and the culture already inherent in the church?"

One of the first things to examine is the values possessed by the planning committee members themselves. We of the turn of the century church must be particularly alert to this stage of the process simply because there is a wide disparity in the basic values held by the members of our churches, as we can see from the incident at First Church Melbourne. The planning committee should ask its members:

What do you think are the three primary functions of a church?

The variety of answers may astonish even the committee itself. The ensuing discussion should prove lively and hopefully enlightening.

The reason for this diversity is that our pews are packed with people who are the product of an age of upheaval in basic values, personal and theological. There is no longer any common thread of agreement as to what is an acceptable philosophy of life. Another reason for the diversity in our values can be found in the make-up of our churches. There is little risk in stating that a typical church in say, suburban New York or Chicago in 1950 would have been comprised of people who had grown up and spent most of their lives in that geographical area. Probably most of the congregation would share the same basic ethnic stock, and many would have been reared in that particular church. Today the opposite is true. The typical suburban church of 1994 boasts a membership hailing from six to eight states and perhaps one or two foreign countries. While most mainliners retain a mono-racial complexion, broad differences in background can be found. Different backgrounds produce different value systems.

In a recent editorial in a national magazine, the editor, David Neff, quotes a <u>Newsweek</u> cover story titled, "Whose Values?"[3] Newsweek's senior editor, Joe Klein, according to Neff, asks the question, "Who is going to fill the values vacuum left after a 30 year spree of unlimited personal freedom and rampaging materialism?" Neff does an excellent job in posing the leading question, "How can we form a value structure in our world when the people seeking values will not vest authority in anyone who attempts to form a value statement?"

---

[3] David Neff, American Babel," <u>Christianity Today</u>, 17 August 1992, 18.

Renaissance or Ruin

Pastors, philosophers, and educators are all seen as having the right to voice their opinions, but these pronouncements are in the end taken as their personal value statements only and viewed as a "statement about the emotional state of the speaker." In other words, any pronouncement about values is rendered as purely subjective and largely moot to any other listener. If Neff's view is true it is especially tragic for the church. Business firms may or may not seek to establish a high value standard. For this sector, it is viewed as optional; advisable certainly, but nevertheless optional. For the church, however, there can be no option. The church is accepted as the "values center" of society. It is our basic business, and this is why it must be broached by the planning group. Raising money for physical plant needs and even program implementation is a peripheral consideration.[4]

Once the planning team tackles the horrendous task of determining if there is a jointly held personal values base, then they must ask the organizational values questions scanned below. All this effort spent on something as intangible as community culture and values may seem to be a waste of time. But make no mistake, if these discrepancies in our deep flow values are not "identified, clarified, and understood," there will be little or no agreement about the organization's future, the expectations of the individual members, or the deep-seated resistance to planning goals by other leaders in the church.[5]

---

[4] A revealing test to determine the most important emphasis in a church can be carried out by asking, "What is our church's most powerful committee?" The trustees are seen almost universally as the real power house in most of our churches. Their function is strictly physical (buildings, property and money). A church with priorities properly placed would see Worship, Education, Spiritual Life, or Community Ministry as the central player, relegating Trustees to a support role.

[5] J. William Pfeiffer, Strategic Planning, XVI.

325

Organizational queries in this scanning values section include:

1. Looking at our current values

2. The church's philosophy of operations

3. The assumption under which the organization operates

4. Naming and reviewing the church's preferred culture

5. Determining future stakeholders

When *looking at the church's current values*, being honest and objective is difficult. Most church members get the "warm fuzzies" (that delightful state associated with feeling secure and loved) at the sight of the steeple, yet have difficulty seeing the dirt on the roof beneath that steeple. Nevertheless, the committee needs to know what values the congregation and its leaders think are important. A look at the budget and the current roster of programs will tell much of the story.

The current philosophy of operations of the church should be critically examined. There may be a glaring discrepancy when the operating philosophy is contrasted to the reality of what the church actually does. The committee may need to inquire among local business people and non-members living in the neighborhood to find the church's "real" self.

The committee needs to ask, *what are the assumptions under which the organization ordinarily operates?* Most church members believe that the church will always be there and open for business. A lady from Landover, Maryland told

Renaissance or Ruin

me once that the regional denominational executive had been warning her church for years that their shrinking numbers would one day cause a catastrophe. Even when the pastor had to be let go for lack of funds, she and her friends felt sure something would happen to keep the 100 year old church afloat. But in 1984, as the Presbytery announced the closing of the unit, she sat in stunned disbelief. Some members actually believe that if worse comes to worst, the denomination will bail out a dying church.

We make other kinds of assumptions as well. Some members actually believe that a stranger walking through the front door will be treated with the same warmth and friendship that they are. Others sincerely think that the pastor is responsible for a church's success or failure. Popular assumptions may be a far cry from reality.

Next, the committee needs to *name and review the organization's preferred culture*. Many churches will deny they have one, seeing themselves as multi-cultural units. As explained in the chapter "The Tribal House," this assumption is almost never valid. The evidence of such a culture is found not only in ethnic name and skin color, but also in the community's behavior. These include: "how it greets or guards itself from outsiders," stories of the good old days when..., its location and what its facility says, the important events of its year, and the stakeholders year after year.

One church renamed itself the Church of All Nations. The members constructed a sign of welcome in six languages and hired a pastor from Nigeria. In truth, however, the church is still an almost all-white church, controlled by a retired pastor who sticks around to "manage" affairs. Some churches say outwardly they are liberal, but are really very conservative. Likewise, many churches belong to conservative denominations and sport a right wing faith statement, but members live a liberal lifestyle.

During the 1950's many German Reformed Churches and churches of the German Evangelical Synod, having come together to form the Evangelical and Reform Church, finally gave up speaking German in their worship services. For the past forty years these churches have been part of the United Church of Christ. Most, however, are still German churches in everything from personality to theology. "Clearly the culture of an organization will either facilitate or hinder both the strategic planning process itself and the implementation of whatever plan that process produces."[6] But the ignorance as to which culture really controls the church is an even greater danger to success.

Finally, *determine the future stakeholds*.[7] Most churches consider only the cadre when seeing a "stakeholder." Push out the parameters. Let us consider:

- ✓ those in the pew, even the ones whose names we do not know,

- ✓ the folks who never show up for a work day,

- ✓ the youth and the non-member attendee?

- ✓ Others in the community who attend no church at all?

- ✓ Professionals and leaders in the immediate community who could become stakeholders in the church's future.

---

[6] J. William Pfeiffer, Strategic Planning, XIX.
[7] J. William Pfeiffer, Strategic Planning, XVI.

These educators, civic leaders, and government workers often see churches as ivory towers.

How can the church get involved (thus creating stakeholders) in the issues of gang control, help for the homeless, controversial community issues, and the rearing of children? In these possible ministry areas are potential stakeholders.

As a grand finale of the Scanning Values, I recommend that once all the questions are brought up and discussed it would be helpful to reach closure by forming a suggested statement of philosophy for the church. This could be the first "going public" for the planning committee. In business and government leadership literature it is suggested that the entire management team joins the strategic planning committee in the process; I do no less. In the church setting, it seems advisable to sponsor a Saturday morning breakfast retreat, or something similar, to involve the entire congregation.

Often the cadre of any group can become so isolated from other stakeholders that they do not hear what is being said by the body. In the business world, this will result in heavy turnovers of personnel and reduced orders from customers. In the church, this situation will result in a slow deterioration in members and friends. By allowing the planning committee a good healthy open dialogue with the entire congregation, a potentially closed system is kept open. As a result the leadership of the church has a chance to hear what the majority of people in the church see as the vital basic ingredients in an overriding philosophy of operating "their" church.

The next question asked by most strategic planners is "what is a philosophy of operations, anyway?" Again, let me use the method of saying what it is not, at least at this stage. It is NOT a philosophy of ministry. It will be later, but not now. It is NOT a mission statement - that comes next. Mission statements say exactly what you intend to do, to or with whom. A statement of philosophy of operations is intended to lay the basic presumptions as to why our church exists. What we want the people to do is tell the world under what precepts they wish to operate. It is the yardstick indicating how we can pursue the course we eventually decide upon.

One example of such a statement, known as the "Five Principles of Mars," comes from the Mars Candy Company. It states:

> 1. Quality - The consumer is our boss, quality is our work, and value for money is our goal.
>
> 2. Responsibility - As individuals, we demand total responsibility from ourselves; as associates we support the responsibilities of others.
>
> 3. Mutuality - A mutual benefit is a shared benefit; a shared benefit will endure.
>
> 4. Efficiency - We use resources to the fullest, waste nothing, and do only what we can do best.
>
> 5. Freedom - We need freedom to shape our future; we need to profit to remain free.[8]

You will note these principles do not specify particular products or activities, but rather lift up ideals on which to base the company's operations.

---

[8] J. William Pfeiffer, Strategic Planning, XVII.

Another version of the same thing, built around a more specific language base, is found in the "Policy Statement of Carthage Machine Company." The result of their Value Scanning process was the following common precepts agreed to by the top management:

1. Carthage Machine Company is committed to continuously improving our ability to anticipate and satisfy our customers' needs.

2. Better satisfying our customers' needs requires that the company and its employees are dedicated to a policy of continuous improvement in all functions and operations.

3. All departments have specific goals that are consistent with this commitment and these goals will be continuously measured.

4. Our progress toward achieving continuous improvement will bring the quality of Carthage products and services to a world class level.

Carthage's effort[9] is much more focused and specific than is Mars Candy's statement of philosophy. Nevertheless, it is not a mission statement. It is still a statement of the philosophy which obviously addresses some major concerns of the stakeholders in Carthage. This same company continued in the process and did develop a mission statement called their statement of "Principles" which is more outwardly focused.

In the church's case there is an inherent danger that the statements on philosophy and/or mission statement, which

---

[9] Patrick L. Townsend and Joan E. Gebhardt, Quality in Action,

follows, will be so idealistic and global as to render the final result as useless hyperbole. The goal is to create a statement of the deeply held beliefs of our local church dealing with the intangible values that everyone in the church takes for granted. These unstated beliefs may vary greatly and can cause tension and gridlock when defining mission, program and procedure.

In the widely diverse community of the church it may be necessary to acknowledge the differences as well as the agreed upon principles. One successful liberal metropolitan church, Plymouth Congregational United Church of Christ, in Des Moines, Iowa has worked under the following Statement of Principles for several years:

> We impose no creeds. We do not insist on uniformity in theology or belief. We think there is room in the church for differences of opinion. We believe in the right of private judgment, and in the possibility of diversity in unity.
>
> Therefore we believe in the freedom of the pulpit, and of the pew. We take as our motto:
>
> We agree to differ
>
> We resolve to love
>
> We unite to serve
>
> When we speak of Plymouth as a liberal church, we mean that we try to keep an open mind toward the truth "known or to be Known to us," and we agree to disagree in the Christian Spirit. With all our differences, we are united in

a common purpose to seek and practice the Christ like way of living for ourselves and for society.[10]

In a church-wide session the questions asked may be

- ✓ Who or what is the basis of the church?
- ✓ Is it faith or is it God?
- ✓ If faith, what faith?
- ✓ Define that faith.
- ✓ Who are we to serve: God, or people, or both?
- ✓ What people?
- ✓ How do we serve them?
- ✓ What do we owe to the people around us?
- ✓ What is our responsibility to God, to ourselves, and to others?
- ✓ Are we be prejudiced or closed to others?
- ✓ Is the church to be a giving community or a receiving community?

---

[10] James O. Gillion, "Liberal and Growth Are Compatible," in Center City Churches: The New Urban Frontier, ed. Lyle E. Schaller (Nashville, Abingdon Press, 1993), 74-75.

Now the planning team should be extremely familiar with the internal forces at work in the church. According to researchers, at this time several questions need to be answered from the data collected. The planning should be able to ascertain:

1. To what extent do leaders and members share a clear and concrete sense of purpose?

2. To what extent does the congregation have a sense of parish?

3. What are the characteristics of the community surrounding the church?

4. Who lives in the neighborhood?

5. What do they expect of the church?

6. What does the church seek of the neighborhood?

7. What are the beliefs of the church's members?

8. What are their values, economic classes, vocations, educational levels, and life styles?

The answers to these questions will allow the planning committee to better realize the congregation's understanding of the ways it is actively relational to the world beyond its doors. Also this information allows the planning team to better know the congregation's makeup and its outreaching history. These ingredients will help facilitate a meaningful statement of current operating philosophy, and the subsequent creation of a realistic mission statement.[11]

When the above questions or any variation of them are answered and the data is compiled, the final statement should be drawn. It could be created using the following outline:

1. Faith

2. Discipleship

3. Responsibility

4. Resources

5. Openness

6. Leadership

7. Ministry

The church can now see itself as it is currently operating.

Many experts believe this one stage of planning is so important that they label it "fundamental to the process." It is the most difficult because it deals with underlying beliefs - both justified and unjustified, both of individuals and of the entire church. It will involve confrontation, it will dig out heretofore unstated assumption that, to date, may have been responsible for congregational shutdown. Because of these mind challenging exercises this stage is often bolted over, or ignored entirely. The benefit of facing this step of development,

---

[11] David A. Roozen, William McKinney, Jackson W. Carroll. Varieties of Religious Presence: Mission in Public Life. (New York, Pilgrim Press, 1988). 97 - 100.

however, is a better understanding of not only each other, including that long time "enemy across the table," but also of ourselves, including that long time adversary in the mirror.

Step Three

The Mission Statement

There were two brothers, each with an entirely different philosophy of life. One lived for fun and personal gratification, and exhibited a lack of purpose. The other held a philosophy of being productive, serving others, and living life under the holiness of God. The first ran a local general store and became known worldwide as a buffoon. The latter became the President of the United States and was known internationally as a peacemaker and godly man. Billy and Jimmy Carter epitomize the wide range of end results growing from two dichotomous philosophies of operation as manifested in the lives of two otherwise closely related people.

Most church members, even lifelong ones, never question or even realize their church has a philosophy under which it operates. They can only suspect that one might exist when they attempt an overview of a series of events and note similar outcomes time and again. The same is true when viewing people. I have no idea what the personal philosophy of either Billy or Jimmy Carter was or is, even though I am personally acquainted and have worked with Jimmy Carter. I have, however, seen the outcome of those philosophies on their personal lives and the impact which each has had on the world around them I can therefore postulate what these principles must have been.

Keeping this in mind, the next stage in the strategic planning process calls for the formulation of a Mission Statement. This document should grow directly out of the statement of philosophy and must agree with it or it becomes a lie, that which Jesus termed hypocritical. This mission statement, like the Carter brothers' public lives, is the worldly thrust and manifested work the church will attempt to complete in the future.

Unfortunately, as most "non-churchgoers" will be quick to tell you, our churches are often seen publicly as prototypical hypocrites by the greater portion of people in the community at large. No person, company, family, or church can long endure unless the philosophy under which that entity exists agrees with the actual mission statement or operating mandate that person or community espouses to the world. The world sees the church as hypocritical, supposedly operating on a philosophy of love, openness and courage, yet we remain missionally closed, culturally segregated, and suffer from paralysis as the result of system-wide fear.

Amelio's Restaurant in Davis Shores publicized that it operated under a philosophy of offering quality to its customers. Its mission statement (advertising) told the world: "Amelio's boasts the finest northern Italian cuisine, served in a delightful atmosphere, and all at very reasonable prices." Amelio's real philosophy, however, was to make as much money with as little effort or outlay as possible. Once a customer walked into the restaurant and witnessed the bedlam among employees, the dirt on the floor, sampled the terrible variety of canned delicacies, and compared the low quality to the high price on the menu, even the weekend gourmet could tell, from the final product, that the mission statement and the philosophy were at odds. Amelio's public image, like that of the church's above, was seen as hypocritical.

Larry Flint, the publisher of <u>Hustler</u> magazine, announced a few years ago that he had turned his life over to God and become a "born-again Christian," yet he continued to publish one of the most disgusting pieces of pornography ever devised. No one was fooled by Flint's pronouncement of a godly philosophy with a mission statement like <u>Hustler</u>.

Billy Carter, Amelio's Restaurant, and Larry Flint all have one thing in common with many mainline churches. Their operating philosophies invite a person to expect one thing, but the reality is quite something else. As for the church, the world expects an open, non-prejudiced, inviting, healing, loving place where God reigns and everyone's confidence is placed in Jesus. Regardless of what our mission statements reveal on paper, in reality our churches are often known to our communities as being closed, racist, nasty (especially to outsiders), warring, hateful places where God is an obstacle kept well at bay by the fact that the Gospel of Christ is replaced by political chicanery and cruel in-fighting.

Amelio's Restaurant is gone as the result of its fraud. Larry Flint has been discredited. Billy Carter unfortunately died rebuffed by his community and greatly estranged from his family. Likewise, the church is facing extinction in large part because of incongruent behavior.

The mission statement coming out of the planning committee must reflect the statement of philosophy item for item, thought for thought, and must agree so well that each interlocks with the other like pieces of a puzzle. After the philosophy of the church is publicized a mission statement must:

- *Develop a clear statement of what business the organization is in or plans to be in. A concise definition of the purpose that the organization is attempting to fulfill in society.*"[12]

The hope for the future is that the church will be obliged in every way to build its programs and exhibit an attitude that reflects this mission statement to the letter.

Specific questions to be answered here, according to Pfeiffer are

1. What function or duty does the organization perform?

2. For whom does the organization perform this function?

3. How does the organization go about filling this function?

4. Why does this organization exist?

Pfeiffer makes an important point often overlooked by many church leaders in asking question number one, *What function or duty does the organization perform?* When asking what function we perform, many of us answer by saying what it is that we do. For example, a Baptist Mission Association for whom I conducted a brainstorming session several years ago asked the question, "What function do we perform?" The association members limited themselves by answering, "We provide denominational support at the local level." In the same

---

[12] J. William Pfeiffer, Strategic Planning, XX.

vein a car manufacturer might incorrectly answer the question by saying, "We make cars."

The difficulty with these answers is they leave no place to go, no place to search for new opportunities, no place to experiment with innovation. Therefore, the planning process becomes a rehashing of the same old thing.

A recommended alternative might be to answer the question in terms of need. The Baptist Association may say, "To help local churches and the greater church continue in dialogue in developing new and exciting ministries." The car manufacturer could say, "To provide people with transportation in an integrated system of reliable, economic, quality products and services."

Many local churches answer this inquiry by saying, "To preach and teach the Gospel of Jesus Christ to all the world."[13] Remembering to look at filling a need, however, churches might venture to try, "To use all just means to introduce the love of God to every person in our community, meeting their needs for salvation, for healing, and caring through personal and corporate ministry." This is not meant to be prescriptive, but only an example of the amplified possibilities coming from the latter statement as opposed to the former.

The first of these mission statements says, "It's done, cut and dried." The second statement forces us on to the second question, *For whom do we perform our function*, in order to answer the first.

Traditionally, the answer to this second question will also be self-limiting and non-committal. Churches often say, "We perform this service for the community." In reality, however, most churches, especially older ones, have little

---

[13] This is the most used statement arising from churches of all denominations.

ministry to the community around them. I suggest answering the question - "What function does this church perform? - not by offering a statement with little accountability, but rather that we force our answer into an action statement, determining exactly for whom and precisely how this elusive function is carried out.

The four questions suggested by Pfeiffer are designed to continually impact on one another by demanding specifics. Therefore, when attempting to answer one question, for example "For whom do we perform this duty or action?" we have also begun to explore each of the other three questions. From this one can see why "The giving of the Gospel to the world" although a common statement, is not helpful. It is not a focused reply and is, in reality, little more than a great platitude.

Most congregations never manage gospel penetration to the state line, even more never broach the county line, and the majority are hard pressed to give an accounting of reaching the town limit, let alone the world. If we are forced to be specific in question one, stating real tasks, "offering salvation, providing a place for healing, and giving one-to-one care," then, out of necessity in question two, we must be specific as to who receives these services. The result of an examination here is often to find out that we, the members, are the only people thus far impacted by our church's ministry. That's a far cry from the world. In this case, an adjusted mission statement should challenge the church to name and strive for a larger, more representative service base.

Pfeiffer's third question leading to the formation of a mission statement, *How does the organization go about filling this function* can be even more challenging. Once specific people have been identified as the future recipients of our ministry, we will be naturally led to list the "things" we are doing or should be doing for them. The Mission Statement can say such things as:

- ✓ what things we will do
- ✓ how often we shall do them
- ✓ at what locations they shall take place.

The committee will venture into the area of real possibilities in mission and will need to be inventive. Also, the program feature of the planning process will now begin to take form.

I have seen churches gather to ask these questions, confident at the inception of the session that theirs was the most ministering church in the community, only to realize an hour later that no one receives their ministry. They discover that there is NO ministry at NO place at NO time. It then becomes the task of the planning team to invent ministry, create places and select times.

Conversely, some churches that have never taken the time to ask these questions will be surprised to discover that there is much being done in ministry even though it has not been put on paper or advertised in the church directory. In this case, the team's function is to expand those ministries for greater involvement and visibility.

As work progresses at this third level the planning team will be drawn to ask *Why does this organization exist?*

Here we are seeking a congregational identity which incorporates beliefs and commitments that hold the congregation together, but which often hold little religious implications. These commonly held ideals motivate its members to make it stand out from others. The answers developed from the last question will go a long way to either validate or challenge commonly held beliefs as to why the church exists.[14] Remember, however, that the primary task of this team is future oriented. The "why we exist" question has an answer easily anchored to the past. The committee's responsibility is to use that historical base and create another highly amplified answer.

One very small troubled church in an urban setting went through this process and found the only reason the church existed was to provide a place of recreation and sanctuary for its members. Several months before, the church had called a pastor who was divorced. In doing this they became aware of the large number of divorced people in their rather populous city neighborhood. During the planning process the team wanted to expand but not change the mission of the church. Consequently the new mission statement gave a new answer to the old question "why do we exist." The revision stated:

> ...providing a place of worship, fellowship, learning, and sanctuary to the many people of our community seeking Christ, including but not limited to people who are divorced and/or others from non-traditional lifestyles, and persons in transition from every ethnic and racial background. We are an open and reconciling church of the Lord Jesus Christ.

As a result of this redefinition of their existence, the church came through a period of growth and rebirth.

Once the planning team inventories the church's long held missional identity and juxtaposes that to the newly

---

[14] Carl S. Dudley, Basic Steps Toward Community Ministry, (Washington, D.C., Alban Institute, 1991), 43.

developed values statement, it becomes an easier task to develop a new mission statement with an *action based ministry component*.

Businesses would naturally wish to create the new mission statement around such priorities as products or services offered.[15] Market needs, technology, productive capabilities, methods of sale, methods of distribution, natural resources, size and growth, and profit/return on investment are also included.

Churches need not be all that different when attempting to form a mission statement. Rather than simply polling the congregation trying to develop some outlandishly general statement that sounds remarkably like Luke 4:18-19[16]. I suggest the planning committee adopt a critical search mode looking for some of the things a strategic planning committee at General Motors would seek to discover.

These revelations will convert into the eight key components that form any mission statement.[17] Translated to ecclesiastical language these eight (in any order) could be:

> 1. *Identify the people we should serve.* Target your prospects by population, lifestyle, and location. Stretch your imagination, explore and search out need.

---

[15] B. B. Tregoe and J. W. Zimmerman, Top Management Strategy: What It Is and How to Make It Work, (NY, Simon and Schuster, 1980).

[16] "The spirit of the Lord is upon Me, Because He has anointed Me to preach the Gospel to the poor. He has sent Me to heal the brokenhearted, To preach deliverance to the captives and recovery of sight to the blind, To set at liberty those who are oppressed, To preach the acceptable year of the Lord. (NKJV)

[17] John A. Pearce, II and Fred David, "Corporate Mission Statements: The Bottom Line," Academy of Management Executives, (New York, American Management Association, May 1987) 109-116.

Renaissance or Ruin

2. *Identify the product you offer and the services you give.* The joy, peace and goodness that come from bringing the kingdom of God to the people with whom you minister is the greatest product anyone can offer. This product takes many forms. To one person you "target" it may mean hearing the Gospel preached leading to genuine personal faith in God. To another it may mean receiving help from the people of God to learn English, to pass a citizenship test, leading to a decent way of life for an entire family. Our product is God's kingdom living. Service will reveal ministry in a thousand forms. The planning committee needs to blend the people with the ministry.

3. *Define your community.* Draw a map of your geographical area, giving it reasonable boundaries. An over optimistic Baptist Church in Camden County, New Jersey defined their community by the river to the east, the interstate to the west, the city line to the north, and the refinery to the south. According to them their "community" included three cities, and two townships of 380 square miles each. NOT! Interestingly, in the same community an extremely pessimistic Methodist church defined its community as three blocks on each side of the church. HORRIBLE!
In determining the geographical boundaries of your ministry area, look at the type of church you are (neighborhood, metropolitan, regional,

suburban community, suburban regional, center city, special mission, rural).[18] Ask from whence your people come, and why? Are there others that should come and from where? Identify other churches of your same denomination. Finally, draw realistic traffic patterns defined by rivers, freeways, downtown, industrial zones, and the like. Remember to place realistic expectations on your physical plant, but don't be overly cautious. The planning team could call for a building to meet specific needs. Many churches are cash rich but building poor. Once these concerns have been broached claim your ministry area, based on the projected data from the queries above.

4. *Identify the core of your abilities to offer ministry.* What are you good at doing? What are you equipped to do? What core technology do you have at your disposal? For these you will need to look at your physical plant, at your staff, at your budget, and most of all at your people. It would be ludicrous for a church of 88 members all above 55 years of age to include a thriving youth ministry program if it didn't have a youth director, an area for recreation, and no money to hire or equip either. A word

---

[18] These terms have been defined by virtually every writer of church dynamics. They remain, however, extremely subjective. The chief factors that influence your church's type are its location with reference to highways, from whence the people come and go, land parcel size, physical plant size, other churches of your denomination in the area, and the homes of you current and projected congregants.

of caution: Do not let these factors limit your plan, if in answering these questions there is an indication of real possibilities in an unexpected area.[19] Budgets, especially, are extremely deceptive. If a real and valid ministry opportunity presents itself as the result of the committee's work, excitement from the congregation or the community will almost always produce the funding.

5. *Incorporate commitment to survive, grow, and prosper.* Most churches are willing to work to survive, brag about growing, but only dream about prospering. All the while they do just enough to survive, refuse to grow, and do everything contradictory to prosperity. The planning committee should offer a definitive component that will lead every member to accept and be enthusiastic about growth and prosperity. One firm incorporated these words, "the company will conduct its operations productively, and will provide the profits and growth which will assure Hoover's ultimate success (Hoover Universal)"[20] You will note the highly directive determinative language - will conduct and will provide. Many churches avoid such binding language. This language

---

[19] The planning committee should be held to real possibilities in deciding these core ministries. Envisioning radical new areas will come later. Current inventories of your physical plant, staff, budget, and membership may be disappointing; nevertheless, at this stage be realistic.

[20] John A. Pearce, III and Fred Davis, "Mission Statements", as found in J. Pfeiffer, Strategic Planning, 131.

should be adopted by the church's leadership as not only a mission statement, but as a directive for the actions and attitudes of church officers.

6. *State key elements in the value/philosophy statement.* This may be as few as three or four words that capture the heart of this previously formed statement. The object is to validate the mission statement as an outgrowth of the congregation's operating philosophy. This adds continuity, increases strength, and prevents hypocrisy. It helps direct the church away from feeling one way about itself and claiming another way before the world.

7. *Identify the church's self concept.* From the discussions in scanning values and developing a statement of philosophy, restate clearly what the church is, as agreed by all stakeholders in the congregation. This action helps put dissension to rest, especially if the overwhelming majority of the people agree on "what we are." These statements should be both brief and realistic. For example, one small hauling firm in New York City wrote, "ABC Trucking is a specialty mover and hauler of small and moderate sized items weighing below two tons available on two hours notice, around the clock." A large charismatic church wrote, "We are the largest Full Gospel, evangelistic preaching/teaching church in the Lakeland area." Everyone should be able to own this statement. One church tried

to form a statement of this type saying, "We are a friendly family church." After having a congregational meeting to decide the context of the statement, it was agreed that the congregation realized they weren't so friendly, so they redrew the statement (a better alternative would have been to restructure the church).

8. *Identify the church's desired public image.* This part of the mission statement may require redoing after completing Develop the Dream, the next stage of the planning process. For starters, however, the team should review all the church has been in the past and boil it down. Now you're ready to state what you desire to be.

For the private sector, this statement is often extremely idealistic. After nine sentences which spoke to market, target groups, products, and the like, one firm ended by saying "To create in our community a strong sense of strength, a good and just business citizen, and an economic force to work for the good of all south Philadelphia people."

For a church, on the other hand, if the committee is not cautious the first nine or ten sentences will automatically ring with idealistic clichés. Therefore this last sentence could simply be more of the same, or it could lead into envisioning what public image could be developed. For example a struggling church in

Bronx New York, a poor urban neighborhood with little or no outreach, boldly stated - "to actively work toward an effective and all-inclusive ministry of service with our neighbors who are poor, disenfranchised, and hurting, bringing the love of Christ to all people in our community through prayer and personal action." This is the place to state what you want the world to see taking place, even if it isn't already.

Once the mission statement fully addresses these issues the planning team is prepared to receive input from the congregation again. Before moving to that next plateau, however, take two weeks to circulate the new mission statement to the congregation. Be prepared to modify it "if" it is unrealistic; not, however, on a negative response from one or two people. Let the mission statement dissolve into the life of the church, digest into every member's psyche, and become the quintessential operating ethic of the prime achievers of the church. Ask the pastor to work the precepts of the statement into a well attended service of sermon, song, and litany. Take away the fear of the new thing. Once members are accustomed to the new mission statement (three or four weeks), then ask them to dream some dreams and envision new visions based directly upon its tenants

Step Four

Develop the Dream
(Strategic Business Modeling)

It has been said by many over the years that it is far easier to get people involved in actually doing something than in planning it. If this old adage is true, this next section, which business consultants have titled "Strategic Business Modeling" should bring forth much excitement. We simply call it *develop the dream*.

The Strategic Planning team should now be able to answer two lead-in questions from the work done and the data collected in the two previous operations:

1. Where have we been?

2. Where are we going?

3. What is the environment in which our church exists?

Now the team is ready to handle the quantum leap of strategic planning - *Exactly how do we get to where we're going from where we're at?*[21]

We shall find the answer to this question in the greatest resource at the committee's disposal, the dreams and aspirations of the people of the church. We have discussed in previous chapters dedicated to leadership, that one of the

---

[21] Benton E. Gup, "Begin Strategic Planning by Asking Three Questions," <u>Managerial Planning</u>, November 1987, 28-31.

talents of leaders is the ability to "inspire a vision" among members and workers. A good leader is one who helps those on his/her team not only to envision the future, but to contribute their dreams to the ongoing planning process. Next, the able leader will enlist these contributors and others into making the dream become a reality.

This key component of daily operational leadership must be no less present on the strategic planning team. The primary difference is that this dream development segment comes on the heels of exercises which have been designed to gather and channel the otherwise spontaneous outpourings of congregational hopes and desires into one driving force.

As the church succeeds in developing a values-philosophy statement, and takes part in the process of building a mission statement, a sense of incompleteness begins to form among the people. For this reason, the Develop the Dream segment tends to be one of the most enabling and satisfying.

A word of warning is necessary. Most churches have gone through this process before; it's not new. Most of the time a mission statement of sorts and a dream session are brought together into one or two planning sessions. What we propose here is greatly different. It comes as part of a four or five month process and is built upon much preparatory work. Therefore, it is advised that the church not use results from older surveys.

I recommend the congregation receive pre-printed forms with each person's name typed at the top, thus fostering responsibility for and ownership of the questionnaire. The document should be headed with a statement that clearly defines the purpose of the planning process. Such a statement might say:

> Keeping in mind our new philosophy of operating our church and reflecting on our mission statement, if you could bring about any new action or program you wanted and have any wish fulfilled, how would you complete each of the following...

Divide the sheet into four headings, two on each side of the paper. The four heading statements to be completed should be:

> 1. I wish my church could do the following one thing for the people around us...
>
> 2. I wish my church would inaugurate the following program...
>
> 3. I wish my church would do the following thing and tell the world about it...
>
> 4. I wish more than anything else the following thing for my church...

One author writing on "Strategic Business Modeling"[22] instructs that this step

> Is not an extrapolation of what the organization is now doing. It is not a long range plan to do more of the same only better.

I recommend the same type of disclaimer surround the congregation's effort.

---

[22] J. William Pfeiffer, Strategic Planning, XXV.

When the results are collected (no more than seven days should be allowed), the team is responsible for collating the results, grouping them together by category, and restating groups of dreams into single statements. The team will need to realize that a great deal of prodding is often necessary to encourage the members to complete and turn in this project. One Free Methodist church had to assign people to go door to door to collect the completed forms. Do whatever is necessary to help *every member* complete and return this questionnaire. The team should be seeking to discover:

- What common dreams and desires can be found among the people, and

- What specific programs can be developed to fulfill these desires.

Modeling becomes the work of the long range planning committee at this point. Using the church's mission statement as a springboard, the committee should *designate specific target areas and design new programs to reach those target zones.* Some examples of target areas may be:

1. *Older persons recently widowed.* There are 20,000 marriages terminated by the death of a spouse in our country each week.

2. *Music and young children.* This requires a full or semi-full time music minister; parents will bring children from great distances to be involved in this type of program.

Renaissance or Ruin

3. *Ministry to single parents and their children.* This usually involves a program with a Parents Without Partners format.

4. *Specific work ministry format.* The church may pick a specific camp or old age home near the church and become a sort of auxiliary to the facility. County or city jail ministry falls into this category. Ministry to traveling Merchant Mariners also qualifies.

5. *Second marriages and blended family ministries.* In an area where fundamental churches are the norm and second marriages are severely frowned upon, a more moderate mainline church could well offer a real haven.

6. *Ministry to gays and lesbians.* This is the most controversial of the alternatives and should be well thought out. Only the more liberal churches would be able to institute this needed specialized ministry. If the church or the pastor harbors any degree of homophobia this ministry will not succeed.

7. *Christian Day Schools.* Churches with unused space, located on major arteries leading to town, or churches in the heart of downtown are well suited to this program. This is a major undertaking and should involve professional staff.

8. *Ministries to the homeless and disenfranchised.* Many churches "left behind" in poorer areas of the cities have become feeding centers, working hand in hand with government authorities to meet this need. This ministry usually should include an open house component for nights when temperatures drop below 40 degrees. (Don't do this unless you work to bring these folks into your worship family and love them as your own. One thing the homeless do not need is another church of upper-middle class people who want to play house on Tuesday at noon, using the homeless as their dollies.)

9. *International churches.* Some urban churches located in areas where 2 or 3 cultures live in close proximity have opted to become bilingual. This unfortunately works better in Roman Catholic Churches who work on a parish system. An alternative could be housing two or three churches, each with its own pastor, meeting at different times and joining once a month for a group fellowship (caution: there can be no reserved spaces). Rest rooms and kitchens must be usable by all. The trustees will need to be equally representative of all the congregations.

10. *Evangelistic center.* A real twist in the normal right to left movement of things would be to look around your community at the other churches. Many older settled communities are

replete with older settled churches. Younger residents have often been reared outside the faith. There are millions of 20 to 50 year olds hungry for the Gospel from a conversion perspective and few churches in some areas meet that need. This choice would require preparatory work in many congregations who might consider this approach too fundamental.[23]

11. *Sunday School centered.* In many older settled communities, particularly in the northeast corridor, the local churches have found themselves with few or no children. As a result, many churches have abandoned Sunday School or cut it to a baby-sitting program. Others close down for large portions of the year. In this setting, one church with a group of dedicated young parents and a pick-up van or bus could offer a vital service to the young families of the area. Older church members will need to offer their full financial and prayerful support.

12. *Teenage recreation center.* In areas that have gone through dramatic changes, large older churches often own huge facilities that are never used. If your church has a gymnasium or pool, but no use for it, open it up to the community. Form an operating board made up largely of leaders from the community. With teen gangs and street crime at an all time high, your church

---

[23] Redeemer Presbyterian Church began in 1989 as an evangelistic mission in Manhattan. Formally this area was seen as un-evangelizable. Redeemer has recorded huge successes.

could save hundreds of lives each year (added note: It will usually stop vandalism on your buildings).[24]

13. *The Mega-church model.* Some churches have found success in following the Korean Assembly of God plan. They decentralize into house churches for Bible study, fellowship and prayer. These groups then come together for massive worship services. The Boston movements in the Church of Christ actually advocates selling off the main church building and renting facilities as needed. This is a growing movement that I feel is radical and dangerous; however, the cell church idea as a part of a greater church has a great deal of merit, especially as a tool for expansion.

14. *The Liberal giant.* We've looked at options that lean toward the conservative scheme; how about the opposite? Look around. If you're in an area where other liberal congregations have gone by the wayside in the path of the conservative swing, you may be the only place left for centrists and those of the theological left. The main thing, here especially, is for the congregation to have its act together. Don't say "we're liberal," and at the same time be exclusionary, racist, sexist and provincial. Be liberal.

---

[24] Many of these suggestions and others originate in Lyle E. Schaller's Create Your Own Future, 113-115.

Actually, my only concern in offering these suggestions is that they will become self-limiting. For every dream your congregation can envision, there are five hundred needs to be met and scores of ways to match them. I have suggested that strategic planning teams take a few days off from their own churches and visit other ministries, especially successful ones, in an effort to see what they are doing and how they do it.

Some programs your team will explore will build your church in number, some will not. The team's only job is to develop its plan in a congruent manner, seeing that the values-mission statement and these prototype programs conform. The team must further incorporate a "proactive futuring" component. Any package developed must allow for free flowing creativity that encourages the seeds they have germinated to mature into a reinvented, regenerated congregation of the people of God.

Step Five

Performance Audit and Gap Analysis

The team is now encouraged to do some pretending, running each prototype program through a trial run on paper. "If we did it, what would happen?" The "performance audit" and "gap analysis"[25] are to be used by the team to prove or disprove the validity of the programs chosen. As the group runs a theoretical prototype through an imaginary performance,

---

[25] J. William Pfeiffer, Strategic Planning. XXVIII - XXXII.

gaps or discrepancies will soon appear; the group must deal with the gaps as they occur.

Using this "What-if" technique, the invasion planning task force under Eisenhower during World War II put a hold on the "D" Day Normandy landings. When visualizing a mock operation, a concern developed that heavy equipment could sink in the sand. It was decided to send in teams of Navy Seals (commandos) to collect and test sand samples to make sure the beach would support tanks and the like. Several beaches were eliminated when this imagined "gap" proved valid.

An example of this procedure can be found in the Church of the Blessed Trinity near Baltimore. In 1986 a planning committee decided to develop a weekend recreation program for neighborhood teens. Blessed Trinity's congregation is white, upper-middle class, suburban, and the medium age is 58 years. The church has no teens and only a few small children. What it does have is a fully equipped gymnasium, an indoor pool, and a fairly substantial amount of money. Like so many other churches, the members do not live near the church which is in a heavily urbanized area with a multi-ethnic population. The average age in the neighborhood is 40 and the people are African American and Korean. Gangs of teens roam the streets because there is nothing for them to do.

The long range planning committee formulated the church's new operating philosophy which stated "...the church as the hand of God to reach out in love to the community it nourishes..." This values statement had gradually developed into a mission statement, approved by the church, which echoed this philosophy with the words "We will inaugurate programs designed to build bridges with our neighbors in the south Baltimore suburbs."

Renaissance or Ruin

Keeping congruency in mind, the committee collated the dreams list around three areas of thrust, one of which highlighted the increased use of the gym facility. Others reflected the overwhelming desire to touch the neighborhood. These dreams and concerns fostered the recreation center scheme. In running the subsequent prototype through the "performance audit" it was discovered that the gym and pool had been given to the church by a wealthy family in 1963 with the stipulation that it be used only by "our church." While the stipulation had no "legal" weight, it was realized that this presented a "gap" between the group's desire and the dream implementation. The committee decided to contact the endowing family and receive a reversal of the stipulation. One contact brought immediate results. The answer was "delighted to see the facility used again."

A second run of the plan developed only one snag. It was discovered that there was no street entrance into the facility. The trustees were then brought in to pre-approve a $1,200 expenditure for a new entrance into the recreation center from the 82nd Street parking lot. This was speedily sanctioned.

Finally, on the third performance audit run it was discovered that no church members could be found to take charge of the day-to-day operation. Also, both the custodian and associate pastor refused to oversee the project.

In order to close this final gap, a board comprised of two church members, the pastor, a local funeral director, and three other neighborhood leaders were recruited. They agreed to oversee the implementation and daily operation of the facility. This included tendering a set of rules and an operating plan that had to be approved by the congregation.

At this point, Blessed Trinity's strategic planning team had taken the mission statement, given it a specific form (drawn from the heart of the congregation), and "proofed" it several times. Several inconsistencies surfaced which were subjected to "gap analysis." Each time, an answer had evolved from a study of the problem. As a result of this methodical approach the dream has moved from a vision into the realm of reality. The Kingdom of God was about to break loose upon the darkened streets of a city in pain.

Step Six

Integrated Organizational Action Plan

Most weekend retreat planning sessions would have ended several stages ago. The bags were packed, and the congregation returned home with high hopes of getting all the hastily thought out plans into action in the weeks and months ahead. The reality is that most of these plans are filed in the cabinet in the fellowship hall and there they will stay forever. The reason? Because there was no mechanism to translate these dreams into reality.

Strategic planning supplies this missing link. The planning team must oversee the conversion of the overall plan into actual programs. The team will closely supervise the implementation, with final responsibilities delegated to either newly formed executive teams (one for each new program), or for lesser programs, the team will work with existing boards and committees in the church.

Strategic planning also contains an accountability factor requiring the planning team to see that the "pieces of the puzzle" come together to form a completed working program. In churches it is assumed that new plans will be executed by existing groups who are responsible for carrying out each part; but that is wishful thinking. The trustees, Christian education, outreach, evangelism, worship, and deacons are maintenance oriented groups. They do not see themselves as inaugurators, they assume that innovation is the job of the long range or strategic planning committee. They are right. It is basically the planning team's job to be the implementors: so let's implement.

The major programs generated by the strategic planning process need to be broken down, by the team, into their "do-able" parts. Then the planning team member representing a particular board should take each part of every plan that aligns to the work area of his/her board back to that board for action. This team member now acts as a liaison reporting back and forth between the operating board, the new program's executive committee, and the strategic planning committee itself. This is done weekly until all tasks are completed. The byword is *follow-up*.

Planning team members should be ever cognizant of their need to be adaptable leaders as they act as go-betweens. The planning committee here is cast in the role of the leader who needs to be adaptable, while the boards of the church are like unto followers, each brandishing its own task maturity with respect to the new program.

This *personal responsibility factor* being borne by the team members holding dual office, i.e. the Strategic Planning Team and a permanent board or committee post, is *a key component in this process*. For this reason it is extremely desirable to see each major board not only represented on the planning committee, but the representative should be a chief stakeholder on the board.

In the case of Blessed Trinity and its recreation center, once the congregation gave its approval to the master plan, the team began to work extensively with the Trustees. They saw that the new entry was completed (time frame 60 days), lighting and pool pumps and other equipment were working well (time frame 30 days), and directional signs installed (time frame 60 days).

They began to work with Church Growth to implement a plan to assimilate any persons who currently had no church, but now began to identify with Blessed Trinity as a result of recreation center involvement. The team began to work with Outreach to develop a concrete plan to handle any calls for help arising out of the new community contact, and/or to refer cases of extreme hardship to several newly developed community resources.

Finally, they worked with the pastor to create a working relationship between the people of the community, the independent board of operation, the city and county authorities, and the people of the church. The team also contacted the church's attorney to procure a copy of legal requirements to which the independent board would need to comply. This covered, in detail, release of liability and insurance coverage needed (time frame 90 days).

A note in passing. Some in the church may harbor feelings that the planning team has become a "super" committee and is intruding into everyone's turf. This <u>intrusion is absolutely necessary</u> for this process to end successfully. If, from ground zero, the right mix of representation appears on the team from a broad base of interest groups in the church, it will greatly belay these objections.

Renaissance or Ruin

The strategic planning committee's job is analogous to the task set before John the Baptist. He came in advance of Jesus as one "crying in the wilderness: prepare the way of the Lord; make straight in the desert a highway for our God."[26] Isaiah, the writer of the original prophesy, continues to lay out the task of both the prophet going before the Messiah and the planning committee leading on before the church. He writes

> Every valley shall be exalted and every mountain and hill shall be made low; the crooked places shall be made straight and the rough places smooth..."[27]

The planning group's task is less a super board and more of a preparation team acting to give the new plans an even chance of survival in what may prove to be hostile terrain.

In the medical setting, a heart surgeon who completes a cardiac bypass procedure would not expect his/her task to be finished once the basic operation is completed. The surgeon will continue to monitor the patient as the cavity is closed, the blood pressure is brought to normal, and the patient goes through recovery, intensive care, post-op, and is out of the hospital for sixty or ninety days. Only then is the patient discharged, and not before.

Likewise, the planning team has guided the church from yesterday through today and is now helping birth the future. They must be allowed this brief time to carry these new programs, which they have conceived, through this birthing process. This step of Integrated Organizational Action Planning is simply the transferring of newly developed programs into the church's existing infrastructure. If done

---

[26] Isaiah 40:3, NKJV.
[27] Isaiah 40:4, NKJV.

properly *the glory of the Lord shall be revealed.*[28]

Step Seven

Plan for Problems

Before going completely public with the new programs, the committee should take one final opportunity to anticipate opposition and implementation problems. These will surface in two arenas and should be addressed accordingly;

- External threats

- Internal threats

This problem search has nothing to do with the viability of the programs themselves, but rather deals with reactions to them.

There will be little *external* pressure against most programs the church will attempt to implement. In the case of Blessed Trinity's recreation plan this was not true. There were neighbors' objections to noise. City governments objected initially because of perceived danger coming from the congregating of so many teens in one spot. These, however, are the exceptions and not the rule. Nevertheless, the committee must anticipate such contingencies and then,

> 1. Develop trigger points to introduce action steps for each contingency

---

[28] Isaiah 40:4, NKJV.

Renaissance or Ruin

2. Agree on which action steps will be taken for each of these trigger points."[29]

You will note this is very similar to the performance audit and gap analysis, except that this stage deals with a finalized working program as it appears to both those outside and inside the church. This *projection of anticipated snags* centers more around objections than around actual problems.

The same two steps should then be taken for the contingencies anticipated under the listing of *internal* threats. In the business world, these would include the death of a chief program facilitator, the breakdown of a particular machine, and like kinds of challenges considered as possible threats in a secular setting. In the church these could include opposition from the church's "No" group. A threat could be posed if a facilitating member moved or became ill, or a key facility needed work at a later date. These problems should not be viewed as presages toward proving "Murphy's law" (anything that can go wrong, will), but rather a list of possible challenges that are better anticipated, and pre-handled, than viewed as evil omens.

The life of the strategic planning committee is now in its twilight hours. At this point the committee and the congregation should be ready to present four or five ready to go programs to the world. The management team assigned to regularly administrate each program is in place, and the hitherto "dream like" *future is about to become a very present reality*.

---

[29] J. William Pfeiffer, Strategic Planning, XXXIII - XXXIV.

Step Eight

Implementation

By this time, six to nine months of hard work have transpired and the strategic planning committee will be anxious to adjourn permanently. The most joyous part of their job is about to take place and they are both deserving to share in it and should consider it necessary to do so.

Any major new program needs a day of grand introduction, of celebration. Every dream carried this far deserves and needs a birthday. This is the day the "dream becomes reality," it becomes the property of the entire church, and the planning team is accorded the accolades they deserve before sliding into history.

The most important test of implementation, however, is the degree to which sponsoring members, especially managers (church officers) integrate the strategic plan into their everyday management decisions.[30] In other words after all the "hoopla" fades, will the trustees, for example, adopt the program with excitement and joy or with lethargy and resentment, determining to "get rid of this burden" as soon as possible? The question remains, will all the boards of the church take continued responsibility for the newly birthed programs, or let them go by the wayside?

To help ensure a long term adoption, I recommend that implementation of the new program(s) take three emphasis. *First*, help as many people as possible get involved with the

---

[30] J. William Pfeiffer, Strategic Planning, XXXVIII.

kickoff planning and implementation. Encourage them to create the greatest "knock their socks off" celebration in the church's history.

Second, on implementation day give credit to all those persons submitting dream sheets that suggested the new ministry or any part thereof. See to it that these people receive recognition as birthing parents of the fledgling program. Also make sure that these folks become permanent administrators and workers in the project. Their ownership will outlive the planning team.

Third, reconvene the planning team two months after full implementation. Have every board and committee head at the meeting. Together they should carry the now operating programs through a brief "performance audit" based on reality instead of theory. They should then subject reality to a "gap analysis" to determine actual shortfalls. Out of this discussion, planned and unplanned problems can be examined, settled, and assigned back to the appropriate church management team for permanent resolution.

The strategic planning process is now at an end. The planning committee cannot and should not remain intact to become another layer of bureaucracy enforcing the status quo. Their work, while being the future today, will soon become homeostasis for the church; becoming tomorrow's past. There will be a tendency for the existing boards of the church to cry for help, giving some impetus to the continuation of the strategic planning team. <u>Their cries should be ignored by the now dissolved team.</u> The infrastructure should and will begin to handle these new programs as part of their normal operating agenda.

Jethro told Moses to "teach the people the statutes." If this has been done and the church infrastructure is God centered in their conduct, if they have learned such leadership techniques as focused brainstorming and adaptable leadership, then they are well prepared to take the work of the strategic planning committee and turn it into ongoing ministry. The job of this team and the goal of this process is to *show the people the way they must walk without carrying them.*

Critics of this almost year-long, very in-depth process will say many things, including the fact that there is too much involvement, it offers too much changing, too many new things, or that you ought to let God just have God's way without human interference. To these we would commend Paul's words:

> Therefore I remind you to stir up the gift of God which in you through the laying on of hands, for God has not given us a spirit of fear, but of power and of love and of a sound mind."[31]

If my original hypothesis is true - that our churches are dying from systemic paranoia, a fear of facing the people of our world as ministers - what better way to "stir up the gifts" then by using the power of God to develop hope and courage. Strategic planning is little more than the

- "laying on hands" to our churches,

- finding new ways to be proactive in programs and ministries,

- using the sound mind God has given us to plan for a bright future in service to God.

---

[31] 2 Timothy 1: 6-7.

Renaissance or Ruin

Strategic planning is one of God's major tools toward the rebirth of our inactive gifts for ministry.

After all is said and done - *this IS the work we must do.*

TRIGGER POINTS

1. What is the real operating philosophy of you church?

2. Does you church currently have a mission statement? How long have you had it? Is there any reality in it?

3. Discuss the fourteen innovative ministry suggestion listed in this chapter. Which ones could you all agree upon? Is there a pattern to your consensus? Can you suggest other ideas for your church?

4. Are you familiar with corporate mission statements (advertising statements) that are outright lies? How do you react to that company once you've discovered this discrepancy?

5. If you could see your church do one great thing, what would that be? Can you all agree on some of these ideas?

CHAPTER XIII

SELECT ABLE PEOPLE

After Jethro had instructed Moses in the teaching of leadership, Moses himself was told to move out of the picture and become an intentional outsider of sorts. Jethro said:

> Moreover you shall *select* from *all the people* able men such as *fear God*, men *of truth, hating covetousness*, and place them to be rulers of thousands, of hundreds, rulers of fifty, and rulers of tens. And let them judge the people at all times.[1]

Using Jethro's words I shall use this chapter to help the church make better choices in selecting its leadership. Some will say "Moses, Israel and most large institutions here have large numbers of people from which to choose, but our church has only 135 active members." Others will make a case that 80% of American churches have active memberships of under 125 and a working core of 15 or 20 people, and that's it. In this situation, many feel that these churches don't have the option of "selecting leaders," they assume the church must accept whoever will take the post and hope it works. To which I reply - "True and not true."

---

[1] Exodus 18: 21-22, NKJV. If this text is translated for teaching leadership in the modern era, *people* should be substituted for *men*.

Let us look at the word "select," understanding that there are two ways of caring out this procedure.

1. Hierarchical selection, and

2. Meritocracy.

First, there is the situation described in Exodus where Moses is instructed to do the "picking." Occasionally, corporate executives do this when they "pick the best person for the job." Theoretically, they fill an empty position choosing the very best candidate for the job. In this case we see *hierarchical selection* at work. The choice in this case comes from the top. Ultra connectional churches such as the United Methodist and the Roman Catholic systems assign their clergy in this manner.

The large church boasting a cadre of 150 or 200 workers (600 plus active members) can more ably assign a small nominating board the task of sifting and sorting the membership to find people that fit their criteria exactly. This type of church can end up with the city's top CPA as treasurer, a retired theology professor as the head of worship, and a manufacturing executive as the head of trustees. Theoretically, this gives the big church the "competitive edge" in carrying out ministry. We will not comment further on a system this large, except to say that while good ministry may be accomplished, this method rarely activates the greater church in leadership. The job and mission gets done most efficiently, but hundreds of people drop out the back door or spend years in the back pew uninvolved.

In a pastor-controlled or a single lay person-controlled church this same method tends to prevail. In a church in Tennessee, the pastor was so firmly in charge that eleven of the fourteen church officers were his family members. This practice is common, especially in the case of independent churches. A local oil distributor controls one Baptist Church in North Carolina. He not only hand-picks the lay leaders, but also the pastors. It is not coincidental that most of the deacons work for his company. Hierarchical selecting may work temporarily, but even in corporate America this method has been dropped in favor of less hierarchical plans. Further, I believe this method is not intended for the church; especially the small or moderate size church.

The *second method, meritocracy,* is a grassroots one. This has been the way healthy churches with congregational polity traditionally work. It has its good and its bad points. While this is basically an ascension to leadership from a base of merit, in the church this is accomplished as much out of spontaneity as any other way. For this reason I often refer to this system as "spontaneous ascension" for want of a better phrase.

It is based on the theory that no one is selected (chosen) from the top, but rather that the system generates leaders spontaneously from the pews. These persons learn by doing, and "qualify" for top church leadership by tenaciously hanging on and performing competently at lower levels. Eventually these faithful enter into an extensive network of other leaders who form the cadre of the local church. This theory is opposite from "hierarchical selection," where the best is selected "in." Here, time and relationships work to select the incompetent "out."

Most corporations that achieve high levels of success in corporate leadership development depend on a combination of these two systems. A beginning employee is subjected routinely to the trials of lower level jobs, ever rising to greater levels of competency by a process of conquering the lower level challenges one at a time. The theory goes that, after a period of years, this process renders that employee knowledgeable and articulate in the affairs of the business, therefore becoming eligible to be placed on the upper level list of chosen people from which the hierarchy selects the officers of the company.

The problem in most churches is that our numbers are so small, and the supply of potential leaders so depleted, that anyone who is willing to just "hang in there" long enough will be assured of being "selected in" regardless of competence, ability or desire. These "in folks" who make the chosen list become more than a core of workers, they become a coterie unto themselves; a clique held together, not by competence or by righteous purpose, but by the exclusion of, or simple lack of other people.

You will recall that earlier we discussed the church as a closed system. Here we see this situation in its embryonic form. After a short period of isolation, the cadre itself begins selecting its members, but only from its own numbers and supporters. Often the people excluded are the competent ones of the congregation.

To solve this riddle we must discover:

    1. How to recognize natural leaders available to serve in the local church.

    2. How to force open the ranks of the cadre allowing and encouraging wider participation.

    3. How to develop leadership where it is not now in practice.

Recognizing Able Leaders

In doing my research, I have noticed that most so-called leaders, secular or church, are not leaders at all, but simply successful followers. Actually, over 90% of the population is in a following mode at any given moment. Many of these people are corporate presidents and the chairs of major civic boards and committees. They, however, become skilled at being exemplary followers when placed in that position.

Leadership is situational. One may be a leader at work but a loyal and energetic follower in a particular social setting. There is no shame in following. There is, however, shame in *failure following.*"[2] In looking to recognize an able leader, then, you may wish to "select out" failure followers.

According to Robert Kelley, the failure follower can be categorized in four distinct ways.

- The alienated follower

- The conformist

- The pragmatist

- The passive follower

The *alienated follower* continually fails because he/she is always troublesome, cynical, and negative. These followers always have a chip on their shoulders, are liable to be headstrong and usually lack good judgment. While being constantly critical of others' lack of adherence to the system, this person challenges rules and laws at every turn.

---

[2] Robert E. Kelley, The Power of Followership, (London, Doubleday, 1992), 103-123.

The *conformist* will accept any task, but lack input of their own. Conformists are continually self-deprecating and are never dependable. They will rarely stick to an opinion or stand with a person, which or who becomes unpopular. These followers avoid conflict and will not stand firm against that which is wrong; consequently, friends and fellow workers find them untrustworthy. Power politicians, on the other hand, covet conformists because they will go along with the company line, acting as *satellites* or *chameleons* when needed. They will compromise the church's very existence to please the clique to which they belong. More than any other single type, these individuals fill seats on committees in the local and greater church.

The third type of failure follower - the *pragmatist*, plays political games and remains ready to shift sides for his/her own enrichment. Each exchange finds them getting the most out of the system for their special interest. The pragmatist is adverse to risk and covers his/her "tail" in an expert manner. They play by rules and regulations as long as it is to their advantage, otherwise only passing attention is paid to the leader's wishes, church policy, the constitution, or the laws of the land. This "politician personality" usually makes it to the top of the church leadership ladder, but upon arrival becomes a "do nothing - accomplish nothing" leader. When the name "Peter Principle" was coined, referring to those who "rise to the level of their own incompetence," it refers directly to this opportunistic, bustling bureaucrat.

Finally, the *passive follower* is characterized by exhibition of the "herd instinct." Like sheep, these people do whatever they are told to do. This may range from cooking potatoes for the Sunday School supper to voting to fire the pastor if told to do so by a "friend." Likewise, the passive follower does nothing unless told to. This would probably include not calling 9-1-1 if he or she noticed a fire in the fellowship hall. Lastly, the passive follower lets everyone else take the responsibility, and of course the blame, for the ultimate outcome of any situation.

By the time you read through these four types of failure followers, you could become discouraged or suspicious of every person with whom you work. Remember, however, our prior statement that - at any given time, 90% of the people in our society are in a follower mode. The secret is to choose *not* to be a "failure" follower.

Also, remember that even those serving in high leadership positions may find themselves being asked to be followers in other settings. I have a friend who pastors the church that S. S. Kresge attended. Mr. Kresge, in his role as CEO of one of the world's largest retail firms, was obviously a remarkable national leader. His vocation prevented him from being a leader in the church, yet his pastor reports that he was one of the most proactive members of the congregation. In other words, this fine Christian was able to switch hats and act as a valuable and successful follower in the church setting:

Every true leader can do this.

There is no disgrace in being a follower. On occasion, even the pastor needs to be allowed the privilege of followership. Danger only arises when a person chooses to work in failure follower patterns, or when a successful follower accepts leadership then fails to exercise that leadership.

This brings us to the successful follower, the type who can become a dynamic leader at the drop of a hat. Kelley refers to them as

- Exemplary followers.

These people do the name "follower" justice.[3] This type of follower is productive to work with if you are a leader, and is able to become a leader easily, already possessing the basic skills needed. *Exemplary followers* are able to focus on organizational goals and commit to the task at hand. They are team players in the best sense of the word - doing a great job whether it be their project or someone else's. They desire to be truly competent at whatever they do. Every job is seen as important to them, therefore they are able to move easily from worship committee, to church secretary, on to moderator, and in the next session serve as a trustee. These people think the good of the organization outweighs their own personal agenda. They are willing to take the initiative to increase the status of the organization while taking pride in being a part of it. Finally, they are open to change, improvement, and growth in the community, ever willing to give some of their turf to another seeking entry.

John Adams, the second President of the United States, appears to have been this type of follower. He did much toward the creation of this country. After Independence, which he worked so hard to achieve, he slipped into the background, serving where he could. He ascended to the presidency, but after serving his term he returned to the Congress to become a distinguished representative. After stepping aside from all political involvement, he continued to be a teacher and a voluntary worker in the building our growing nation.

In the church setting *an exemplary follower has and lives by faith*. They will be in love with God; they likewise will love people. Exemplary followers may not be "walking - talking" evangelists, but no one doubts that they are aware of

---

[3] Kelly 125-147

Jesus' presence in their lives. In the congregation, these followers will exhibit an openness and an unselfishness which, while perhaps quietly lived, will nonetheless speak loudly of their faith.

The answer, then, to the first question posed: *How do we pick leaders from our midst?* is

☐ *Pick the exemplary followers* - they possess everything needed to be great leaders.

Opening Closed Leader Systems

The second question is *How can the ranks of the core church (cadre) be forced open to allow and encourage wider leadership participation?* The first thing to understand[4] is that in no case do power cores (cadre) wish their ranks expanded. This should not be seen as insidious or premeditated, but in all instances, deny it as they will, groups are comfortable with their own composition.

First, I suggest you share the information found in this book concerning power dynamics, closed systems, and follower - leader patterns with all the leaders of the church. A defensive reaction can be expected. This should be followed by a frank and open discussion of this behavior pattern and how it impacts the church. Once responsible people become aware of this tendency to close their system, and recognize the symptoms in their own group, a willingness, even an urgency often develops to take corrective action.

At this point the pastor and the nominating committee should begin to work, to search for new folks to help broaden the base of leadership. This phase of the process should begin long before nominating season. The nominating committee

---

[4] See Chapter III, The Powers to Be.

needs to begin a search of church membership, asking who would be willing to serve in leadership. This will bring few if any results, but it will alert everyone to the need.

The next step is to personally approach neutral members who hold no office and "sell" them on the idea of getting involved and taking committee positions. Have written, "honest" descriptions of the jobs available for the candidate to explore with an expansion-minded leader.

Finally, and this is the toughest step, when nominating season comes, some of the long-term leaders should step down for an agreed-upon period, usually two or three years. This is an extreme, but most likely necessary sacrifice for both the leader and the church.

<u>Many positions in the church may then sit unfilled.</u> Don't panic! Don't fill them haphazardly! If necessary, let them go empty for a quarter of a year (treasurer, moderator, and financial secretary excepted). Keep reminding the congregation of the situation, but don't "crisis manage." Although it will require extraordinary discipline, let the situation continue. Sooner or later, some of the least likely people will begin to respond to the emergency. Encourage the "step down" leaders to become the mentors of the newly elected officers. Encourage the step down leader/instructors not to ridicule or "showoff" how much they know, but rather to be "teachers." This rather elaborate and demanding procedure calls for the pastor and the nominating committee to agree to work closely for perhaps an entire year.

Do not be surprised that after such an alteration, the workings of the church will change significantly. Whenever you add new leaders to the group, methods and input will change.

A few years ago, as women began to fill corporate positions, it was found (ridiculed at first) that women conceptualize leadership differently than do men. Women lead by story telling, building and seeking community; i.e., through relationships. Men, on the other hand, seek facts, make their point and decide quickly. Men establish hierarchy and goals very quickly. After two decades in the business world, women are adapting to the male scene and changing accordingly. However, the business world itself is also changing and adapting; it is becoming more female in its collective personality, more relational, more people focused. All entities involved (men, women, and the corporate world)[5] are impacting on one another. The same thing will happen to the church as new blood becomes part of the core structure.

As new leaders enter the church infrastructure, change will occur. The more closed the core has become, the greater the objections to these changes there will be. You will hear:

- ✓ You can't do that.

- ✓ We've never done that before.

- ✓ We tried that once and it didn't work.

<u>Strife and tension will replace the peace and harmony of former meetings, but</u> things will begin to happen. The new faces will be - *stirring up the gifts of God*.

If the ranks of the core church are to be open, it will require the dedicated effort of strong, well differentiated lay leaders, a confident pastor leader, and several well informed intervenors. All of whom are willing to use their powers in a

---

[5] A perfect example of a relational triangle as covered earlier. Edwin Friedmen, <u>Generation to Generation</u>.

prophetic way. These avant-garde leaders will need a loyal group of "exemplary" followers. The pragmatist, the passive follower, the conformist, and the alienated follower will be all too ready to challenge such an effort. Don't forget that the tightly woven mesh of relationships that were responsible for the original success of the local church will now draw together to prohibit such endeavors.

If, however, there are those who are willing to risk those relationships to bring about the rejuvenation of the church, the congregation will respond in a very brief time. The victory of openness over closedness should also lead many "failure followers" to become "exemplary" ones.

Something From Nothing

The third issue to be addressed is that of helping the non-leaders of the church become leaders - not position holders. *How can we develop leadership where there is none?*

For the answer, recall that Jethro instructed Moses to teach the leaders of the people to obey the statutes and the laws, and to show the people the way they should walk. Jethro then launched both Israel and us on a community building journey by calling for a return to a faith relationship with God. We continued on our journey finding ourselves standing for our people as leaders, and we found the prerequisite to leadership is to acknowledge God's hold on our lives. We were also encouraged to accept God's word as the basis for our existence. We expanded that journey to include leadership development methods and planning processes for the local church. We discovered that the initial task is to elevate all position holders, long term or new, to the level of a leader *selected "by" God* and *selected "of" God.*

Jethro also taught Moses that to institute this selection process, "by and of God," he needed to take responsibility and select leaders hierarchically - this would relate to "by God" because Moses was charged as God's prophet. We concluded that the spontaneous ascension method of selecting leaders takes place in the local church by special committee, planning group, or nominating committee. Now we need to add the most important criteria of all. The newly chosen leaders must also *select God* in order to qualify for selection by the church - this would relate to the commandment - "of God". In other words - the church's leaders must above all - *fear God*.

Fear of God, put simply, means -

the candidate must be a person whose life indicates he/she worships, stands in awe of, believes in, and surrenders to - God.

This confirms God's selection of the candidate.

Virtually every denominational handbook, discipline, book of instruction, or faith statement includes this condition as a prerequisite to leadership. The Book of Worship of the United Church of Christ for example, asks that candidates stand before the congregation and make a faith pronunciation upon accepting leadership.[6] The United Methodists do the same, as do both major Presbyterian bodies.

Yet as nominating committees meet, the subject of a candidate's faith is never broached. The invitation is made by the committee to the chosen candidate without asking if the person would be willing to recite the faith statement, and do so in genuine belief.

---

[6] Book of Worship, 1986, United Church of Christ Office of Life and Leadership, see Members Reception page 61, and Commissioning to Lay Ministry pages 427-428.

No consideration is given to the question -

do the nominees believe in Jesus Christ, and do they act like it.

Jethro never told Moses to search for accountants to be treasurer, nor did he demand only woodworkers be in charge of trustees. What he did demand was that *every leader be a true believer, living in obedience to God.*

It is possible that less than 50% of the Protestant and Catholic lay leaders in America pay deference to God or hold to a genuine belief in the faith system they serve.[7] I estimate a lessor number enjoys a contemporary - animated relationship with Jesus Christ. New candidates and incumbents alike, should be selected not only from the church's sponsors, but also selected on the basis of their ongoing relationship with God.

Jethro next demanded that these leaders be people *of truth.* This means not known as liars, but it also means not seen as hypocrites. The selected ones need to select a Christ-like lifestyle, both within community and without. There is no worse shame than for a pastor to visit the workplace of a church officer, only to find out that everyone there is "astonished" to find that their co-worker - your leader - is a church member.

This demand of Jethro's also precludes from leadership the pragmatic follower type (the scheming, profiteering politician) as well as the conformist type (two-faced, non-authentic, cowardly). Persons living this truthful lifestyle will accept the job and will do the job. They will be an

---

[7] From my experience, I will guess that nearly the same statistics apply to the clergy.

"exemplary follower" and will go on to be an open and honest leader.

Jethro continued, teaching that the candidates must *hate covetousness*. Persons who choose to want their own way, to demand things go by their rules only, to disregard the rules of the organization (all symptomatic of the alienated follower), have no place in leadership in a Christian church. Covetous people are takers - not givers; hoarders - not sharers; demanders - not askers. Covetous, selfish people would never receive the respect of their followers because they would never be able to tender respect to them first.[8]

These requirements, if conspicuously published and consistently adhered to, will go a long way in disqualifying many in the church (including current insiders) from being selected for leadership. This situation has only one way of being overcome. Jethro insisted that the entire congregation be led into leadership availability. He told Moses to - *select from ALL the people* - not just the insiders or the ones who camped close to Moses' tent.

In the mainline church, where "religious type" people are often suspect anyway, it may be considered unkind to disqualify people from leadership just because they don't "actively" believe in God. By the same token, in more conservative bodies it is often unseemly to pass over a believer who "is on fire for God" because he is judgmental or she is combative in group settings. These persons being considered for disqualification could be a best friend or perhaps a relative, a factor which further exacerbates the situation. There is however, nothing kind or productive to either the candidates or

---

[8]   The Adaptable Leadership theory as covered in Chapter Ten of this book is little more than respecting the place your follower is in and being willing to love him/her enough to build his/her respect for themselves through a process of building task skills and task maturity.

the congregation in placing people in positions and asking them take responsibility for an institution to which they cannot offer their allegiance.

It is not suggested here that God is limiting in the selection of persons for church leadership. No person, no matter how unskilled or under-educated, is excluded from leadership. The physically handicapped, the person of lower I.Q., the man or woman who is overweight or severely underweight, the trained and the untrained are all called (selected) by God for leadership in the Kingdom. The only thing required God leaves in the candidate's own hands and control. That qualifier is to *select of God, follow God,* and *be not covetous.*

Jethro ended his great dissertation on leadership by warning Moses to let the leaders - *Judge the people at all times.* In today's language "Bug-off and let the lay leaders do their own work!"

Many times, seemingly more qualified long term leaders interfere and overrule the new trainees. They throw their weight around and intimidate newcomers to leadership. We pastors can inadvertently do this to entire congregations. Usually the pastor is the best qualified religious teacher, preacher, worship leader, and church administrator in the body. The very awareness of this by the pastor and among the people often results in a one-person worship service and a one-person administration.

Qualification is however, an elusive and ever changing quality. The least effective church treasurer I ever knew was an accountant, but not a believer or an active church member. My selection for best treasurer was a part-time bank teller who loved her church and her God. The least competent church clerk I worked with was a trained, mature executive secretary, but an unbeliever. The best clerk was a homemaker who never finished high school. The two least effective, do-nothing pastors I have ever encountered, both hold doctorates from prestigious universities; while ironically, four of the best six, most effective and dynamic pastors on the scene today, hold only the most rudimentary credentials.

The bank teller, the homemaker and the four pastors have but a few things in common. These are:

- They all love the Lord Jesus Christ

- Each cares deeply for the people of their churches

- All are very active in their churches

- Every one is active in ministry outside their own church

- Each has a burning desire to succeed for God.

I was privileged to be a leader for some of these people. I was equally proud to be a follower for several of the others. In all these cases I knew that the Holy Spirit was active in their lives and that I had worked with a Christian.

TRIGGER POINTS

1. Looking at Exodus 18: 21-22, do you see the leadership in your church spread over ALL the people? Draw an organizational chart showing how power and leadership work in your congregation.

2. How are leaders chosen in your church? Who has the most say?

3. Looking back over this entire book, list several actions that need to be taken to move your church into the Twenty-first century. Prioritize these.

4. *Take Action - Be Persistent - Don't Give Up.*

POSTLUDE

The sun disappeared from the western sky of Sinai as Jethro concluded his world-changing discourse to Moses. Placing his aged hand upon the younger leader of the new generation, he said in closing,

> If you will do this thing, and God so commands you, then you will be able to endure, and all the people will also go to their place of peace."[1]

With this, the wise one retreated from the troubled Moses.

Israel had come to the end of an era, an era that had lasted for 431 years. Jethro, unlike Moses, had been able to comprehend the gravity of the thing with which Moses was dealing. New ways would have to be sought and implemented, and greater involvement would have to be achieved. If this did not happen the people would not survive the transformation. It would be the responsibility of the leadership to accept the new era, define its environs, adapt to it, and eventually conquer it. The Hebrews were doing more than traveling eastward two hundred miles. They were beginning a trek that would carry the world from pre-history to history, from no relationship between God and people to a time of blood kinship that would link God and humans together forever.[2]

---

[1] Exodus 18:23, NKJV.
[2] In the life and person of the Lord Jesus Christ.

Our turn-of-the-century church is likewise finding itself at the end of an era. Like Moses and the people of Israel, we are about to transcend more than the artificial limits of a century; indeed a millennium. We are moving into a new and unexplored age. As we progress through the *fin de siecle*, we will leave behind the modern era, the industrial age, and that five-hundred-year period during which all humanity has concentrated on the development of the new world, the American continent.

This transition period is being labeled the "postmodern era." It will be a vital transition despite its innocuous sounding name. The very foundations of modern civilization are being threatened. There are strong and powerful forces that are working diligently, attempting to make this a backward passage into a new Dark Age. They are using the fear of the people brought on by migration, crime, and changes in the international setting to manipulate society into accepting their message of regressive social revision.

Radical religious fundamentalists[3] in every country are

---

[3] AM and SW radio stations, carry extremist programs twenty-four hours a day. One station in New Orleans airs a nightly program with focus on getting guns into the hands of "as many good Christian people like us" as possible (supporters of the show are all ironically white). They fight to undo the Brady Law and other government regulation; implying the US government should be overthrown. Other air much of the same message. A "prophet" from South Carolina warns of impending doom in our cities. He challenges order "in the name of Jesus," warning people to flee the cities, moving into the hinterland. His target audience is white, middle class, third generation and up - "real" Americans. The ones to flee from (left behind to face the wrath of God) are black, brown, yellow, and other new Americans. A slightly "dressed-up," but essentially identical form of fear laced Christian revisionism is pumped daily into millions of homes via the 700 Club and the Jerry Falwell programs. What most people don't realize is that none of the above has anything whatsoever to do with Evangelical Christianity or the Gospel of Jesus Christ.

Renaissance or Ruin

broadcasting propaganda around the clock, many calling for armed revolution to get their way. Their message, whether Christian based or Islamic, is basically the same:

> fear of foreigners, separation of races, racial and ethnic superiority, absolute control of government and law by the chosen elders of the faith, laws directly out of the Bible or the Koran (including stoning), and the revocation of all the rights of women, returning them to their former slave-like condition.[4]

These messages of doom and hate advocate that the absolute control of the family will rest in the male head, and the rule of law will be replaced by a demand for absolute obedience to religious councils enforced by Lords of the Holy War.

SCARED ? - *I hope so!*

Because you and your church may be the only thing that will stop such a presage from becoming reality. We, however, will have nothing to contribute, we will be impudent, unless our churches wake-up and embrace the new world in which we live.

As we journey forward through this period of change we meet obstacles never before encountered. A major challenge facing the mainline church is to *hold the tenets of its faith* intact while *venturing forward into a world not yet born*.

- ♦ How will we offer spiritual leadership in this new era?

- ♦ How will we frame our faith in this new land of promise?

---

[4] H. Wayne House and Thomas Ice. <u>Dominion Theology Blessing or Curse</u>. (Portland, OR, Multnomah Press, 1988). 63 - 138.,

Jethro told Moses that the first order of business was to endure. Many have voiced prophesies of doom for the church, citing the trend away from church. They interpret this to say that people have "gone non-religious." They say this is the precursor of a faithless society in the postmodern era .

Leonard Sweet disagrees sharply:

> Postmodern people have not become less spiritual. They are both less religious and more spiritual, less oriented toward "organized religion" (the church has yet to comprehend how this culture hears this phrase) and more disposed toward what used to be known as "spiritual things." But postmodern people have not become less spiritual...Postmoderns are not less interested in religion than ever before, indeed they are exploring new religious experiences like never before. The church has simply given them less interesting religion than ever before. The "unchurched" (an ugly word) are actually more religious than they were a decade ago, their 2,500 metaphysical bookstores bursting with religious erotica and esoterica. Old-line Christianity has entered a glacial age of coldness and despair, exuding all the beauty of ice, in the middle of a spiritual heat wave.[5]

If traditional Christianity is to thrive, it must first heed Jethro's advice we need "to endure." In order to do this we must see our faith as clearly as possible. No church which continues to treat its faith relationship with apathy and/or ignorance will continue. We must also see our world as clearly as possible, and celebrate our presence in that world.

---

[5] Leonard L. Sweet, Quantum Spirituality, 36.

Examine, first, your faith. Anglican theologian Bruce Wilson employed an informal experience with astounding results that speaks to this issue. He asked the same two questions of a large group of churched and unchurched people. First he asked "what immediately comes to mind when you think of someone who is *very religious*?" He received identical answers from all the participants - "churchy, rigid, pious, otherworldly, judgmental, Bible basher,' and 'old."

Next, he asked the same people what comes to mind when you think of someone who is *very human*? He was astounded by the answers he received - "caring, understanding, warm, kind, forgiving,' and 'helpful."[6] These results make it apparent that we need to examine everything about living our faith experience - from worship to social action programs - to determine why people see our faith as rigid, unforgiving, cold, and judgmental. All of these are contradictory to the quintessential Christian message of love, excitement, forgiveness, and warmth.

Compare the worship, educational programs, and belief intensity found in the growing evangelical and charismatic churches to the lumbering, decaying mainliners and you will see that faith shared with verve, joy, warmth, and excitement is highly effective in bringing those outside the church into the body. According to one California Assembly of God pastor, whose church grew from 12 members in 1969 to 3,000 by 1986, there are three differences in the corporate faith life of these postmodern successful enterprises as compared to the old-line denominational churches.[7]

---

[6] Joseph G. Donders, Risen Life: Healing a Broken World, (Mary Knoll, Orbis Books, 1990), 92; as quoted from "Homiletics", (North Canton, OH, Communication Resources Inc., 4:4. Oct. - Dec. 1992), 33.

[7] Lyle E. Schaller, Different World, 64-65.

1. *A person's personal religious experiences take the place of the promise of God as the central validation of one's faith.* Each person is led by the leadership to understand that Christ is Lord, letting Him take command of each person's life. Entry level into fellowship is not baptism as a baby, which is not experienced nor can it be remembered, but rather there persists the demand for all candidates to come personally to the cross and experience Christ's death as a deed done for them. Baptism follows for each person not as a sacrament (mystery), but as an ordinance (ceremony) marking an occasion when "something" important took place in that person's life.[8]

2. *God's Word - the Bible and music have become primary.* Music here is a teaching tool which echoes the scriptures often letter for letter. It is praise centered, not theology centered. It is pleasing to the ear of the a twentieth century dweller with no thought given to the tastes of the 1740's. The Bible is believed, relevant, exciting and written by God. There is no consideration of a dead German theologian's arguments concerning the validity of the manger scene or the virgin birth.

---

[8] It may seem that I am attempting to decry pedo-baptism, but such is not the case. I am trying to provoke the reader into seeing how far we have gone, in the traditional church, in our effort to minimize a personal faith journey for our members. If that is proving antithetical to success, I suggest we examine ways of reintroducing experiential religion to our congregations.

3. *The new churches espouse a theology of glory emphasized over the cross.*[9] This is as much as anything a product of the age of the members. The newer churches are filled with young people who are looking for empowerment in their lives. They are seeking God to supply the needs they have here and now and are less preoccupied with salvation in this next life which seems, in many cases, as a paradise compared to their present existence.

These churches address the need to overcome drug and alcohol addiction, to survive as a single parent, to overcome the heartbreak of divorce from the person you love, to have God present when all have abandoned you since you've contracted AIDS, and to receive extraordinary power to support a family on a marginal income with no health insurance and even less hope. Thanks to the cross these new believers can indeed look forward to eternal life after death; their main problem is getting through this life in one piece.

---

[9] I take issue with this statement. It is true that the new charismatic churches lean toward "power and glory" as their central theme. This becomes the outgrowth, the by-product of Jesus suffering on the cross. For many other newer groups, however, especially evangelicals, including the growing Baptist groups, the cross has been reset in the center of the faith and everything revolves around it. The cross (not gold ornamented and gem laced) for these most active purveyors of faith in the new era, becomes not only the focus of the faith, it becomes the sole requirement.

4. *God is seen as imminent, while the old mainline theologies concentrate on the transcendence.* This relates closely to the comments found above. Here God is seen as a living breathing partner, not as a throne-dweller on the other side of the universe. If you get sick - you ask God to heal you - *and God does!* If you need strength - you ask God to carry you - *and God does!* If you need miraculous power to overcome - you ask God - *and it's as good as done!*

If you accept the Assembly of God pastor's comments and my commentary, you come to the conclusion that basically, people are flocking to churches that offer and encourage a one-on-one animated and personal relationship between God and each individual. You would probably come to the conclusion that the turn of the century "new age" people are hungry, fearful, anxious, and suspicious of political institutions to whom they cannot relate. You may suspect that many of the people seeking a relationship with God feel the need to no longer "go it alone." They do not wish to "keep the faith," but rather desire to "live the faith." You may envision a population racked by major wars, political disenchantment, racism, bigotry, lying, substance abuse, and a generation in ruin due to amoral living, open sex, and promiscuity. You will see men, women, and children desperately seeking a personal knowledge and relationship with God seeking the cure for years of God being pushed further and further out of everyday life.

Now that we've looked at our environment, we must look at ourselves. This book has gone far to accomplish that end. I join Bishop Richard B. Wilke, Dr. Leonard Sweet, Lyle Schaller and others who love the church and its people, in

Renaissance or Ruin

risking severe criticism in order to identify the major wrongs that I see. The world sees these faults; only leaders of the mainline churches are blind to them. This is why a strong, open, new lay and clergy leadership dynamic is absolutely essential.

The goodly portion of new generation churches are seen as dogmatic but exciting. They are demanding, but they are ministering. They are known to ask brazenly, but they are also known as generous givers.

We old-liners, on the other hand, do not minister, we do not lead, and we do not share. We are widely seen as closed communities. Is this what our generation is to do with one of the greatest gifts God has ever given the world? Will we or should we then endure?

Our leaders need to be encouraged to look at the world as clearly as possible. Carl Dudley warn that "our familiarity and our prejudices will bind us to the past and blind us to our problems."[10] Thousands of our churches each year spin their wheels attempting to serve a world that no longer exists. The cure for this communal myopia is to deal with facts and look at the world as it really is. Our congregations need to examine themselves and begin to live in and with the real world.

We are told that this new world, being born of many people from many lands, is "yearning for a sacred way of living on the earth." Many sociologists and theologians tell us that postmodern era dwellers "are hungrier for spirituality than ever before, and enjoying it less in their churches and synagogues."[11] In short, if our faith communities are to endure, our leaders, lay and clergy, will need to become innovationists, challenging a

---

[10] Carl Dudley, Basic Steps, 1.
[11] Leonard J. Sweet, Quantum Spirituality, 37.

system of religion which, to the world around us, has become fatuous, at least, and dangerous at most.

Our future as a people of faith does not depend on God's will for our survival. Our rebirth does not depend on the whims of a fickle world or on changing demographic patterns. Our endurance and victory depends solely on our leaders' ability to become holistic, many-sided, completely open, and fully inviting. Our leaders and congregations will need to become both "antennas and transmitters"[12] the messengers between the people of this changing world and the God who desires, above all, to love human beings into the promised land. *The church must be willing to be the Sinai over which our people pass from bondage into a place of peace.*

Our pastors have been trained to be "caretakers" of a status quo worshipping, hold-the-fort, dying community of an over-the-hill race of people. Our congregations huddle around their decaying tribal houses, attempting to fend off the imaginary onslaught of invaders to their land. If we are to prosper and be a vital force in a world that needs us desperately, we must train pastors and other leaders to be coaches who teach, lead, and move the community forward to be all that it can be.

Finally, our pastors, lay leaders, and members must proclaim that the faith that Jesus taught, the love that God has shown and the power the Holy Spirit offers are the major ingredients in building the Twenty-first century world. Christ alone has given an all inclusive religion based on love, edification, acceptance, understanding, mercy, and spiritual growth. We of the traditional Christian church offer the one major link, open to all humans, for full and unhindered communion with God.

---

[12] Leonard J. Sweet, Quantum Spirituality, 47.

> The centrist, all-inclusive, eclectic theology of mainline Christianity could be the only faith system able to carry the blessings of the modern era intact into the next century.[13]

It is true, the human race is about to cross a monumental threshold. The entire world has been focused on one major project for the past 500 years - the building of the western world. This great task which transcended the enlightenment, the great awakening, the industrial era, and the modern era, has now come to an abrupt end.

Not a village or hamlet in all the world has remained isolated from the impact of this progressive movement. The villages of Bavaria, the Steppes of Russia, the plains of the Serengeti, the islands of the Aegean, the coasts of India, the streets of Paris, and the cliffs of the Yangtsee have all given thousands of their young, ever separated from their homelands, in order to forge a new order that had never before existed.

The religion of the carpenter of Nazareth has likewise been enhanced by its merging with the cultures of these diverse peoples. In turn our belief system has changed the world. When the message of Jesus, as interpreted in our pluralistic setting, has been shared, the world is changed for the better.

---

[13] Having lambasted the radical right, it is proper to acknowledge here the perniciousness of the radical religious "left." This dangerous force has found a home in the mainline churches and now constitutes a threat to our existence, not from armed intervention as in the case of the right, but from forcing the adoption of immorality as a way of life. I do not give as much emphasis to this group, because their message of social sickness has not received wide spread acceptance in the church. God's message for world healing and universal justice falls between the radical right and leftist factions.

The task of the mainline church is far from complete - it has just begun. We should be - no, we *must* be - ready to accept leadership in this floundering world.

If we allow our great ecclesiastical institutions to disappear because of apathy and fear, we may be leaving the world to a dark future. The next century could turn out to be an era of backwardness and ignorance, boasting a reductionist religious philosophy based on superstition, terror, and injustice. Our cities could all but disappear and international law could give way to ethnic states of competing war lords. Life as we know and appreciate it could come swiftly to an end. However, if we overcome our fear and apathy, reclaiming the faith that Jesus left us to share, then through that faith God can create a world without war, poverty, and racism.

We are at a great crossroads

We can follow prophets of doom and the people of hate
or stand on the promises of God.

We can stand still and die
or can make this new world come to pass.

We can if we truly believe -
come to our "place of peace."

When Jethro's job was completed, he disappeared out of the pages of history. He left Moses and the leadership of Israel with a choice:

- Either rebirth the nation
or be destroyed in the desert.

Renaissance or Ruin

Jethro then went away into his own land.

    That same challenge faces our people today:

- We will either choose the *Renaissance* of our church, our faith, and our society, or we will let them fall into *ruin*.

The choice is yours.

                                         Amen.

BIBLIOGRAPHY

Adams, Arthur Merrihew. 1978. Effective Leadership for Today's Church. Philadelphia: The Westminster Press.

Adorno, T. W., E. Frenkel-Brunswick, D. J. Levinson, and R. N. Sanford. 1950. The Authoritarian Personality. New York: Harper.

Allen, Joseph L. 1984. Love and Conflict. Nashville: Abingdon Press.

Bass, B. M. 1985. Leadership and Performance Beyond Expections. New York: Free Press.

Bennis, Warren. 1989. Why Leaders Can't Lead: The Unconscious Conspiracy Continues. San Francisco: Jossey-Bass Publishers.

Blackmore, James H. 1984. Second Acts. Raleigh: Edwards and Broughton.

Blanchard, Kenneth, and Norman Vincent Peale. 1988. The Power of Ethical Management. New York: Ballantine Books.

Boyatzis, R. E. 1972. A Two-Factor Theory of Affiliation Motivations. Unpublished Ph.D. dissertation. Harvard University: Department of Social Relations.

Bright, John. 1981. A History of Israel. 3rd Edition. New York: Westminster Press.

Burns, James MacGregor. 1978. Leadership. New York: Harper and Row.

Chadwick, Norma. 1991. The Celts. 2nd Edition. London: Penguin Books.

Cox, Harvey. 1984. Religion in the Secular City. New York: Simon and Shuster.

Dudley, Carl S. 1978. Making the Small Church Effective. Nashville: Abingdon Press.

_____, Carl S. 1991. Basic Steps Toward Community Ministry. Washington: Alban Institute.

Edelston, Martin, and Marion Buhagiar. 1992. "I" Power: The Secrets of Great Business in Bad Times. Ft Lee. NJ: Barricade Books.

Edwards, David L. 1978. Christian England, Its Story to the Reformation. Grand Rapids: Eerdmans Publishing Company.

Forbes, Cheryl. 1983. The Religion of Power. Grand Rapids: Zonderman Corporation.

Ford, Leighton. 1991. Transforming Leadership. Downers Grove, IL: InterVarsity Press.

Friedman, Edwin H. 1985. Generation to Generation. New York: The Guilford Press.

Grant, Michael. 1990. The Fall of the Roman Empire. Revised Ed. New York: Collier Books.

Hahn, Celia Allison. 1994. Growing in Authoruty, Relinquishing Control. Congregations, vol. XX, no. 2. Washington: The Alban Institute.

Harris, John C. 1977. Stress, Power and Ministry. Washington: The Alban Institute.

Haugk, Kenneth C. 1988. Antagonists in the Church. Minneapolis, Augsburg Publishing House

Hersey, Paul. 1989. Leader Effectiveness and Adaptability Description. Escondido CA.

Hersey, Paul, and Kenneth H. Blanchard. 1969. Management of Organizational Behavior. Englewood Cliffs: Prentice Hall.

House, H. Wayne and Thomas Ice. 1988. Dominion Theology: Blessing or Curse? Portland OR: Multnomah Press.

Johnson, Paul. 1991. The Birth of the Modern. New York: Harper and Collins.

Kelley, Robert E. 1992. The Power of Followership. New York: Doubleday Currency Books.

Kouzes, James M., and Barry Z. Posner. 1988. The Leadership Challenge: How to Get Extraordinary Things Done in Organizations. San Francisco: Jossey-Bass Publishers.

Leas, Speed, and Paul Killans. 1973. Church Fights: Managing Conflicts in the Local Church. Philadelphia: Westminster Press.

Macoly, Malcom. 1981. The Leader. New York: Simon and Schuster.

McClelland, David C. 1975. Power: The Inner Experience. New York: Irvington Publishers.

MacMurray, John. 1932, 1938. Freedom in the Modern World. London: Faber and Faber.

McCrum, Robert, William Cran and Robert MacNeil. 1986. The Story of English. London: Penguin Books.

McGregor, A. M. 1960. The Human Side of Enterprise. New York: McGraw Hill.

Mann, Robert, and Julie M. Staudenmier. 1991. Strategic Shifts in Executive Development. Training and Development. Alexandria: American Society for Training and Development Volume 45, Number 8.

Mead, Loren B. 1990. Reinventing the Congregation. Action Information. Washington: Alban Institute.

Micewski, Andrzy. 1984. Cardinal Wyszynski: A Biography. San Diego: Harcourt, Brace, Jovanovich Publishers.

Moltmann, Jurgen. 1977. The Future of Creation. Philadelphia: Fortress Press.

_____. 1979. Hope for the Church. Nashville: Abingdon Press.

Munoz, Ronoldo. 1990. The God of Christians. Maryknoll: Orbis Books.

Overstreet, Bonaro W. 1954. The Unloving Personality in the Religion of Love. Edited by Simon Doniger. Religion and Human Behavior. New York: Association Press.

Peck, M. Scott. 1983. People of the Lie: The Hope for Healing Human Evil. New York: Simon and Schuster.

_____. 1987. The Different Drum: Community Making and Peace. New York: Simon and Schuster.

Peters, Tom, and Nancy Austin. 1985. A Passion for Excellence: The Leadership Difference. New York: Random House.

Pfeffer, Jeffrey. 1981. Power in Organizations. Boston: Pitman Publishers.

_____. 1992. Managing with Power: Politics and Influence in Organization. Boston: Harvard Business School Press.

Pfeiffer, J. William. 1991. Strategic Planning: Selected Readings. San Diego: Pfeiffer and Company.

Pondy, Louis R. 1978. Leadership is a Language Game. Leadership: Where Else Can We Go? eds. Morgan W. McCall, Jr., and Michael M. Lambardo. Durham: Duke University Press.

Richards, Lawrence O., and Clyde Hoeldlke. 1980. A Theology of Church Leadership. Grand Rapids: Zondervan Publishing House.

Roozen, David A., William McKinney and Jackson W. Carroll. 1988. Varities of Religious Presence. New York: Pilgram Press.

Roth, Cecil. 1964. The Spanish Inquision. New York: W. W. Norton Co.

Rowe, I., R. Mason and K Dickel. 1985. Strategic Management and Business Policy. Reading, MA: Addison-Wesley.

Sawyer, David. 1986. Work of the Church: Getting the Job Done in Boards and Committees. Valley Forge: Judson Press.

Schaller, Lyle E. 1966. Community Organization: Conflict and Reconciliation. Nashville: Abingdon Press.

_____. 1971. Parish Planning. Nashville: Abingdon Press.

_____, and Charles A. Tidwell. 1975. Creative Church Administration. Nashville: Abingdon Press.

_____1987. It's a Different World! The Challenge for Today's Pastor. Nashville: Abingdon Press.

_____. 1990. Choice for Churches. Nashville: Abingdon Press.

_____.1991. Create Your Own Future. Nashville: Abingdon Press.

_____. 1993. Center City Churches. Nashville: Abingdon Press.

_____. 1993. Strategies for Change. Nashville: Abingdon Press.

Steiner, G. A. 1979. Strategic Planning: What Every Manager Must Know. New York: Free Press.

Sweet, Leonard I. 1991. Quantum Spirituality. Dayton OH: Whaleprints.

Thompson, J. D., 1967. Organizations in Action. New York: McGraw-Hill.

Townsend, Patrick L., and Joan E. Gebhardt. 1992. Quality in Action, 93 Lessons in Leadership, Particapation, and Measurement. New York: John Wiley & Sons.

Walls, Dwayne E. 1971. The Chickenbone Special. New York: Harcourt Brace Jovanovich, Inc.

Wilke, Richard B. 1986. And Are We Yet Alive. Nashville: Abingdon Press.